Fragmentation o
Middle East

THE MAKING OF THE MIDDLE EAST

Series editor Roger Owen

Already published

In preparation

Fragmentation of the Middle East
The last thirty years

Georges G. Corm

Professor of Development Sociology
Lebanese University, Beirut

Translated by Selina Cohen, Raj Isar
and Margaret Owen

HUTCHINSON
London Sydney Melbourne Auckland Johannesburg

Hutchinson Education

An imprint of Century Hutchinson Ltd

62–65 Chandos Place, London WC2N 4NW

Century Hutchinson Australia Pty Ltd
PO Box 496, 16–22 Church Street, Hawthorn,
Victoria 3122, Australia

Century Hutchinson New Zealand Ltd
PO Box 40–086, Glenfield, Auckland 10,
New Zealand

Century Hutchinson South Africa (Pty) Ltd
PO Box 337, Bergvlei 2012, South Africa

© Editions La Découverte, Paris, 1983
© English translation Hutchinson Education 1988

Set in Linotron Times
by Input Typesetting Ltd, London

Printed and bound in Great Britain by
Anchor Brendon Ltd, Tiptree, Essex

British Library Cataloguing in Publication Data
Corm, Georges G.
    Fragmentation of the Middle East.—
    (The Making of the Middle East series).
    1. Middle East, 1945–1980
    I. Title II. Series
    956′.04

ISBN 0 09 173237 9

Contents

Preface

The task of analyzing the development of the Arab Near East in a way that fairly and soberly grasps the changing, complex reality of the region is a risky, if not foolhardy, undertaking. To the difficulty of coherently setting out the various political, religious, economic and cultural elements at work in the unfolding of events is added another obstacle: the constant presence of prejudice and passion from which no observers, whether from the East or the West, are ever immune.

The Near East is that place where the love-hate relationship between East and West, which has existed at all levels since time immemorial, finds expression. As a frontier march between the two, historically the Near East has always possessed an importance dis-proportionate to any changes of course of the cultural, economic and religious currents which order East-West relations.

In the eighteenth and nineteenth centuries, the route to the Far East, so vital to the British Empire, created an 'Eastern Question', which – though the joy of essayists, diplomats and historians – indirectly sparked off the First World War. Today, oil, so indispensable to the continuing dominance of western economies, has turned the Arabian Peninsula into a strategic region, and certain barren and underpopulated kingdoms and principalities into strutting peacocks, while the simultaneous existence of Palestine and Israel dramatically symbolizes the conflict-ridden ambivalence of East-West relations in all their historical, cultural, religious, economic and political dimensions. Last, but not least in importance, the Near East is the cradle of the three great monotheistic religions, all branching off from the same stem and each with its share in its turbulent and bloody history; in our own secular century of technical and scientific progress, we are at this moment witnessing yet another act of that particular drama.

To the amalgam of prejudices and passions of the region's historical and cultural heritage, the twentieth century has added the formidable distortions of ideology, introducing new obsessions into the perception of events and of the realities behind. Furthermore, modern media techniques have endowed ideology with a sure manipulative capacity that no governing or administering power can now do without. And when manipulation itself becomes infused with these prejudices and passions, the way opens to the worst – fanaticism or totalitarianism or both.

Since the beginning of this century, the amalgam has, alas, too often governed the images Arabs and Westerners have formed of one another. Western Christianity's historical heritage, guilt-ridden about Jewry and scornful of Islam; the political passions aroused on one side or the other by decolonization; the persistence of underdevelopment and humiliation despite oil wealth; the enormous economic and geopolitcal stakes – all these are basic ingredients in the primitive sentiments ruling over opinion on both sides of the Mediterranean, and too often making for economic and political decisions that consequently intensify conflicts and destabilize a region so vital to the equilibrium of the world.

The aim of this work is therefore to denounce these sentiments, seek to reduce prejudices and replace passionate feelings by reasoned observation. To achieve these objectives, it will be necessary to try and grasp the too often ignored social and cultural reality of the Near East, generally reduced to the sensationalist fantasies of journalists or commentators or to sociological or politcal typologies that are mere mirror images of Western beliefs and perceptions of the East.

Such a task may well seem inordinately ambitious. How can one person claim to understand the truth about the Arab East as it is in our day in competition with an accumulated Western scholarship with its erudite traditions of Orientalism and knowledge of the area? Above all, how to penetrate the opaque complexity of Arab society which itself sees no image of its own existence other than through the three related, distorting prisms of modern ideologies, frustrated anti-Westernism and cultural attitudes out of phase with complex modern conditions?

Understanding the reality of Near Eastern society is by no means a simple exercise. It requires an acute awareness of the existence of those distorting mirrors through which East and West apprehend one another's contorted grimaces. In addition, it is necessary to clarify this reality and to place it within a historical framework being created in front of our eyes, but the significance of which is not yet obvious. For what is one to make of a history constantly punctuated by military coups, plebiscites, palace revolutions and successive military defeats, and too often read through the only available means of interpretation, namely notions of under-development and of imperialism, or the fomenting of plots by the big powers and their secret services?

One is therefore in danger of falling into a sterile form of reductionism, in which men, even the greatest, events, and spontaneous social movements are seen as no more than playthings in the hands of obscure social forces situated in Washington or in Moscow, or indeed identified as freemasonry, international Jewry or Pan-Islamism. What people take to be the causes of an event or phenomenon are at least as important as the nature of the event or the reality of the phenomenon, because these beliefs decisively influence the behaviour of the particular society and the attitudes of its leaders.

It is accordingly important to try and grasp the reality of social and cultural experiences, and then to situate them in a historical perspective without the various reductionisms that jog the observer's elbow from all sides. It is not that the great powers and the obscure forces they can unleash are necessarily absent, merely that their influence is really effective only if geared to an autonomous local context in which certain favourable components are present. Therefore, it is necessary to probe for the true explanations and in so doing delimit the precise shares of autonomy and of determinism.

This book is neither a purely academic nor an entirely popular presentation, but an attempt to interpret events in the Arab Near East so that they are, as far as possible, equally coherent to Westerners and (Arab) Easterners. Because there is a close overlap of East and West in this border zone known as the Near East, this venture into ecumenicalism is first and foremost an exercise of the rational faculties rather than of the passionate emotions.

There is a lot to be said about the notion of an Arab Near East, which offers the convenience of a dual geographical and ethnopolitical precision, making the subject easier to contain within appropriate limits. Here, 'Near East' will refer essentially to the countries belonging to the League of Arab States on the eastern borders of the Mediterranean, namely Syria, the Lebanon, Palestine and Egypt.

Libya, Tunisia, Algeria and Morocco are best defined geographically as 'North Africia'. These Mediterranean Arab countries will be thus excluded from the immediate field of analysis but will certainly be brought into it whenever they exercise a direct influence on the development of events in the Near East.

The countries of the Arabian Peninsula are to be considered more as the Middle than as the Near East, but, because of their oil wealth, are not only fundamental to the socio-cultural development of the region, but also indispensable partners in the development of events in the Near East. For this reason they cannot be ignored and must, to a large extent, be integrated into the analysis. Indeed, a whole chapter will be allotted to oil and to the historical formation of the Saudi monarchy, which has become central to the balance of power in the region.

Iraq and Jordan, both natural geographical extensions of the Arabian Peninsula, constitute a hinge between the Near and the Middle East, and will be mentioned as and when they play an important role in the Near East itself.

The Mediterranean Sea is what really makes the essential difference between these two Easts, for it is on its shores that East and West converge.

But to speak of an Arab Near East is to exclude Turkey and Iran. Although the former is Near Eastern by virtue of its Mediterranean situation and the latter Middle Eastern by its position astride Asia Minor and the routes to Central Asia,* and although both are Islamic, neither is an Arab society. In the past their destinies have been linked to those of the Arabs, but for a long time they have developed separately, even if mutual influences continue to make themselves felt; these will be mentioned each time they make a definite imprint on the Arab Near East.

There remains Israel, the underside of doom-stricken Palestine, the awkward meeting point between East and West, which the international bodies are not able to assign to any geographical region, but which by force of circumstance has become the absent omnipresence in the development of the Arab Near East. It is therefore to it that the penultimate chapter of this book will be devoted.

Being a zone of the convergences and divergences of great

*Central Asia = Soviet Muslim Republics + W. China + Mongolia + Tibet.

civilizations, religions and political empires, the Arab Near East cannot be understood in a simplistic manner, Exhausted from the weight of its own history and from the devastating shock of the Mongol invasions, for four hundred years, from the beginning of the sixteenth century to the beginning of the twentieth, it lay supine under Ottoman domination and then, unprotestingly, became the happy hunting ground of French and English armies for a quarter of a century. Following the Second World War came the intoxication of freedom and a compulsive fascination with the American empire to the West and the Russian empire to the East. Launched into the hitherto unimaginable after all those centuries of sleep, it could no longer distinguish between the dreams and reality, existing somewhere between military defeats on an unbelievable scale and divinely willed manna of oil spouting up out of its hidden deserts and turning it into a gigantic money-making machine riveting the attention of the rest of the world since 1973.

In these circumstances, the incoherence which strikes observers of events in the Arab Near East is hardly surprising. Modern media function rather like an enormous microscope that enlarges for peering eyes the fleeting moments, the crowd scenes, the blood spilt by assassins, the images of civil war and terror, the sumptuous palaces of emirs and the devastated towns.

This work seeks to give these events a balanced place in the complex and difficult development of Arab society in the Near East. It also attempts a perspective of those men who both lead and are led by events, the Arab political leaders who had always aroused strong feelings either of hostility or of admiration in both East and West. It is not always easy to decide whether to view them as builders of States and standard-bearers of modernity, or as by-products of still-decadent societies, manipulated by forces they have no control over: a problem that can only be resolved rationally in terms of an explanatory model such as this book attempts to set up.

To this end, I have chosen to embark on a historical approach designed to situate the major events that have shaken the Near East over the last thirty years. The nationalization of the Suez Canal in 1956 and the 1978–9 Camp David Agreement establishing peace between Egypt and Israel are the two great dates of that period of the region's history during which Arab society has been shaken not only by the two wars of 1967 and 1973 but also by oil wealth and a resurgence of religious fundamentalism with a terrorist coloration. During this same period, Near Eastern society has also been torn between calls to revolution and radical, secular and modern change on the one hand, and the desire for order, stability, tradition and bourgeoisification on the other. And finally, this same society, so eager for unity, fraternity and social justice, has more than ever before been fragmented by centrifugal forces, ideologically and politically divided, and overwhelmed by the burden of an oil wealth not only huge in itself but regionally and socially very unequally distributed.

Yet the historical itinerary is not as chaotic as might seem at first sight. This book attempts to look beyond the apparent incoherence of events and to reconstitute the rational dynamism they contain. The periodization of the past thirty years which broadly demarcates some of the chapters is to some extent arbitrary and intended simply to provide benchmarks in the exploration of the terrain.

Moreover, within each chapter the complexity of events calls for flashbacks well outside the period covered and sometimes as far back as the beginning of the nineteenth century. This applies to the three great axes of change and consequently of heightened tension in the Near East. Thus, the Nasser period cannot be seen in a historical perspective without evoking Muhammad Ali, the Viceroy of Egypt, who, from 1805 to 1948, revolutionized Near Eastern customs and institutions. The Lebanese civil war is hardly intelligible outside its true setting of the deep upheavals experienced by Lebanese and Near Eastern society of the nineteenth century, particularly the troubled and bloody decades of 1840–60. Finally, to understand the astonishing oil saga and the religious experience of the Saudi Arabian kingdom, we must return to the end of the eighteenth century, which marks the beginning of the history of the Wahhabis, the first important movement of Islamic religious fundamentalism in the modern Middle East.

We can only fully apprehend the strait-jacket in which the creation of the State of Israel has confined the whole of the Near East by further entering into the traumatic and conflict-ridden history of Judaeo-Christian relations in the West. The penultimate chapter seeks to set out the three-cornered, potentially explosive relationships that link Arab society to Western and to Israeli society, as well as to the Jewish communities of the Diaspora. For the fate of this region of the world, so vital to international peace and prosperity, is unquestionably linked with the moves towards harmony and detente within this so far discordant and ill-fitted triangle. The last chapter will attempt to gauge the significance and repercussions of Israel's invasion of Lebanon in 1982.

Within the framework of a simple historical narrative, it has obviously been impossible to do more than trace the broad outlines and main themes in the Near East's last three decades. It was a considerable temptation to provide detailed descriptions, to include exhaustive accounts of all the cultural and social elements, all the focal points and underlying symptoms that give a framework to the general picture, but this would have involved producing a work of academic type or, more simply, weakening the framework itself. Burdening a text with notes and quotations is not in any case an infallible proof of objectivity or of a scientific approach.

In short, the object of this work is to offer, in an easily accessible form, a vision of the Near East other than the one of all-pervading irrationality too often presented. For a vision in which misunderstandings, passions and ideology cease to dominate one side or other could in time, however distant, also become the reality of a Near East reconciled with the West and with itself, and of a West reconciled with itself and thus with the Near East. Only in terms of such reconciliations could the Israelis find their right place between East and West, to become a meeting point between the two littorals of the Mediterranean and no longer a running sore in the Near East, paralysing its relations with its Near West, Europe. Realization of that vision would also enable Islam to be itself at last and Arab society to exercise free choice in its ideological and cultural affinities.

Only the history of freedom is of moral significance to humanity. Wherever alternatives of choice exist, there is always a place for freedom. Even if history is only a collection of precious moments, however rare, when choices existed, it cannot be pure folly to hope that certain alternatives should remain open to the Near East. At this meeting point of different civilizations, the forces of tyranny and freedom, of decadence and civilization, have always confronted one another. The Arabs vaguely sense this without however being able to express it in a clear and reasoned manner; they have been the victims of despotism for too many centuries. But the West, with the strength of its brilliant technical civilization and all the rationality acquired by the practice of freedom, should both know and express this point more clearly and forcefully.

Unfortunately, too much selfishness and thirst for power, and too many historical traumas associated with Judaism and Islam govern its Near Eastern policy.

One can but hope that this double impotence in the West will give way to a more creative dynamic before all alternatives have disappeared and the Near East and the Near West are condemned to the reign of tyranny.

Introduction

Precise conceptions of Arab identity

Some basic conceptual explanations must be given to begin with in order to dissipate the numerous prejudices which prevail, in the East just as much as in the West, concerning Arab identity; there is in effect a complete confusion of race, ethnicity, religion, culture and nationality. The lack of precision in words in French and other Western languages, and also in Arabic, leads to an amalgamation of ideas which should remain distinct if a complex social reality is to be coherently understood.

Obviously there is no Arab race as there are black, white or yellow races. Neither is there an Islamic race to which the Arabs might belong. The Arabs, originally from the Arabian Peninsula and the Syro-Mesopotamian desert, are of Semitic stock; their precise ethnic origin, as for most peoples, is little known and is the subject of diverse hypotheses, a matter for specialists. Syro-Babylonian texts point to their existence in the nineteenth century B.C. As with all peoples whose way of living is rooted in antiquity, the ethno-cultural blueprint of the Arabs of the twentieth century, just like that of the Greeks, the Italians or the Iranians, has undergone profound changes. Conquests and invasions gave rise to particularly complex mixtures of populations and cultures in the Arab case; today's Arab society rests on extremely rich and diversified ethnic and cultural foundations. These foundations, not always properly embraced, or ordered in the collective consciousness, serve as a hidden catalyst to the powerful internal centrifugal forces which tear Arab society apart. The distinctive and continuous historical criterion of Arabness has been, since antiquity, the existence of the Arabic language, and not religion as is all too often believed, implicitly or explicitly, not just in the West but also in large sectors of Arab society itself. In the course of their history the Arabs have in fact been adherents of diverse religions; until now not all Arabs are Muslim and Islam has a far greater number of followers in the Indian sub-continent, central Asia and South-East Asia than in the Arab world.[1] On the other hand, their attachment and faithfulness to the language are incontestable. It could even be asked whether the fidelity of Arabs to Islam is not in large measure, and in certain of its most obvious aspects, due to the strength of the historical links which unite the Arabs to their language. This question will be addressed later.

As with religion, neither can the sense of a common history or a continuous attachment to a geographic region be the decisive criterion for an Arab identity. The geographical movements of Arab society in the course of history were in fact very great and the different peoples temporarily or permanently assimilated underwent historical evolutions which were different, or at least specific to them, with shifting centres of power, often several at a time.

Historical complexity of Arab identity

The pre-Islamic period

Originally composed of nomadic tribes, except in the south of the Arabian Peninsula where a rich urban civilization flourished, the Arabs before the Islamic conquest had infiltrated the Mesopotamian (Iraq) and Aramaean (Syria-Palestine) areas and created small kingdoms like that of Queen Zenobia at Palmyra or the Nabatean kingdom at Petra. On the eve of the appearance of Islam, the Arab tribes were subject to diverse cultural and religious influences. Some were Jews, others Christians, a few Mazdeans, but quite a number had remained pagan: Mecca was a great centre of pagan cults. Certain tribes were under the sway of the Persians in the shape of the Sassanid Empire, others were subject to the Byzantines who dominated the whole of the Middle East. North Africa was also at this time under Byzantine dominance; originally Berber, its population was Jewish and Christian. The Donatist heresy was rampant there; in Egypt, the local population, though strongly Hellenized, also practised a specific form of Christianity, the Monophysite, and had conserved the language of the Pharaohs, which, written in the Greek alphabet, was called Coptic, the name still applied today to the important Egyptian Christian community.

In fact, in Asia Minor as in North Africa, the particularisms of the populations were expressed through the different forms of Christianity and independence sought by the local churches in relation to Byzantium. Too often there is a tendency in the West, as in the East, to forget that Christianity flourished first in the Middle East and that the history of the Arabs before and after Islam was very much affected by Eastern Christianity. In the West the obligation to affirm the primacy of the Roman church led to the rejection of Middle Eastern Christianity, including that of Byzantium; among the Arabs, the power of Islamic religious ideology always sought, owing to the force of circumstances, to cause the pre-Islamic past to fall into oblivion. This was not something specific to Islam but rather a characteristic of monotheism found just as much in Judaism and Christianity; Christianity was forced to destroy all vestiges of pagan civilization. It was not until the Renaissance that European society was again linked to the Graeco-Roman sources of civilization.

A knowledge of the pre-Islamic history of the Arabs is indispensable to an understanding of the contemporary evolutions of Middle Eastern states. This history shows the working of the powerful centrifugal forces, evidence of the varied local particularisms, which the great empires that always dominated this area of the world were never able to diminish. The diversity of Eastern churches, persisting until today, added to which is the diversity of heterodox Islamic sects, provides the most striking expression of these forces. Religion and power are thus intimately entwined in the Middle East, not so much for specifically Islamic reasons, but because of historical traditions very much older than Islam. A region of great geopolitical importance, the Middle East has always been dominated by rival empires, some rooted in the depths of Asia (Babylonians, Persians, Seljuks, Mongols, etc.), some in the Mediterranean world (Greeks, Romans, Byzantines), some relying on the unity of the Nile valley (Pharaonic Egypt). The local population of Asia Minor and North Africa, always subject to these great empires, where religion played a leading role, often expressed their opposition to the central power in the form of religious particularism. As for the Arabs, nomadic tribes who were often traders, or populations settled in the framework of small kingdoms on the borders of the great empires, they were constantly torn between the diverse and contradictory cultural, political and religious influences to which they were subject.

The fragility of Arab power in Islamic civilization

These are the basic data which explain the vision of the Middle East as a region of schism and heresy where traditions and geopolitical data are deeply engraved on the collective psychology. The appearance of Islam and the Arab conquests seemed for a moment, under the Umayyads and then under the first Abbasids, firmly to unify the Near and Middle East in a glittering civilization into which the conquered peoples would willingly be integrated, close as they were to the Arabs in ethnic and linguistic origin. In reality Arab power was from the very start extremely fragile. It was first threatened by rivalries to succession even within the Prophet's own family; this gave rise later to the great schism between the Shiites on the one hand, followers of Ali, the son-in-law of the Prophet, who did not recognize the legitimacy of the Umayyad dynasty, and the Sunnites on the other hand who did. Arab dominance was subsequently called into question by the conquered or peripheral populations who were ethnically and linguistically different from the Arabs; the Persians, Berbers and Turks.

Of course the Arabic language played a role in classical Islamic civilization equivalent to that of Latin in Roman Christendom; it was the language that was the vehicle of culture in classical Islamic civilization. But if the Turks[2] and the Persians adopted the Arabic alphabet, they nevertheless preserved distinct languages in order to support the maintenance of their own ethnic and national personalities, even though during the classical period of Islamic civilization the religious link had seemed for a short time to blot out particularisms. The same phenomenon can be found in Western Christendom.

In fact, as far as the Arabs were concerned, from the middle of the ninth century A.D., Abbasid power disintegrated. It fell more and more under the influence of Persian elements and was forced to place itself for protection in the hands of Turkish military forces or to rely on the goodwill of foreign dynasties; meanwhile more and more non-Arab kingdoms and sultanates were forming, not recognizing the authority of the Abbasid caliphs except for form's sake. Dynasties, kingdoms and sultanates were henceforth to be made and unmade against a double backcloth of ethnic rivalries between Arab and non-Arab elements and religious rivalries between different Shiite sects on the one side, often presenting aspects of socio-political radicalism, such as the Qarmatians, and Sunnism on the other side representing the orthodoxy of a weaker and weaker central power. The only effective centre of Arab power in the tenth century was provided by the Hamdanites who governed northern Syria. Andalusia, conquered in the name of Islam by the Berbers of North Africa, remained under Umayyad sovereignty until the eleventh century, power returning then officially to the Berber dynasties and being progressively dismembered, thus opening the way for the Spanish reconquest at the end of the fifteenth century.

Scarcely recovered from the shock of the Crusades, the Arab Middle East underwent the terrible Mongol invasions in the twelfth century. Baghdad was taken and destroyed in 1258. A number of Middle Eastern towns rich in history and culture suffered the same fate, thus delivering a fatal blow to Arab civilization. The Mamluks, slaves of Turkish origin, brought down the Mongols and re-established order and peace in Egypt, Syria and Palestine. They were overcome in their turn at the beginning of the sixteenth century by the Ottoman Turks whose ascendancy continued until the end of the eighteenth century and whose power would not disappear until the twentieth century. All these dynasties originating in Central Asia practised a rigorous Sunni orthodoxy which forced the Shiite sects which had flourished and multiplied from the tenth to the thirteenth centuries to become completely clandestine; they also put a stop to the rich philosophical movement which had until then characterized Islamic civilization. As early as the Ayyubids (1174–1260), a dynasty of Kurdish origin founded by Saladin who drove the Crusaders from Jerusalem, a Sunnite restoration took place in Egypt, Syria and Palestine. It was not until the Safavids emerged in Iran (Persia) in the sixteenth century that a renaissance of Shiite power would be seen.

Islamic power and the problem of integration

One can see, then, how chaotic the history of the Arabs is, both before and after the appearance of Islam. One can also see how much it overlaps with that of other peoples who encircled the Middle East: Persians, Greeks, Byzantines, Turks, Kurds, Berbers. One can appreciate the complex accumulation of religious and cultural influences to which the Arabs were subjected. Absent from political history for nearly nine centuries, one can understand the difficulty of re-entering the modern world for the Arabs as they emerge, scattered far and wide and in separate states, from centuries of foreign domination. This domination stifled any collective consciousness of the ethnico-national type but left intact the local particularisms of all kinds. The non-Arab Islamic empires or kingdoms which ruled the Near and Middle East as well as North Africa were never in fact integrators or assimilators. Islam itself is not a centralizing or nationalistic religion, contrary to the appearances it can give.

First and foremost Islam recognizes the legitimacy of the existence of monotheistic religions, especially Judaism and Christianity; it also recognizes the legitimacy of the pre-Islamic religion of Persia, Mazdaism. In this, Islam is different from Western Christianity which until recently did not grant any legitimacy to other religions. Moreover, despite its Arab origins, on which the text of the Koran lays much stress, the universalist character of Islam can be seen from afar: within the community of believers there must be no difference between Arabs and non-Arabs. Here there is a difference between Islam and Judaism which, more often than not in the course of history, has sought to combine religion and ethnic adherence. This is why in most Arab countries there are non-Arab ethnic minorities or non-Islamic religious minorities which have survived intact through the ages despite all the historical upheavals, thanks to a structural acceptance of pluralism very specific to Islam.

Minorities in the Arab world

Ethnic minorities

The two principal ethnic minorities are the Kurds, mainly in Iraq and Syria, and the Berbers in North Africa. Certain groups within these minorities are 'Arabized'; that is to say they have abandoned their languages and adopted Arabic while preserving a distinct ethnic consciousness. Kurds and Berbers as a general rule adhere to an Islamic faith derived from orthodox Sunnism. There are, however, some Muslim Berbers whose allegiance is not Sunni, the Mozabites of Algeria. By the same token there are several Kurdish tribes in Iraq who are Christian. In the Arabian Peninsula there are minorities of Iranian stock, notably in Kuwait and Bahrain; they are obviously Shiite.

It should be pointed out that there remain in most Arab countries numerous Turkish, Circassian, Albanian and European families whose origins go back to the Crusades. In Iraq, there is a Turkoman minority which is fairly important since it comprises about half a million members.

Religious minorities[3]

Non-Islamic minorities

Non-Islamic religious minorities are found in the two parts of the Arab world, the Mashriq and the Maghrib. There are no Christian minorities, however, except in Egypt and in the area of the Near and Middle East (Iraq, Syria, Lebanon, Palestine). They are almost entirely Arabized at the level of language and culture. They are the Copts in Egypt (7–8 per cent of the population) and different Christian communities connected with the Eastern churches in the other countries (8–10 per cent in Syria, 45–50 per cent in Lebanon, 9 per cent in Palestine, 3 per cent in Iraq). In Iraq there are still some Christian communities which are not Arabized or partially Arabized: these are the Assyrians who speak Syriac. In Syria, three villages near Damascus, where Aramaic is still spoken (NB it is actually Syriac which is still spoken – MEO), constitute more of a curiosity for tourists than an ethnic phenomenon.

It should also be pointed out that there are small Armenian communities in these same countries. This is a case of minorities both ethnic and religious.

The Jewish minorities, formerly very important, especially in North Africa, Iraq, Yemen and Egypt where their existence goes back to pre-Islamic times, have greatly decreased since the creation of the State of Israel. The eradications of the Jewish communities in Algeria is due to the Cremieux decree which in 1870 offered Jews the possibility of taking French citizenship. The Zionist movement later used all possible means of pressure, including the simulation of terrorist attacks in Arab countries with a strong Jewish minority, to trigger off a massive movement of immigration to Palestine after 1948, the date of the creation of the State of Israel. This was totally successful in Iraq and Yemen where as early as 1948/9 the Jews left *en masse* for Israel. It was only partially successful in Morocco and Tunisa where a relatively important number of Jews still live (about 30,000 in Morocco and 20,000 in Tunisia). The Jewish community in Egypt was forced to

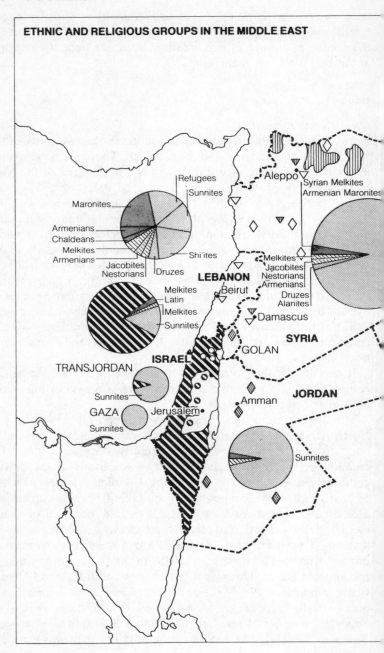

ETHNIC AND RELIGIOUS GROUPS IN THE MIDDLE EAST

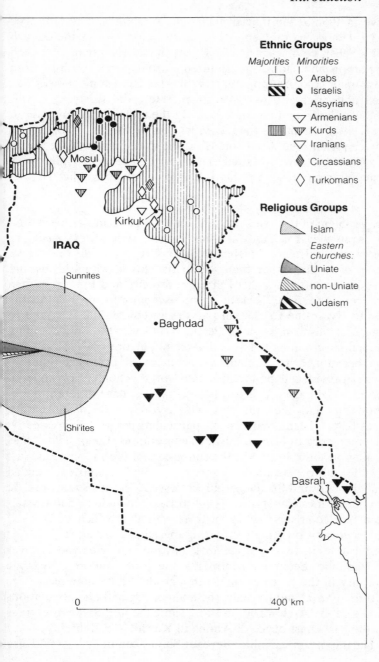

Ethnic Groups

Majorities *Minorities*

○ Arabs
◐ Israelis
● Assyrians
▽ Armenians
▼ Kurds
▽ Iranians
◈ Circassians
◇ Turkomans

Religious Groups

Islam

Eastern churches:

Uniate

non-Uniate

Judaism

IRAQ

Mosul

Kirkuk

Sunnites

Shi'ites

•Baghdad

Basrah

0   400 km

leave in 1956 at the time of the triple invasion by Israel, France and England, at the same time as the members of the French and English colonies living in Egypt; many Egyptians of Israeli persuasion had, however, acquired European nationalities from the time of colonization. Remarkably, the Zionist movement had been able, right up to 1948, to operate quite freely in Egypt, propagandizing and raising funds. On the basis of this emigration, Israel often maintains that there was an exchange of population between it and the Arab countries: the Palestinians to the Arabs as against the Jews to Israel. This is evidently a convenient way of avoiding any responsibility in the Israeli-Arab conflict.

Islamic minorities

The problem of the existence of Islamic religious minorities within the Arab world is quite another matter. It is always easier to accept the existence of something different outside one's own group of origin rather than within it. This is why schisms and heresies are often fought with more ferocity and bitterness than rival religions. Islam is certainly no exception to this rule: as the heir to Byzantine Caesarean papistry in the Middle East and to state Mazdaism in Sassanid Persia, Islam was the only common denominator among the very diverse populations it had gathered together under its emblem. Attachment to orthodox Sunnism always provided a powerful means for the holders of imperial power to fight against the centrifugal forces of the different populations, as had been the case with Byzantine dogma in earlier times before Islam. With Islam, particularisms were expressed by the emergence of diverse religious conceptions, the principal ones turning on the role of Ali, the son-in-law of the Prophet, the last of the four so-called 'righteous' caliphs who succeeded Muhammad, and his line of direct descent and his successors. In Christian times Christological quarrels, often violent, had crystallized particularisms, giving birth to churches which denied the Chalcedonean doctrine concerning the nature of Christ.

Shiism, in its two chief variants, Zaydite in Yemen and Twelver in Iraq and Lebanon, represents the most important Islamic minority in the Arab world. Although the Shiite holy places are in Iraq at Najaf and Karbala, the main centre of Shiite populations is outside the Arab world, in Iran. There are also Shiite minorities on the east coast of Saudi Arabia in Kuwait and Bahrain.

The important Ismailite (Sevener Shiite) community should also be mentioned; its adherents are spread throughout various Asiatic countries, among them Syria, and their spiritual leader is the Agha Khan.

Shiism is violently opposed to Sunnism on the question of the organization of power in Islam and maintains a deep-seated historical dispute with Sunnism. Shism does nevertheless share with orthodoxy a complete respect for the Koranic text and for the most part for Islamic law. On the other hand, Shiite doctrine includes the eschatological belief in the return of a 'hidden' Imam, something which is entirely rejected by Sunnism. Despite the rigorous Sunnite restoration of the twelfth century, Shiism managed to keep itself going by the practice of 'concealment' (*batiniyya*), which legitimized an external adherence to the official religious doctrine while preserving specific beliefs by concealing them.

Kharijism (sometimes called Ibadism) should also be mentioned; this challenges historically both Sunnite caliphal orthodoxy and Shiite doctrine and is prevalent in the Sultanate of Oman and among the Mozabites in Algeria.

Wahabism, which is predominant in Saudi Arabia and Qatar, cannot be classed as an Islamic schism; it is rather a fundamentalist and rigorous doctrine and practice at the extreme of Islam.

Other Islamic sects derived from Shiism are on the other hand clearly heterodox. It seems that the harshness of the persecutions they have suffered have pushed them towards a syncretist esotericism, long impervious to any knowledge on the part of a non-initiate. The chief sects of this kind are the Nusayris (nowadays called the Alawites) in Syria and the Druzes in Syria and Lebanon. The former represent approximately 9–10 per cent of the population in Syria, the latter 6 per cent of the population in Lebanon and about 3 per cent in Syria. One should also point out the existence of the Yazidis in Syria who, it is said, are worshippers of the 'devil'. These sects have succeeded in lasting through the centuries among a considerable number of others which today have disappeared. A celebrated work of the eleventh century, *The Book of Religious Communities and Sects (Kitab al-milal wa-al-nihal)*, by the Imam 'Abd al-Qadir al-Baghdadi, lists six philosophical religious tendencies which were the source of heresies which had engendered forty-five sects.[4]

Hidden away in scarcely accesible areas in order to escape persecution, these minorities of Islam in the Arab world have thus been not only politically but also economically underprivileged. This is often also the case with ethnic minorities or certain Christian minorities. Thus their 'liberation' is achieved nowadays in turbulence. It was first helped by European colonization with obvious ulterior motives of dividing in order to rule, then by the institutions of the modern independent state, notably the army, the school and the creation of political parties.

A minority established as a state: Israel.

The creation of a Jewish state in Palestine was clearly a great shock to the psychology of Arab society in the Middle East. It was an enterprise which presented a serious challenge to subsequent events, setting as it did a very dangerous precedent in a region where ethnic and religious minorities retain an important dynamic role. In the eyes of unitarian nationalist Arabs, Israel would separate the Mashriq from the Maghrib and encourage divisions within Arab society. In the eyes of Islamic fundamentalists, the Israeli success, that of a state built on religion, provided the futility of the secularism and modern nationalism the Arabs adopted, forsaking fundamental Islam. Finally, in the eyes of the minorities of the Middle East, how could a Jewish state not be an example to follow should the occasion arise, if circumstances permitted?

Arab minorities outside the Arab world

The existence of Arab minorities outside the Arab world must also be pointed out. One example is in the region of Iskanderun and Antioch in Turkey which was a Syrian province until 1938 when France, the mandatory power, surrendered it to Turkey in exchange for that country's neutrality in the conflict with Nazi Germany. Official maps of the Syrian Republic still delineate the frontiers with Turkey along former lines. A fair number of the Arabs of this region, which Turkey is doing its best to 'Turkify', are Christian, Antioch having been historically one of the holy places of Eastern Christianity. In Iran, in the region of Khuzestan (also called Arabistan), the Arab minority, mostly Sunnite, comprises about two million people. In Ethiopia, the Eritrean populations are mostly Arabic-speaking and Muslim. On the other hand, it should be mentioned that in Sudan, a good part of the population, that in the southern provinces, is neither Arabic-speaking nor Muslim. Similar problems arise in Somalia and

Mauritania; it is hard to know how to treat them in the framework of this book which concentrates on the Arab Middle East.

Geographic diversity

Added to these complex ethnic and historical data are the data of geography and environment which bring a new dimension to the diversity of Arab society. Here again, in the absence of a centralizing state, the ways of life and the regional means of production remained totally heterogeneous and impenetrable: nomadic life in the desert regions; the countryside overburdened with taxes and forced labour in the irrigated plains; isolated villages living in self-sufficiency on the meagre resources in the mountainous zones; lastly towns, monopolizing culture, the economic surpluses of agriculture, small-scale production and of course political and religious power. It was not until European colonization, the setting up of modern states and the integration of the Arab economies into the international economy that this diversity would be reduced, usually maladroitly.

In the light of this extraordinary geographical and historical diversity, one can see how misleading is the superficial image of a homogeneous Arab society with a monolithic collective personality. This is even more the case when one speaks of Islam. This myopia does not afflict just Westerners; it is also the achievement of the Arabs themselves whose contemporary thought obliterates the contradictions and the diversity of the historical past and of geographical places, in order to valorize sometimes the national link, sometimes the religious link, the swing of a pendulum which never comes to a standstill. The dynamics of this movement have till now scarcely been studied.

The questions that should be asked concerning Arab identity

In conclusion, it remains to point out the difficulty of setting down a list of the nature of the questions that should be asked concerning Arab identity in all its dimensions.

1. There is no doubt that from the Atlantic Ocean to the Arabian-Persian Gulf, an Arab culture permeates society, whatever the diversity and the particularisms of the local populations. If the Kurd in the Middle East and the Berber in North Africa, with their different variant dialects, can remain incontravertibly in existence,

then the Arabic language and culture are an indestructable link. The diffusion of education, the means offered by the modern media and the progress of the press and publishing in Arabic provide a circulation of culture among Arab states; the effects of this are bound to be felt in the end. The problem here is the content of this modern Arab culture, in particular in its relation to religion, to philosophy and to the exercise of power, but also to the culture of the industrialized world.

2. To combine Arab identity with Islamic identity, which often leads people into speaking of an Arab-Islamic civilization or an Arab-Islamic personality, is in our opinion a phenomenon with pronounced ideological aspects expressing the confusion of Arab intellectuals faced with the decline of Arab society. It is true that Western orientalists are also nowadays very fond of ambiguous concepts, after having dwelt for a long time exclusively on Islam, obscuring the reality of the peoples of Muslim faith as well as the diversity of their ethnic personalities. When a non-Arab asks an Arab what his national identity is, he immediately answers that he is an Arab, not that he is a Muslim. This would not be the case at the level of a more elaborate discourse between an intellectual or a political personality and a non-Arab, whether Muslim or not, because the combination of national with religious identity offers many advantages. It was the Koranic prophecy which made the Arabs into great conquerors and great civilizers, a movement which left its mark on world history. The combination of the two identities is thus for the politician an element of prestige and legitimacy counterbalancing dictatorial and oppressive practices as well as the reality of underdevelopment; for the intellectual who refuses to see the reality of his society it is an easy and demagogic compensator in a hollow discourse for a wrongly assumed modern Arab identity. And for a very good reason, since the rift is immense between the splendours of classical Arab civilization, animated by the breath of the nascent Islam, and the misery of underdevelopment and multiform dependence on the West. In the rivalry of the Arab elites in power in the different states, the call to Islamic legitimacy is also a weighty factor when things are going badly.

3. However, it is the unitarian Arab view, and not the Islamic, which motivated the great events linked with decolonization, in particular during the Nasser period, even if today, yielding to the combination of circumstances, certain people endeavour to

visualize recent history through an Islamic prism. Since the nineteenth century, important tendencies of thought have striven to realize a national identity which would not be a prisoner handcuffed to a religious identity. They reached their height in the 1950s and the 1960s and their hero was Nasser. It was the failures of Arab society faced by the Israeli challenge and the exigencies of modernity and economic independence, as well as the inability to achieve Arab unity, which provoked the violent reflux of secularism and the resurgence of Islamic fundamentalism. Nor should it be forgotten that in the course of the last ten centuries, from the decline of the Abbasid Empire to the arrival of Muhammad Ali in Egypt at the beginning of the nineteenth century, Arab identity was totally obliterated in favour of Islamic identity, maintained in a position of exclusivity by the foreign conquerors in order to establish the legitimacy of their domination. It is not easy to efface the secular importance of the ideological means used to ensure the permanence of a system of political domination that has been called by Marxists, somewhat excessively, 'Asiatic despotism'. Thus it is not surprising that in the current reflux of modernizing and secular ideas, provoked by the failures of contemporary Arab society, there is a forceful resurgence of nostalgia for the Ottoman Empire, in other words for metaphysical and ideologoical comfort which ensured an imperial Islamic unity, formerly world power.

4. The problem is all the more complex in that there are, in the blueprint for Islam itself, secular traditions of rigorism imposed by the non-Arab dynasties in order better to establish their power. The Islam of the conquering Arabs was at first an Islam of philosophical and cultural opening up, the source of the very beautiful intellectual and scientific blossoming which, strengthened by Syriac, Aramaic and Persian contributions, could allow the preservation of the great achievements of Greek civilization, later taken back by Europe. The result was a multiplication of religious sects and philosophical schools, constantly putting the fundamental dogma of Islam in danger. Also, the history of Islamic civilization is one of fundamentalist reactions intended, as in Christianity, or earlier in the history of monotheistic religions in Judaism, to ensure the unity of power and religion in the face of all the centrifugal forces. From the beginning of the ninth century, reaction established itself. It was consummated in the twelfth and thirteenth centuries when Turks and Mongols definitively snatched

preponderance in the political domination of the Middle East from the Arabs and Persians, themselves in bitter rivalry. The Sunnite restoration, which began in fact in the eleventh century, led to the closing of the door of religious exegesis and the prohibition of philosophy, thus blocking any possibility of evolution.

5. Every now and then, in reaction against this rigorist Islam, but much more rarely in agreement with it, as with al-Ghazzali (1059–1111), one of the great masters of Islamic thought, there developed mystical Islam, called Sufism. A complex and underground world, since it is almost totally ignored by sociological observation, the Sufi orders (*turuq*) have always played a very important role in urban and rural life in the Arab Middle East.

(a) The heart of a veritable popular 'freemasonry', the Sufi orders seem to have played an important compensatory role among the underprivileged in the face of the omnipotence of 'canonic' law (*sharia*) and the ultra-conservatism of its application by the official clerics, the '*ulama*', in the service of political and military power. Muslim mysticism has fascinated many orientalists, among them the celebrated Massignon who devoted a part of his work to the study of the life and passion of al-Hallaj (858–922), a great Muslim mystic who died in cruel circumstances and in whom it is quite easy to see the image of Christ in Islam. Apparently on the way to disappearing in the twentieth century, under the impact of accelerated modernization, the activities of the Sufi orders seem to be flourishing anew once more, notably in Egypt.[5] The fetters and tensions of modernization, in particular as a result of oil wealth, are certainly largely responsible for this.

(b) It remains to be seen how the transition will be made from the current violent popular dissatisfactions in the Middle East among the Sufi orders to activist cells of the Muslim Brotherhood, in other words from mysticism to politics. One English anthropologist has outlined a description of a similar transition in Egypt at the beginning of the century, showing the decline of a Sufi order and its local cells to the profit of Hassan al-Banna, the founder of the Egyptian Muslim Brotherhood.[6] Today, one can easily envisage a double renaissance, parallel and complementary, of orthodox Sufism and rigorous activism; we will indeed see at work in this book all the forces which help to swell the rigorist torrent. In any event, for Iran, whose evolution traditionally influences Arab Shiism, it is ultra-orthodox rigorism, personified by Imam Khomeini, which has overturned everything in its way, in spite of the existence of Shiite trends with secular aims, philosophically, mystically and socially broad-minded.

6. But among Arab intellectuals, those who are currently making a noisy demonstration of Islamic identity are scarcely interested in the mystical or philosophical aspects of Islam. Only the aspect of political mobilization arouses their passion: their fascination with power takes precedence over all calm reflection. They are often the same people who were fervent Arab nationalists, then leftist socialists, who today find themselves at the forefront of a Utopian Islamic nationalism, fundamentalist and transethnic. It often happens that these intellectuals become 'Westernized' in the extreme and live in a manner closer to that of Parisian salons or big American universities than that of fundamentalist religious brotherhoods. The reform of Islam and its re-opening to the great trends of modern thought, which was the preoccupation of the Arab thinkers of the *nahda* (renaissance) from the beginning of the nineteenth century, has thus ceased today to be a topic for consideration. On the contrary, the fundamentalist and rigorist idealization of the Islam of the earliest days is an obsession which has developed with the occlusion of Arab society and the recession of nationalist secular ideology. Moreover, little is found in the Arab world of the Iranian variant of Islamic Marxism, although certain signs of it are evident in the thought of the Libyan president.

7. It remains to say that it is hard to conceive in the long term the way Middle Eastern Arab society will swing, caught as it is in religious rigorism and culturally closed to the industrialized world. Naturally, the attraction of Khomeinist Iran is a strong one for the society first blocked by European colonization, then swamped under the weight of sudden oil wealth unevenly distributed and too rarely used judiciously. However, the attraction of modernity remains, in our opinion, still just as strong, even if the disappointments of the last quarter of a century have affected its most telling expressions, such as those of Boumedienne or before him Nasser. The weight of historical factors must, however, be borne in mind, in particular the obliteration of the Arab personality for six centuries in empires where power rested with non-Arab elements who had immobilized the progress of religious thought in order to make rigorist Islam a fundamental element of political legitimacy. The current recession of modernizing and nationalist Arab ideology is thus potentially dangerous if the obstructions to

modernization persist in Arab society and if the religious fundamentalism of the state practised under the influence of the oil-producing Arab countries continues to be reinforced. The danger is aggravated by the recession of the nationalist and secular view in Turkey which was, with Egypt, one of the principal bastions of modernity.[7] The crushing victories of Judaic state fundamentalism in the Arab Middle East, embodied by Israel, are also an important element in this problematic of identity, as is the passive attitude of Western countries towards the excesses of the Zionist phenomenon.

8. The problematic of Arab identity in fact hinges on one principal axis: the reappropriation by Arab society of the integrality of its history after so many centuries of effacement of ethnico-national personality and faced by the confrontation with modernity, particularly difficult for the Arabs. The omnipotence of oil, which is also that of the West in the Middle East, the failure of unity, the defeat in regard to Zionism, do not make the task any easier at the moment.

For marginalized and disinherited social strata, as well as for an intelligentsia dreaming only of power, it is understandable that in the present context it is extremely tempting to be content, on historical grounds, with choice morsels; the grandiose epic of Islam annihilates the past and the future. The danger in this is obviously very great: the war between Iraq, supported by the countries of the Arabian Peninsula, and Iran must in part be interpreted in this context; it proves that the Arabs are well aware of the danger, even if the opportunity afforded by this war or the way it is being conducted raise many questions in the very interior of the Arab world. Israel on the western flank, Iran on the eastern, two ambiguously bleeding situations for the Arabs where religion, ethnicity and culture crudely test a contemporary Arab identity which is still to be found.

1 From 1956 to the death of Nasser

The end of a hero

A hero's death being often more significant than his accession to power, a historian can arrive at invaluable, if incomplete, insights from the way a nation reacts to the death of its leader. Over the past thirty years, two men have made a deep impact on the destiny of the Near East, their lives and deaths punctuating the distinctive moods, obsessions, fashions, hopes and resentments of each epoch. Both were Egyptian, from that land of Egypt which is both motionless and vital, eternal yet so fragile, 'begging' but 'proud', and 'violent' but 'pitiable'.[1] Like twentieth-century Pharaohs, both wanted to change the course of history, the second seeming so far to have succeeded, the first to have lamentably failed.

Yet the reality of the Near East is not so easily grasped, for one cannot help but contrast the unusually simple funeral of Anwar Sadat, the Egyptian Republic's second President, assassinated in the autumn of 1981, with the tremendous farewell the Egyptian people gave their first President, Gamel Adbel Nasser, at the same season, eleven years earlier.[2]

'Colonel Nasser', as certain Western newspapers took pleasure in calling him, was however disastrously defeated in the third Arab–Israeli war, which was so catastrophic for the Arabs. In a six-day *Blitzkrieg* in June 1967, Israel conquered the whole of Egypt's Sinai Peninsula, Syria's formidable Golan Heights and the west bank of Jordan (so infused with sacred history that some see it only as the biblical Judaea and Samaria), not to mention the old city of Jerusalem, containing the principal holy places of Islam, Christianity and Judaism.

By the autumn of 1970 the Israeli army had still not retreated an inch. Some months earlier, despite the gibes of the Palestinian Resistance and the Arab left, Nasser had agreed to an initiative by the American Secretary of State, William Rogers, to try and break the political and military deadlock in the Arab–Israeli conflict. Then, just as he seemed about to be setting off for Canossa, the Egyptian President, visibly exhausted, died of a heart attack. Amidst a merry-go-round of Arab Heads of State, he had been striving in vain to stop the bloodshed in Jordan, where King Hussein had decided that he would no longer tolerate the armed presence of the Palestinian Resistance, through the various organizations of which the Near East Arabs then hoped to regain their lost dignity.

And yet this man of defeats, who had earlier lost another war in the Yemen, and accepted Syria's secession in 1961 (Syria had been united with Egypt in a fit of enthusiasm in 1958), could still draw wild emotion from the crowds on the last harrowing journey to his final resting place. The intolerable grief displayed at his burial was like that of half-grown children abandoned by an adored father, though many might have wondered what inheritance this father had left to warrant such intense mourning. In the West it was merely interpreted as yet another expression of that mystical, mysterious and somewhat irrational 'Eastern soul'. But the anti-Nasser forces in the Arab world, and there were many, saw in the grandiose funeral merely the final gesture of a demagogic regime mobilizing the crowds in the vain hope of diverting attention from its own record.

The Arab Right, however, had said the same thing about that extraordinary day, 9 June 1967, when the Egyptian President had taken his first journey into the land of darkness. At about 6 p.m., his face distraught with grief and brimming with tears, Nasser had announced on all the radios and televisions of the Arab world the full extent of the defeat by Israel, from the depths of despair admitting his own guilt like a Christian sinner and his willingness to atone. Immediately people began to fill the streets of Cairo, and in Damascus, Baghdad, Amman, Beirut and Algiers innumerable crowds also gathered to summon their hero to stand firm at his post and not to bend in the face of adversity. Such extraordinary scenes being rare in the history of the nations, this too was seen by many as mere manipulation by State apparatuses at bay.

In search of a lost voice

But has anyone in the West ever taken the trouble to listen to an Eastern people? It is as if, by definition, Eastern people did not have souls. Grand abstractions like the Orient, Islam etc. no doubt have one. But the people themselves are viewed only as the playthings of their own potentates or their colonial masters, in the past good for nothing but for supplicating their sultans and petitioning their occupiers, and now for coming out onto the streets for a bribe of a few piastres or at the incitement of some demagogue or manipulation by the modern mass media.

Such is the all-too-common image of Eastern peoples, one that encourages the reader to take refuge in reductionist abstractions, whether stereotypes of ethnic or religious prejudice, political ideology and conventional wisdom. It is true that the people in the East – unlike those of the West – are deprived of a modern political language, organized and institutionalized in a well-defined periodicity. But this is all the more reason to be tuned in to those privileged moments when, absolute power suspended, society can express itself with the violence of an unleashed torrent and in a few brief instants give voice to emotions bottled up during long years of silence.

In the case of Nasser, the grief was all the more intense because the Arab people lost a magician of collective emotion, whose words over the course of seventeen years had expressed certain of his society's deep impulses and who had himself been carried along by them. With the help of the modern media, it had been a bravura of language, without precedent since the Koranic prophecy itself, a performance which came to an abrupt end for the Arabs with the loss of their hero. The grief was as great as the silence into which Arab society from then on was in danger of sinking.

As remarked on at the time, only the loss of the great diva of Arab song, Om Koulsum, aroused the same intensity of grief. The comparison does not end here with the role of language, which would merely reproduce the facile cliché of the fascination words hold for Arabs. The parallel emotion aroused by the deaths of the hero and the heroine actually corresponds to double frustration historically present in Arab society: that of freedom and political dignity as well as of love and sex. For these silent people, whose voice for a moment they personified, the words of Nasser and the singing of Om Koulson bore a profound reference to centuries of domination and political tyranny on the one hand, and on the other to thousands of years of patriarchal tradition and emotional and amorous conformity.

Sadat's speech, characterized by a somewhat pronounced stammer, despite its warmth and very popular accent, merely kindled a nostalgia for the metallic timbre of the Nasser voice roused by the breath of that collective emotion. Furthermore, Sadat rarely spoke in front of crowds, preferring meetings of political high-ups, or of Western press correspondents, in front of whom he so liked to smoke his pipe, reassuring symbol of Anglo-Saxon civilization. On these occasions he usually remained seated. Nasser used to speak standing up, like a Pharaoh, in open spaces and always in a suit and tie, symbols of a non-military modern man. Sadat used to dress up: sometimes as an admiral, sometimes as a field marshal, sometimes in a *galabiyya* (the Egyptian peasant costume) and sometimes as an English gentleman. It was not by chance that he entitled his autobiography *In Search of an Identity*.[3]

But it is not yet the moment to paint comparative portraits of these two men who have become symbols of two such apparently contradictory, yet nevertheless complementary, eras. Beyond the striking difference in their outward personalities, both were actually products of the same impatience, from similar social backgrounds and trained in the same military academy. Together they had exercised power since 1952.

This already indicates the complexity of human beings and of the social forces that bear them along and which they express. For Sadat, too, represented the innermost being of an Egypt which could give an open-hearted and massive welcome to Richard Nixon only four years after the great bereavement of 1970, the loss of a man who had for so long symbolized resistance to the same imperialism of the capitalist West Nixon was personifying so well. In the absence of a broader view of the deep-seated complexities of these peoples without an organized political language, it is tempting to regard such behaviour as inconsistent, childish and irrational. But one must go much further back to understand the passage from Nasserism to Sadatism with its complementary contrasts and break in continuity between the two eras. To do this, we must once again turn to the voice of Nasser, which so sublimely made all Egyptian and Arab society quiver.

A laugh about a canal

Everything began with a political speech or, rather, a laugh, which a quarter of a century later still rings in the ears of a whole generation of Arabs. For Arab society the twentieth century began with a laugh. It did not begin as the historians say with the collapse of the Ottoman Empire in 1918–19; nor in 1945, following the global ebb of European influence due to the Second World War, which politically liberated a substantial part of Arab society from colonial domination and gave birth to the League of Arab States. On the contrary, the Arab twentieth century, which is only the fourteenth century of the Hegira (the beginning of the Islamic calender)[4] began on 26 July 1956 in Alexandria, ancient city of Mediterranean history, when Nasser announced to the Egyptians that the Suez Canal had been nationalized and that the Egyptian technicians who had taken over from the foreigners were ensuring the normal passage of ships. With a mixture of joy and emotion the Egyptian President then started to laugh. The Arabs are reputedly never seen laughing, yet here is the Caesar-like Head of State of a people downtrodden for a thousand years laughing in the middle of an important political speech – an occurrence unheard of but fitting to the occasion. The reintegration of the Suez Canal into the country's national assets was equivalent to a paralytic suddenly regaining the use of a vital part of his body. All the jubilation of Arab society was in that laugh.

It is never sufficiently appreciated just how much transport routes mean to the economy and society of a country, particularly a Mediterranean country wedged between Africa and Asia. A prestigious French historian once aptly referred to the sixteenth-century '*espace-mouvement*' (an area of active internal movement).[5] How better to describe a transport route that links Europe and the Atlantic world to Africa and Asia like a jugular vein of international commerce, and is an alien body across Egypt. Though a symbol of Egypt's geographical and economic dispossession, the Suez Canal was nonetheless built in the last century under the auspices of a sovereign, the Khedive Ismail, who dreamed of integrating the country into the circuit of the world economy and turning it into a St Simonian workshop of technical progress. Ismail was Albanian, a member of the aristocracy of the declining Ottoman Empire. Once nationalized, the Suez Canal became the symbol of Egypt's entrance, in its own right, into the modern world of prosperity and progress which until then had remained the sole preserve of the great powers.

The nationalization of the Suez Canal was clearly an event of immeasurable importance that triggered off a series of changes through which we are still living. It made Egypt and the Arab world the spearhead of the claims of the Third World. It was its influence that in substance led to the creation of OPEC,[6] the nationalization of oil and the four-fold rise in its price – even if the torch had meanwhile passed from Gamal Adbel Nasser to another Arab Caesar, the Algerian Huwari Boumedienne, who in 1974 forced the leaders of the world to discuss the economic despoliation that was crippling two-thirds of mankind.

A like connection links the nationalization of the Suez Canal in 1956 and the Extraordinary/Special Meeting of the United Nations General Assembly on Raw Materials and Development, convened in 1974 on the Algerian President's initiative, and then with the Conference on International Economic Co-operation held in Paris between 1975 and 1977.[7] The link continues to subsist through various negotiations on a New International Economic Order designed to give the downtrodden and underprivileged peoples in this world a greater equity and justice. What are now referred to as the 'North-South' negotiations can thus be traced back to this nationalization, which was the first clear expression of the right of peoples to the use of their own natural wealth, including the advantages of a favourable geographical location.

The whole question of the Canal was indeed one of national repossession and economic health. For Nasser, the young President with a military background, was the son of a postal official, and in Egypt, as elesewhere in the underdeveloped world, post offices, like the army, are symbols of modernity and progress. The new President was obsessed with the idea of leading Egypt out of its backwardness into economic health and of integrating it on an equal footing into the industrialized world's path to progress and prosperity. Nationalization and, as a matter of priority, the construction of a huge dam on the Nile at Aswan, which would produce the energy necessary both for industrialization and to irrigate the millions of hectares so essential to the survival of a people experiencing a population explosion.

The transmigration of souls: the Pasha and the Colonel

In the light of that purpose, Nasser was but a reincarnation of another very great figure of Egyptian history, Muhammad Ali, who, first as Pasha and then as Viceroy of Egypt from 1805 to 1849, was every bit as controversial. For Muhammad Ali also dreamed about, and almost succeeded in, bringing what was then a sleepy and anaemic Egypt straight into the nineteenth century. In the space of a few years he turned it into a great hive of industry, changed the land tenure system, built irrigation dams and canals and introduced the farming of cotton.

Simultaneously, he built himself an Arab empire, occupying Syria and Lebanon and sending an expedition into the heart of the Arabian Peninsula to knock sense into the recalcitrant Bedouins, who, a century and a half later, were to establish that extraordinary oil super-kingdom, Saudi Arabia, on which the stability of the Western world now rests. And, with his armies at the gates of the Taurus, he threatened even the Sublime Porte. Then the whole venture collapsed like a house of cards, because of a change in the international situation, whereby a colonial and reactionary Europe decided in collusion with the Tsarist Empire that it definitely preferred a worm-eaten Ottoman Empire to an Albanian Pasha who seemed uncomfortably like an Arab Bonaparte.

Nevertheless, at the beginning of the nineteenth century, when Europe and North America were the only places in the whole world to show any vitality or dynamism, Muhammad Ali's achievements were extraordinary. Over and above his economic achievements, which neither Colbert, the Meiji of Japan,[8] Marx, Lenin, Stalin, nor even Keynes would have impugned, he outlawed religious discrimination against non-Muslim minorities, developed education along secular lines, modernized the administration, nationalized religious property, dismissed those ulema[9] who opposed his secularization policy and abolished the traditional Ottoman system of taxation.

It is true that the Pasha of Egypt came from the Empire's military caste which was predominantly Balkan in origin, and so that for him Europe and Christendom were not distant and mysterious lands of religious infidels. In fact, he showed open and active sympathy for the Christian Arabs of Egypt and Syria and was also the first Muslim Head of State to integrate Christians into Islamic armies, notwithstanding that soon after the Muslim conquest Islamic doctrine both in law and practice excluded them from military posts and from conscription. In this respect, Muhammad Ali belonged to a line of Ottoman reformers who, from the beginning of the eighteenth century, had become sensitive to the Empire's backwardness in relation to Europe.

It was from this line of descent that the Young Turks emerged at the end of the nineteenth century, their exemplar being Mustafa Kemal, who resolutely turned his back on inter-ethnic Islamic solidarity in favour of secular nationalism. Those first Arab nationalist military officers who turned away from Islamic solidarity with their Turkish co-religionists at the beginning of this century to dream about Arab unity are in effect nourished from this same source. Despite certain features particular to him, Nasser was also in this tradition.

Geography and opera to the rescue

Geography, that neglected ancestor of the modern social sciences, can now lend a hand with the historical continuity we seek in the effort to see beyond the apparent ruptures that great historical events inevitably provoke. It can never be stressed fully enough that the Ottoman Empire was a Mediterranean empire,[10] the centre of gravity of which was always closer to the West than to the East. For this reason Mediterranean Islam must not be lumped automatically with the Islam of the Asian continent, any more than southern Christendom, whether Catholic or Orthodox, should be with that of the North.

The chaotic history of the Near Eastern Arabs over the last century is partly the outcome of this subjacent conflict, barely visible through layers of scholarly abstractions, between the Islams of the Mediterranean and of the Asian continent. President Sadat is the best known of its victims. He was never quite sure whether he was a peasant from continental Eygpt and close to the Islamic fundamentalism of the Muslim Brotherhood, or an occidentalized gentleman from the magical and cosmopolitan Alexandria, the atmosphere of which Lawrence Durrell[11] captured so beautifully.

President Nasser never seemed to have been in any doubt. Like Muhammad Ali, he wanted the economic progress and political independence of the industrialized world, and if the West would not help he would get it from the East. Subjected to repeated assassination attempts by members of the Muslim Brotherhood, he rapidly removed all trace of their presence from Egypt's political, social and cultural life. His successor, by contrast, reintroduced the Muslim Brotherhood and its sympathizers into political life and gave a free rein to their influence – a mistake he would pay for with his life.

At all events, the dynasty Muhammad Ali founded in Egypt was, with a few exceptions,[12] resolutely modernist and pro-European. It was with the European powers that the Pasha of Egypt had negotiated the establishment of his dynasty, in compensation for having to abandon his political and economic achievements in the Near East. But in their desire to give Egypt all the trappings of a European monarchy, Khedive Said (1854–63), and especially his successor Ismail (1863–79), reduced their country to financial bankruptcy, which only further increased their dependence and paved the way for British occupation. Verdi's *Aida*, which was first performed in Cairo, was commissioned by Khedive Ismail to celebrate the construction of the Suez Canal. Could one dream of a more beautiful marriage between East and West or a more romantic meeting of lips than those symbolized by the two shores of the Mediterranean? *Aida* alone is witness enough to the mutual attraction of East and West, to which could be added Mozart's *Il Seraglio*, which, like so many other musical and literary masterpieces too numerous to cite, gracefully credits the Ottomans with such noble feelings.

But many will judge this an unhealthy and dangerous love, the partners too unequal for the man-eater the secular, colonizing West had become not to devour the languid flesh of the long-somnolent East. This is indeed often said in various ways, whether by simple anti-imperialist imprecation or by calls, elegant and rational or brutal and fundamentalist, as the case might be, to an otherness specific to the Arab partner. Recently such feelings have also been more subtly expressed in a general denunciation, by an American-Arab expert in English literature, of all aspects of the East-West relationship, in a work deriving from the authority of the late Foucault, master analyst of the power of words. From Dante's malediction against the Prophet of Islam, through Flaubert, Nerval, Renan and others who have cogitated over the Near East, to Lord Cromer, Britain's implacable Proconsul in Egypt from 1884 to 1907, everything has flowed into a mould of totalitarian language which has congealed into an immutable caricature of the East.[13]

Said's book, a best-seller in the East as well as in the United States, provides a good example of those complicated prisms referred to in the Introduction through which East and West view one another. The complexity reveals itself above all when an Arab in search of an Arab identity speaks from what he believes to be a Western model, but also when a Westerner in search of the exotic speaks from what he takes to be an Eastern model.[14] Irrespective of whether it is an attack from an Occidental standpoint or a defence from an Oriental one, what is inevitably produced is all those exaggerations and abstractions, by-products of intellectual structures held at all levels in a tight vice of ideology. In this respect, the most sophisticated scholarly book may often be no different from the hasty judgement of a journalist conditioned simply by the prejudices of his own environment.

Development and imperialism

For this reason, when we try to account for the weakness of Nasser's achievement, we are as embarrassed as when judging the failure of Muhammand Ali. Moreover, the former seems to have taken up the work of the latter with a perfect parallelism. Their love of dam building, proof of mastery over nature, their fascination with industry and the technical progress that pointed to the future and their attempts to marginalize religion in sociopolitical life opened the way to secularization, so far an indispensable ingredient for the exercise of freedom. In this sense, the two men were both unquestionably in love with the idea of 'development' and were therefore sons of the European Enlightenment who could never have revived the despotic model based on religion which has so often dominated the East, but which for many centuries, it must not be forgotten, was also that of the Christian West. Their work, like that of Mustafa Kemal Atatürk, went much further than the reforms undertaken by the last Ottoman sultans in the nineteenth century. The 1839 Ottoman reform was manifestly a late response to all that Muhammad Ali had already achieved in Egypt, Syria, the Lebanon and Palestine. The reform of 1856, which reaffirmed and enlarged the principles of the first, had been obtained only after strong pressure from the European Powers, anxious about the possible consequences for

European stability of a too-rapid disintegration of the Ottoman Empire.[15] They were never applied with much zeal or fervour.

Muhammad Ali and Nasser, on the contrary, aimed at a complete revolution to lift their country permanently out of its backwardness and underdevelopment, and both committed themselves fully to this task. Both came up against Western nations that had become World Powers prepared to tolerate nothing short of controlling a strategic centre for international communications like the Near East. In neither case is there any need to resort to explanations that blame imperialist conspiracies for their failures, because the facts speak for themselves.

Muhammad Ali was perhaps wiser. With his industrialization uncertain and his armies exhausted, he made the most of a bad situation by withdrawing to Egypt before suffering military catastrophe and, having gained recognition for his dynasty, submitted himself to the will of the big Powers. He allowed his state-owned factories to be dismantled and monoplies and custom controls to be abolished in compliance with the Balta-Liman Treaty imposed in 1838 by England on the Ottoman Empire in order to nullify the first feeble impulse of the Near and Middle East towards industrialization. His descendants, also in search of modernism, were to leave to Europe the task of developing Egypt along colonial lines.

Nasser's heir, Sadat, was to do the same. The 'open door' economic policy, *infitah*, for which he was so reproached by the Egyptian and Arab left, was merely a replica of that of Said Pasha and Khedive Ismail, in which Western capital and technology were welcomed into the country without any restrictions. The resultant racketeering and scandals have been described in meticulous detail by an important historian of the industrial revolution.[16] This description, which could be applied to the Sadat period, also fits the Saudi Arabian monarchy, now sick from a surfeit of oil, as Egypt was from that of cotton in the nineteenth century.

Muhammad Ali was, after all, merely an Albanian officer who succeeded in becoming Pasha and then Viceroy of Egypt. Nasser was an Egyptian, the son of a people humiliated to the full and crushed by poverty. He was the first native Egyptian ruler of a nation that had been farmed out to foreign dynasties for centuries. How could he be wise? Muhammad Ali came to power in an age of conservative regimes: Ottoman, Russian, British and Austro-Hungarian empires, and French and Prussian monarchies. Nasser

lived in a time of republics and revolutionary resistance movements, of the humble who were everywhere challenging the
powerful, of triumphant socialism among the Chinese, Vietnamese and Korean masses in the Far East and in Cuba, only two
hundred kilometres from the American mainland. He became one
of the great driving forces behind those Third-World celebrations
in the form of meetings of non-aligned countries, which began
sedately in Bandung in 1955 and culminated in a gigantic triconti-
nental samba in Cuba in 1966.[17] How could this Egyptian president
have been wise? Was he making history or was he being swept
along by it? Did he really know where he was going, where these
grandiose events were leading him? It seems pretty clear that he
did not.

The anatomy of the Nasser message

Cultural misperception and self-education

Nasser came of that urban petty bourgeoisie of peasant origin so
well depicted in the work of that star of the Egyptian novel,
Neguib Mahfouz.[18] His cultural horizons and social environment
and the general condition of the Egyptian people, divided between
a blatant but at times a very cultured plutocracy, often of Balkan,
Turkish or Circassian descent, and the solid mass of the peasantry
with a thin layer along its fringes of lower middle-class government
employees, all went into the making of this figure seeking to
navigate without compasses in seas neither he nor his advisers
succeeded in charting. Could he have as well chosen a different
entourage and sent back into their barracks those army colleagues,
mostly of his own social background, with whom for a decade he
had shared the dream of regenerating Egypt?

It was General Muhammad Neguib's last-minute decision which
provided cover for those 'free officers' who, in July 1952, without
bloodshed, forced King Farouk into exile, the last descendant of
the Albanian dynasty founded by Muhammad Ali. As a puppet
of the English, Farouk had governed Egypt in scandalous luxury
and unbridled libertinism. Nasser had refused to accept or see any
virtue whatsoever in any member of this mostly landed plutocracy,
despite its culture and experience of power. He rejected it
outright, persecuted and humiliated it. Unlike Sadat, who was
more sensitive to the traditional values of the social hierarchy in

the Egyptian countryside, Nasser personified the defiance of the small people of Cairo who, in their poverty and cultural isolation, hated the splendour and luxury of those well-heeled Pashas, also so much at ease with the colonial rulers with whom they had shared power and wealth.

This was how, after the ousting of the easy-going General Neguib in 1954, it began, that incredible story of love and passion between Nasser and the urban crowds not only of Egypt but of the whole Arab Near East. Despite all the rebuffs the people received during the Nasser era from an untrammelled bureaucracy greedy for power, a magic current always passed between this leader (deep within himself so unstable?) and the millions of Egyptians and Arabs. For President Nasser's speeches were always a marvellous quadrophony, engendering splendid moments of collective emotion when large sections of the Arab nation narcissistically saw his words as coming from themselves.

'Fascism', cried Western observers, for whom the relationship between governors and governed was a serious business that demanded rules and codes. 'Destructive demagoguery', accused the conservative social forces of the Arab world, who thought it highly unwise to fly in the face of a Western power and saw no good in socializing poverty. Nevertheless, although no one denied the fascination that Nasser's speeches held for the masses, few have tried to look beyond the spectacular aspect of this phenomenon, which, to date, is unique in contemporary Arab history.

For Nasserism was neither a political doctrine nor a social philosophy; it was simply the way in which a young and inexperienced Caesar, from a culturally isolated background, did his thinking out loud in the simplest language in front of the crowd and searched for and found at the opportune moment from among the various alternatives the solution to one or other of the thousand problems of underdevelopment, dependence and poverty. The democratic speech counterbalanced a brutally authoritarian practice of power, but it was exactly what all those thousands of listeners would themselves have said had they been in their leader's place, that is to say, in the institutional and cultural void created by centuries of oppression.

Because Nasser would spend hours patiently explaining, his speeches were remarkable for their self-education. He explained the nature of investment, the need to save in order to invest, the divisions of society along social and economic lines, what imperialism was, how it worked, how it infiltrated itself. He explained how to industrialize, how to finance the enormous costs of a high dam; what population increase was and its impact on economic development; what socialism was and the difference between it and communism; what nationalism was; how religion must not be confused with national expression and must not interfere with civil and political life, and so on. It is clear that the Egyptian president had to make an enormous effort to become better informed, to develop his own knowledge and be able to transmit it.

The democracy of language and the secularization of thought

But it was not only the educational content of his speeches that was important. It was also, and perhaps above all, their form. Nasser was actually the first responsible Arab politician to use everyday language, or, more exactly, language midway between the educated rhetoric understood only with difficulty by the illiterate or barely literate crowds and the idiom-packed dialect of the local popular tongue, which is often incomprehensible to non-Egyptian Arabs. By abandoning the pompous, still phrases of literary Arabic, the political leader removed the distance between himself and his audience, lines of communication between them opening up and improvization permitting the tribune to adjust his words better to the emotions aroused in the crowd.

At least on this level, the Nasser inheritance was largely positive. In abandoning a language so lofty in tone that it had remained the monopoly of a small cultivated elite in favour of a more practical and realistic one within the reach of the average person, the Egyptian president confirmed and completed what the Arab press had begun at the end of the last century. Democratic work, no doubt, though in all likelihood not undertaken consciously. Admittedly, certain North African leaders, particularly Bourguiba and Ben Bella, spoke in a popular Arabic, but this was in the dialect of the Maghrib, understood with difficulty in the Near East.

Nasser's speeches could not, however, form the basis of a political creed, which is why Nasserism has failed to survive outside a few Lebanese parties associating themselves with his name. It does indeed personify the continuing, irrepressible desire for political independence, industrialization and improvement in living standards. In this respect it is an exemplar of Third World discourse, of which Nasser, along with Nehru and Tito, was a grand precursor. The philosophical material in Nasser's speeches was, however, too flimsy to constitute a body of doctrine. It consisted of a refusal to choose socialism in its entirety and with all its consequences, of a utopian affirmation in an essentially poor and oppressed environment, of a non-exploitative capitalism confined to small property owners, and of the need of a 'third path' between capitalism and socialism. These were all elements in social and political philosophy which nowadays would make for a brilliant career in the Third World.

But Nasser at least avoided the absurdity of 'cultural revolutions' (not to speak of red, green and blue books) imported from mysterious China, as well as sterile and hallucinatory proclamations of a specifically Arab Islam, or, so much in vogue at the moment, of an Islam sufficient unto itself for the purpose of bringing about the prosperity of all the peoples.

His speeches, which have recently been studied[19] with all the available tools of modern linguistics and content analysis, reveal the remarkably secular structure of his thought, especially when he spoke on religion and the nation, quite contrary to the common image of him in both East and West, in which he tends to be seen either as an unsuccessful Islamic conqueror or, as the addicts of a conspiracy theory of history would have it, manipulated by the all-powerful Soviet Union. Over and above his lengthy economic expositions, one is struck by the frequent use throughout his speeches of the word 'to build' or 'to construct', a natural corollary of secular thought turned towards the future in an optimistic vision of inevitable progress.

Oh beloved West!

In this sense, Nasser was unquestionably not at all a man of the East, confined mystically within a circular vision of history in which divine Providence reigns supreme, but a man of the West. He simply set out to seek in the Slav East what the West was prepared to accord him only grudgingly and in an atmosphere still too heavy with the old paternal colonialism his people no longer tolerated. The West exacted too high a price from him who by rights should have been treated as a favourite son. He paid the price, but it hurt him and the Egyptian people deeply. It is not so difficult to understand why he was so deeply mourned, and yet that same people became delirious with joy when Sadat achieved what his predecessor had failed to accomplish, the accolade with the West, so visible, a symbol of progress and prosperity for these impoverished but proud people.

The extraordinary visit to Jerusalem in November 1977, so clearly approved of at popular level, can only be explained in this context. The Suez Canal having been successfully crossed by the Egyptian army during the October 1973 war, honour was saved. Morever, from 1975 the Canal was to be reopened to international shipping. In the meantime, the price of oil, life-blood of industrialized countries, had quadrupled. Future wealth assured and humiliation forgotten, the Arabs believed that they could rediscover the West. Anwar Sadat, Nasser's heir, would be the man for this rediscovery. He displayed the same panache and went to the same extremes as his predecessor, who, by snubbing the capitalist West, had thrown Egypt, and with it a good portion of the Arab Near East, into the arms of the opposing socialist West.

In this respect, the two men were as alike as twins, Nasser going to extremes in setting up a bureaucratic and corrupt form of socialism, and Sadat by opening Egypt up to a savage, racketeering and no less corrupting form of capitalism. But both policies revealed the same phenomenon: the immense anguish of two men, both sons of the people, confronted with their country's poverty and humiliation, but also with the historic opportunity a ruler cannot afford to miss. Aristocracy or upper middle classes rarely suffer such anguish and if they do possess an organized language through which to channel expression and harness emotion.

The death of Nasser does indeed mark the end of an epoch, but not of the tragedy. The charismatic leader gone, the Arab Near East actually rapidly changed its political stance. Governed on the Left during the Nasser period, it imperceptibly but surely moved to the Right in the 1970s. Flamboyant anti-imperialism and passionate socialist, secular modernism were replaced by open or disguised pro-Western policies, religious fundamentalism and the speculative killings to be made out of a huge and sudden oil wealth. But the basic tragedy did not change: outside a narrow circle of oil dividends, mass poverty and the humiliation of the Arab world's weakness and fragmentation continued in the face of the geopolitics of powerful nations, which remained sublimely indifferent to the legitimate historical and economic demands of the Arabs, particularly in regard to the Palestinian cause and to the orderly control of their own natural resources.

This political swing becomes the more difficult to define as one leaves Egypt, land of cohesion and continuity in the Arab Near East and enters a world of the opposite, those regions of schismatic ruptures and of resulting political-religious dissimulations that no conqueror or religion or civilization could ever assimilate on a long-term basis, despite the indelible imprints each has left. Governed successively in antiquity by Babylonians, Egyptians, Assyrians, Persians, Greeks and Romans, and in the Christian era subjected to Byzantium, Persia and then to the various Islamic empires, the people of the Near East, and to a large extent also those of the Arab Middle East, have never abandoned their religious and tribal diversity, of which the Old Testament, like the Koran, gives us a thousand eloquent testimonies.

In certain cases this diversity was complicated by an ethnic diversity which foreign conquerors introduced into the area and which the dismemberment of the Ottoman Empire accentuated. Its most visible manifestation is found in the plurality of Eastern Christian Churches that had broken away from Byzantine christological dogma and in the numerous Islamic sects, either schismatic like the various Shia sects or a more complete esoteric break with Islamic doctrine, like the Druze, Alawis and Yazidis. Added to these are contrasts between urban and peasant attitudes, between people of the mountains and those of the plains, between the nomadic and the settled, as well as memories of a tribal past, however distant, still alive among the settled people.[20]

In this complex and unsettled society, already so rich in centrifugal forces, modern ideology in its different varieties and notably nationalism and Marxism became an additional source of diversity. Its politics consequently seem absurdly complex to the observer accustomed to coherent national entities articulated in familiar social groups and developing in an ideological world of definite rules. This also explains why the political swing of the Arab Near East away from anti-imperialist, pro-socialist attitudes and behaviour towards positions more conciliatory, if not openly favourable, to the Western capitalist world (so clearly visible in the case of Egypt) remains subtly obscure for the rest of the Near East. The events in Lebanon in 1975–6 provide a good example of this. But even beyond the variety of events, whether it is the radical revolutionary aspirations of certain Palestinian or

Lebanese movements, or the powerful conservatism of the oil monarchies so extraordinarily influential in the region, all combines to increase the socio-political chiaroscuro.

2 From the Khartoum summit to the October War: 1967–73

'Sadatism' or the polarization of contradictions

Historical periods, like social structures, overlap, never ending abruptly and never letting it be sure that their end is final. It takes centuries to make such judgements; modernity is thus never acquired permanently. Hence the difficulty of analyzing a historical period that only adds up to a few decades, and likewise the unpredictability of events occurring at the points of contacts of epochs and cultural currents and the opacity they present to interpretation.

Sadat and Nasser symbolize two epochs in which elements of continuity offset those of sudden change. Examples of the latter are found in the outer manifestations of the two men's personalities and thus of the two epochs they personified; the former, however, are more hidden and more difficult to discern with, as it were, the naked eye. President Sadat himself actually embodied the contradictions of this chaotic Near East, both contributing to their exacerbation and ending as their victim. His epoch, however, is not yet closed, and events today are as unpredictable as ever. It should perhaps be regarded more as an interlude, as a theatrical intermission during which the controversial producer disappears and the scene-shifting takes place amid total confusion.

'Sadatism' was not a 'doctrine', as an internationally reputed Egyptian Marxist thinker for a long time claimed in a weekly column in *Al-Ahram*, Egypt's most prestigious daily newspaper.[1] Sadat also entrusted several Marxists with important posts and sometimes ministerial portfolios, a gesture inconceivable in the Nasser period. At the same time, a pious man who in his youth had been an admirer of the Muslim Brotherhood and a friend of its great figure Hasan al-Banna, he allowed this Brotherhood, decimated by Nasser, to reconstitute itself. He also wanted to Islamize Egyptian legislation, thereby undoing the secular work of all his predecessors since Muhammed Ali, while at the same time advocating a return to liberal democracy, civil liberties and a multi-party political system.[2]

How could this advocate of total ecumenicalism between the three great monotheistic religions have allowed to blow up under his rule, among his own people, the bloodiest clashes in centuries between Copts[3] and Muslims. How could he pray under Israeli flags at the al-Aksa mosque in Jerusalem, Islam's third most holy place, while debarred from going to Mecca, its most holy place in the heart of Arabia? How did this leader of Egypt, the centre of the Arab world and headquarters of the Arab League, this inheritor of non-alignment, which Nasser, through force of circumstance, had created on the Left, manage to cut himself off from almost all the Arab countries to cultivate a simple-minded anti-Sovietism and to allow the United States to undertake military manoeuvres in Egypt? How could this man of modest social origins, whose name was associated with all the socialist measures of Nasser's Egypt, promote his country's return to the international circuit of parasitic racketeering of such unhappy memory in Egypt's history, which in a few years called in question the social changes Nasser had brought about for a fairer distribution of the national income? Was it just political clumsiness? Clearly not, for the man had shown himself to be as astute a political animal and as passionate about Egypt's glory as his predecessor had been; like Nasser, he had made the most extravagant gestures on its behalf, though also the most dangerous, and had likewise sought a radical solution to underdevelopment and poverty.

Like Nasser, however, Sadat functioned by intuition. The former had felt the wind of Third World rebellion and had done a great deal to increase it; he had foreseen the advantages of the cold war between the USSR and the United States; and had thrilled to the gallantry of a socialism idealized and so far unsullied and unassailable. He made it his setting and kept unchanged, although towards the end of his life, when he agreed to discuss American initiatives for settling the Arab–Israeli conflict, he realized, too late that an epoch had passed. Sadat, on the other hand, understood that socialism was no longer in fashion, which did not displease the rather conservative temperament of this son of a peasant; that the exigencies of a peaceful coexistence no longer allowed him to take more from the Russians than they had already given the Arabs in terms of armaments and political support; that

Islamic ideology, having been chloroformed for half a century by secularism and nationalist fervour as much as by the hopes of modernity embodied in the great works of development was recovering its senses; and that a double monarchistic/republican impetus, from the new oil and financial power of the kingdom of Saudi Arabia and from the young Arab Republic of Libya, had given this ideology a powerful means of expansion. This double Islam, conservative and puritan on the one hand, revolutionary and Leftist on the other, but on the whole fundamentalist and therefore eminently political, could not but suit this man, who loved his rural roots and whose faith was therefore characterized by regular manifestations of piety; and could not but fascinate this devout Muslim who was nevertheless an admirer of the Christian West and who risked everything to make peace with a Jewish State that had so often inflicted humiliation on the Arabs.

Sadat unquestionably carried within himself all the contradictions of the two epochs which telescoped into each other and which he himself experienced intensely. Just as Nasser was for the preceding period, he was a key figure, an accelerator of events, for that central interlude in the destiny of the contemporary Near East through which we are still living. But history does not like being hurried, as it has shown so many times by those terrible reactions which invariably follow turbulent periods of rapid change. At its deepest level, a society never totally accepts change, whatever the momentum imparted in any period either by the pressure of a foreign culture, or by the dynamism of its own elites or by the combined action of both. Neither does it accept the natural passage of time, which tarnishes the brilliance of its great historical rhythms. The histories of Europe, China, India and Japan offer a thousand examples of this; the Near East, that other great zone of civilization, is no exception to the rule.

So far we have been occupied with Egypt, pivot of the region by virtue of its thousand years of human, geographical and historical cohesion. Thanks to this cohesion, in recent times it has produced leaders far surpassing in stature the sovereigns, kings, princes, Heads of State and party leaders of the rest of the Near East. In contemporary history only Mustafa Kemal, the Turk, and Boumedienne, the Algerian, have made as much of a mark, but neither belongs directly to the Arab Near East.

The spectacular nature of Sadat's gestures and his tragic end at least provide good illustrations of the fundamental change undergone by the Arab Near East between the mid-sixties and the mid-seventies. The region which under the Nasser influence seemed in 1966 a great zone of economic progress, progressivist revolution, modernism and anti-colonialism, became in less than a decade a land of tensions, contradictions, terrorism, religious fundamentalism, extreme wealth and appalling poverty. The misfortunes of the Lebanon and the perpetual wanderings of the Palestinian nationalists in search of a State are sufficient to prove this point.

To render these dramatic changes fully intelligible we must take into account the emergence of the Arab oil world, already beginning to take shape in the mid-1960s and to move to the forefront of the Near Eastern stage. The centre of this oil world lies among the Wahhabis, the puritanical Bedouins who have not only become the wardens of Mecca, in the heart of Islam, but also the depository of the industrial West's life-blood, for without its oil Europe would collapse. We arrived at a new and difficult meeting point between East and West, to be discussed later in Chapter 3. To establish the main theme of those changes, it is necessary to return to the bitter defeat of 1967 the Arab armies suffered at the hands of Israel.

The Khartoum summit *impasse*

Yes to the West, no to Israel
The defeat of 1967 was not only of Arabs against Israel. It also marked the collapse of the Arab Left *vis-à-vis* the conservative forces, that is to say essentially of the Arab nationalist, socialist, populist and Third Worldist Egypt of Nasser *vis-à-vis* the Pan-Islamic, pro-Western and conservative Saudi monarchy. This now forgotten aspect of the events of 1967 is at least as important as Israel's occupation of new territories. It manifested itself in Khartoum at the end of August 1967 at the fourth summit of Arab Heads of State since 1964, when, in evaluating the effects of his defeat on inter-Arab relations, Nasser let Saudi Arabia's pro-Western arguments triumph over those of the 'hard-liners' of the Left, extremely hostile to the imperialism of the big industrialized capitalist countries.

The hard-liners were Syria, at the time under a Leftist leadership, to which we shall return later, and Algeria, which from its own experience saw no reason why a cease-fire had been accepted and a people's war not launched against the Israeli enemy. Syria boycotted the summit completely, which Algeria abstained from attending. The Palestine Liberation Organization (PLO) followed the hard line but could not afford to stay away from or boycott this important meeting. It was in Khartoum that the Arab countries in fact capitulated, not to Israel waiting impatiently since 9 June for the conquered and humiliated Arabs to come and propose peace, but to the Western countries. For if the battle against Israel had been lost, the war against the Western powers, which had over-armed that neo-Spartan republic, had not yet begun, and in this war oil, the most formidable of weapons, was in the hands of the Arabs. But the Arab oil-exporting countries, headed by Saudi Arabia, would not hear of interrupting oil supplies to the West for such an act could constitute a *casus belli* to which they feared to expose themselves. Apart from the 'socialist' republic of Iraq, these countries were monarchies or ultra-conservative emirates that feared the Soviet Union like the devil; all those years they had been subjected to Nasser's snubs, which, furthermore, had enabled the Soviet Union to establish itself solidly in the Arab world. However militant in other respects, Algeria was also none too enthusiastic about stopping oil exports, for it was embarking on an intensive industrialization programme for which all its resources needed to be mobilized.

The Arab Heads of State meeting in Khartoum thus decided that oil would not be used as a direct weapon against the Western Powers protecting Israel;[4] the latter could thenceforth with complete peace of mind let the Jewish republic keep its conquests. In Khartoum, the Arabs therefore deprived themselves of the only weapon that could oblige the West to force Israel to withdraw from the occupied territories. Captured by the attractions of peaceful coexistence, which offered substantial economic advantages, the Soviet Union was more wary than it had been during the Suez expedition of 1956 of playing the role of dispenser of justice to the oppressed people. Alexei Kosygin, head of the Soviet government, met the American President Lyndon Johnson on 23 June 1967 at Glassborough in the United States only a few days after the humiliating defeat of the Soviet Union's Arab friends, Egypt and Syria. Although it had been their sole provider of arms, the Soviet Union did not let its own indirect defeat affect the summit, which seems to have taken place in a very amicable atmosphere.

Certainly, Khartoum gave consecration to the refusal to have anything to do with Israel, since the Arab countries undertook not to sign an armistice, nor to recognize or engage in peace negotiations with Israel. On the other hand, the tacit recognition that the Western powers dominated the Arab world was, to a similar extent, total at Khartoum. Giving up the only weapon, namely oil, with which the Arabs could pressurize the West into forcing Israel to evacuate the occupied territories, in effect contributed towards confirming the occupation. The summit thus created a deadlock fraught with consequence, the lessons of which President Sadat fully learnt, firstly by getting rid of the Soviets and totally integrating Egypt into a network of American interests and then by going directly to the Israelis for talks. The Khartoum equation of yes to the West, no to Israel was untenable, as all subsequent events in the Near East were to demonstate.

Oil, a social security system and not a weapon

Meanwhile, the Khartoum summit had established the total victory of the Arab 'moderates', led by Saudi Arabia, Morocco and Tunisia, against the 'extremists', essentially Syria and to a lesser extent Algeria, the PLO and Iraq, the future 'Rejection Front', especially when Sadat signed the peace treaty with the Israeli enemy in 1978. From then on, the Saudi monarchy and the oil sheikdoms headed by Kuwait became the true arbiters of the Arab situation. A remarkable fact about the way things developed was that two conservative oil monarchies, Saudi Arabia and (pre-Gadaffi) Libya, as well as one emirate, Kuwait, would in future pay regular subsidies to the victims of the confrontation, i.e. those countries with territories occupied by Israel. Using oil revenues to finance reconstruction of the economic and military potential of the Arab countries attacked by the Israelis, namely Egypt, Syria and Jordan, could be interpreted as 'positive' utilization of the oil weapon.

Such generosity obviously had a price. In Khartoum President Nasser signed an agreement with King Faisal of Saudi Arabia engaging himself to withdraw Egyptian forces from the Yemen, where they had been bogged down ever since an obscurantist monarchy had been toppled by a republican *coup d'état* in 1962. The Egyptian intervention in this case had contributed towards generalizing a civil war in which Egyptians and Saudis were really fighting through Yemenite proxies to dominate the Arabian Peninsula. The retreat from the Yemen was in fact the *coup de grâce* to Nasserite Jacobinism. In future the only opponents of the all-powerful, conservative, pro-Western Islam of the Saudi Arabian Wahabis, would be the revolutionary romanticism of certain Palestinian Resistance movements and Syrian 'Leftism', which had been brought to heel in 1970 by General Hafez al-Assad's celebrated *coup d'état*. Algeria remained a hard-liner but was too far away to exercise any direct influence over the Near East. As for Iraq, as we shall see, it had enough on its plate what with Kurds and Iranians, to make its 'rejection' anything more than a point of principle. Whatever any rejection may have signified, thanks to a fabulous increase in oil revenues, this whole world was to fling itself headlong, in the 1970s, into an indiscriminate modernization in which the most favoured partner was as always the West, through the big multinationals.[5]

Moreover, the Khartoum summit had also laid the foundations for a sort of system of 'social security', based on subsidies from the oil-rich to the 'confrontation' countries, this representing a first step towards Arab economic solidarity, which gained special momentum after the four-fold increase in oil prices in 1973. In fact it was there that the decision was taken to create an Arab Economic and Social Development Fund, although it actually materialized only in 1973. Arab economic solidarity is, moreover, a formidable weapon in the hands of the oil-rich countries, for it is they that largely finance the institutions that give it concrete form. Nevertheless, the benefiting countries become accustomed to living off subsidies and to a style of life not usually justified by the inadequate efforts of their own internal development.

All this somewhat anticipates subsequent developments, but for these to be fully intelligible it requires a clear understanding of the Khartoum summit, which marked an important turning point in Arab Near Eastern history. It was, in fact, in Khartoum that the actual repercussions of the Arab–Israeli conflict and of the June 1967 defeat became clear. It was here that Nasser finally abandoned the Arab revolutionary and the nationalist strength that he had till then symbolized for the purpose of making peace with his former enemies, notably the Saudi monarchy and the other moderate countries. While the Israelis were waiting in Jerusalem for the Arab contingent to come and sign a peace treaty, it was made in Khartoum without them. But the Israelis very quickly got into the act, consolidating their occupation by annexing Jerusalem and colonizing Sinai, the Golan Heights and the West Bank of Jordan.

The Egyptian President had hardly any alternative. With the Suez Canal, the big earner of foreign exchange, henceforth closed and his army's military equipment, particularly aircraft and armour, largely destroyed, his power could not have survived without financial support. Furthermore, the situation at the domestic level was even worse. The army command, headed by Field-Marshal Amer, great satrap of the regime, was in almost open rebellion. Nasser just managed to restore the situation by arresting the Field-Marshal and his principal acolytes. The day after the Khartoum summit ended, Field-Marshal Amer committed suicide, the final scene of an antique tragedy, for Nasser and Amer had always been companions and had joined not only their political destinies but also their families.

It was thus really a reprieve, in the context of a withdrawal into what by force of circumstances had become exclusively Egyptian interests, that President Nasser obtained at Khartoum, as much to consolidate his regime at the domestic level as to rebuild his army. This enabled him to launch a 'war of attrition' along the cease-fire lines on the Suez Canal which restored his reputation but had a devastating effect on the Egyptian economy, because of the extent of Israeli reprisals. In addition, the Soviet military became increasingly involved in the Egyptian defence system, for, cut to the quick by the traumatic experience of 1967 when tons of Russian military equipment fell into Israeli hands, they insisted on retaining exclusive handling of sophisticated equipment. At the political level, however, the Soviet Union, then in full peaceful coexistence with the United States, agreed not to go beyond verbal support for the Arab cause and supply of only defensive military equipment. It was again a deadlock that led President Nasser in 1970 to end the war of attrition and to accept an American peace initiative.

This was a far cry from the situation in 1956 when the cold war atmosphere and the resolute intervention of the American President, General Dwight Eisenhower, turned the easy military victory of the combined forces of Israel, France and England against an under-equipped Egyptian army into a political defeat. In reality, the victory had been that of Egypt, which, only three months after the aggression it had experienced had obtained evacuation of all the occupied territories. In the case of the 1967 aggression, this time solely the act of Israel, the defeat was as much political as military inasmuch as despite their policy favouring Western interests, and despite the Soviet Union's automatic support of the Arab position, the three countries whose territories were occupied failed to obtain Israeli withdrawal. Even the Hashemite Kingdom of Jordan, pillar of Western influence in the Near East, failed to get proper negotiations under way to retrieve the West Bank, a chunk of Palestine that had escaped Israeli occupation in 1948 when the Hebrew State was founded and which Jordan had since administered until the Israelis occupied it in 1967.

At this level also, the Khartoum summit clearly confirmed the Arab defeat, and as far as the Palestinian struggle was concerned engaged the Near East in complete deadlock. It is to the credit of President Sadat that he broke the deadlock by triggering off the October 1973 war and then by the visit to Jerusalem and the Camp David peace negotiations. In the aftermath of the Khartoum summit, with all its implications, Sadat did not really have much choice. Having engaged in a gallant last-ditch stand against Israel, he could not allow himself the luxury of turning his back on the impossible equation of 'yes to the West *and* yes to Israel'. Having done this, he was forced out of the oil-financed 'social security' system initiated in Khartoum, for a summit of Arab Heads of State held in Baghadad in 1978 declared him an outlaw in the Arab world.[6]

An ambiguous alternative: Leftism

But if Khartoum was so negative in result, was it not perhaps contrary to all that has been said, that other alternatives existed? Those Left-wing Syrians unwilling to tarnish their revolutionary purity by attending the Khartoum summit, were they not right? Did those Palestinian Liberation Fronts advocating all-out people's war, and which made Jordan a field of spectacular experiment before being wiped out by King Hussein's troops in 1970, not have a valid alternative? At this point it is necessary to recall the quarrel and the debate for a long time of central concern to the Arabs, both intellectually and politically, that were settled by force during the 1970s, first in Jordan and then in Lebanon, two States of particularly vulnerable structure.

To set this quarrel in its historical context, we must look

outwards into the rest of the world. Internationally the years between 1965 and 1970 were, in effect, a time of great revolutionary excitement. The Chinese Cultural Revolution glowed with all its fire. Vietnamese resistance to the enormous American war machine flaunted a heroism which fascinated the masses in the great capitals of the Western world. In Latin America, Che Guevara had left Cuba to prepare the way for popular guerrilla warfare in the jungles of Bolivia, where he was killed at the end of 1967. In Paris there occurred the unprecedented spectacle of May 1968. In Czechoslovakia, in this same year, it was the Prague Spring. In 1970, in Chile, there was the epic of Salvador Allende and Popular Unity. In short, with all its ups and downs, the end of the sixties saw a strong wind of libertarian activity blowing through four continents and everywhere challenging the established order.

Far away from the compromises of Khartoum, many in the Arab world lived for such moments of ultra-Left elation. The traditional forces of the Left, that is to say essentially the parties claiming to go back to the spirit of Nasser and the communist parties, were from now on considered as 'petit-bourgeois', 'revisionist' and having sold out to the Soviet 'State bourgeoisie', that sacrificed revolutionary cause of the world's peoples, in favour of peaceful coexistence with the imperialist super-Power, the United States. All over the Arab world dissidents within the communist parties began to look to the Chinese model of popular liberation warfare. A spate of divisions occurred in the Palestinian movements, creating numerous factions each claiming to be more Left-wing than the other. The more Right-wing nationalist parties were also attacked by the Left-wing virus and emotionally discovered the Marxist gospel.

It is true that these extreme-felt conversions cannot be seen exlusively as the instant fruits of an international ideological craze. Even outside the relatively limited intellectual circles of the communist parties, Marxist ideas had in fact enjoyed a certain revival since the beginning of the decade. This began with the Iraqi revolution of 1958 which brought General Kassem to power. Until his downfall in 1963, he relied increasingly on a particularly active communist party which underwent a remarkable expansion during his rule. The revival continued with the radicalization of the Nasser regime in Egypt, following the break in Egyptian-Syrian unity in 1961. This break was accentuated by the war in the Yemen, which, as we have already indicated, set Third World socialistic Pan-Arabism against Saudi Arabia, the leader of the pro-Western Islamic style of Arab conservatism. Finally, Algerian independence proved the success of guerrilla war against a regular army, while the self-management socialist populism of the Algerian government also favoured integrating a Marxist vocabulary into the prevailing ideology.

It was, in fact, the military defeat of 1967 and the international context in which it occurred that caused the Palestinian political parties to take a double ideological leap, firstly from nationalism, tinged with socialist tendencies, to classical Marxism; and then straight afterwards from classical Marxism towards the different variants of ultra-Left Marxism that reviled the Soviet Union and the 'petit-bourgeois' Arab regimes allied to it and blamed the USSR for the crushing defeat by the Israeli enemy. Emphasizing the international context of these accelerated ideological swings were the close ties established between some of the Palestinian resistance movements and South-East Asian liberation movements (especially in Vietnam), and also those in Latin America and Iran. But even more important were the ties with ultra-Left revolutionary movements in the industrialized countries, the Red Brigades, the Bader-Meinhof group and the Japanese Red Army, which even carried out a suicide commando operation on the Israeli airfield of Lod.[7] We find here a new kind of encounter between East and West, in which common frustrations are expressed through violent action against all the symbols of the established order. Even in Iraq at the beginning of the seventies a dissident communist group went underground in the south of the country in the hopes of organizing a popular uprising. The experiment failed almost from the start.

This wave of Leftism reached its highest point in Jordan, when, during the summer of 1970, the Popular Front for the Liberation of Palestine declared that certain parts of the Kingdom of Jordan controlled by their guerrillas were 'liberated zones', and then proceeded to hijack four aircraft belonging to international airlines. Abu Iyad, second-in-command of the normally moderate organization al-Fatah, announced that the Jordanian capital Amman was to be transformed into the 'Hanoi of the Palestinian revolution'. That was the last straw. There follow the famous 'Black September' when the entire military apparatus of the Palestinian resistance was driven out of Jordan by the regular

Jordanian troops only to reconstitute itself in Lebanon, where Arab ultra-Leftism continued its career from 1975 in a bizarre alliance with Islamic conservatism. This foreshadowed the alliance between the Iranian Marxist Left and the Islamic clergy which toppled the powerful Pahlavi throne in 1979 despite having had its progress blocked in 1976 by the Syrian regular army.

Syria: the enfant terrible of the Near East

At this stage we must go back a little, to the role of Syria, the *enfant terrible* of the Near East. Since 1949, when the first military *coup de'état* took place, it was the cradle of the Party for Arab Revival (al-Baath), which in all likelihood holds the record for internal factions, purges and secessions out of which new ruling organs emerge to claim true legitimacy.

As already mentioned, we are now in a country of schisms. The great christological quarrels marking the consolidation of Byzantine orthodoxy were fought out in these lands, whose mountains, some centuries later, would provide shelter for all the Islamic sects rejecting the dominant Sunni orthodoxy.[8] Paradoxically, Damascus was also the capital of the first great Arab empire, that of the Umayyads, in the seventh and eighth centuries. The Syrians of the twentieth century have never forgotten this, and, true to the prestige of their past grandeur, were the foremost in calling for that Arab unity which turned, in the doctrine of the Baath, into a sort of mysticism. The period under consideration here, the years between 1965 and 1970 were equally heavily laden with ultra-Leftism. At all events the group of officers controlling the ruling Baath party under the aegis of General Salah Jahid was very sensitive to 'People's war' rhetoric and to the 'rallying of revolutionary popular forces' in the Arab world. It is also true that in the government were three civilian doctors[9] who had belonged to a medical mission to the NLF in Algeria.

Shortly before the outbreak of the June 1967 war, the Syrian Baath set up the 'Saika' movement, a military wing of 'the avant-garde of the war of popular liberation', an organization regrouping the Palestinian cadres of the party. It was the operations of these guerrillas that had caused a dangerous mounting of tension with Israel in the spring of 1967. Subsequently, Saika was to play a more important role in the PLO, where it continued to represent the interests of the Syrian State. Its participation in the events of

Lebanon was continuous. Its dreaded leader, Zuhair Muhsin, ended up by being assassinated in 1980 in Cannes on the French Riviera, which says much about the limits of revolutionary romanticism as practised by State apparatuses or their by-products.

Unity of popular forces against the petit-bourgeois regimes responsible for the defeat of 1967, and wars of popular liberation by partisan armies in the style of Che Guevara, the Vietcong, and the peasants of the NLF, rather than regular armies which ended up corrupted by the exercise of power – this, in substance, was the message Arab ultra-Leftism put across during the years of decline of the Arab nationalist movement precipitated by the defeat of 1967. Let us not judge too quickly a movement which, by definition, was ambiguous, but which amongst the Arabs, as elsewhere, brought together the son of an upper middle-class family, the frustrated intellectual, and the son of peasant or worker who dreamed of social justice after centuries of being trampled on. That this ultra-Leftism included a number of minorities, as did the orthodox Marxist movements, should not in reality change our appreciation of these currents, for the dream of brotherhood and ideological consensus still remains highly respectable. Yet this change of appreciation occurs among many Western observers, who see the presence of numerous Christians, Shias, Ismailis, Alawis, Druzes and Kurds in the leadership of these movements as proof of their social marginality and thus of non-representativeness – an opinion furthermore shared by many conservative Arabs and notably the sympathizers of fundamentalist Islamic movements. Arab conservative forces, particularly the Saudi monarchy, have never missed an opportunity to attack these movements because their leaders belong to Christian or non-orthodox Islamic sects.[10]

Events in the Near East since the beginning of the 1970s can only be fully understood if the analysis takes account of the constant efforts by conservative and pro-Western forces in the region to put an end to this dangerous marginality. The Khartoum summit had already rescued the Nasser regime which in its fervour had dragged the Arab world to the Left. In its obsession to be still further Left than Nasser, from 1965–6 onwards the Syrian Baath government opened the way to ultra-Leftism, which explains its absence from Khartoum. Some years later, however (in 1976), it would be at the Riyadh and Cairo summits, which looked for ways of ending the Lebanese conflict, in which the extreme Right and the extreme Left of the Arab world had been fighting each other savagely for seventeen months through Lebanese and Palestinian intermediaries.

The ambiguities of Arab unity

The significance of a certain type of Arab ultra-Leftism should not, however, be exaggerated. Apart from the Palestinian experiment in Jordan, and the running sore of Lebanon, it remained more of an ideological fashion among Arab regimes, used more for strengthening themselves amid their local populations and in relation to sister countries than a reality lived in depth. In the case of Syria and Iraq during the 1960s, it was an ideology which, under the label of popular struggle, could legitimize creating civilian armed militias that could come to the help of the Baath party if it came to be threatened or insufficiently backed up by the regular army. For these two countries especially it was an effective means of combating the uncomfortable memory of Nasser's attempt at unity with Syria from 1958 to 1961, which ended in a break that left the whole Arab world bitter. Thus, the mid-1960s saw an absurd situation in which the pro-Nasser forces in Syria and Iraq were generally thought of as Right-wing conservative, whereas the Baath elements were seen as the harbingers/standard-bearers of social radicalization. In these two countries, in fact, in an attempt to counteract the increase of Marxist or ultra-left radicalism, many conservatives came to embrace Nasserism, and particularly the representatives of traditional religious forces who feared the secularism of social radicalism and the atheism of all Marxist-inspired doctrine; of the same opinion were bourgeois elements in commerce and industry who feared the tendency towards nationalization and expropriation of property by a socialist government.

Nasserism thus served to bring together the forces of the Right in their silent struggle to oppose the communist parties and the more radical tendencies at play in the Baath party. This paradoxical situation provided Egypt with a means of perpetuating its influence, seriously weakened by the breakdown of Arab unity. Local forces opposed to the Baath party's absolute power and to the development of communist parties found indispensable respectability under the Nasser umbrella. As a support to this analysis, observers could not fail to notice that even within the Baath party, the Right was far less anti-Nasserist than the Left.

An ultra-Leftism in the service of parties which had themselves obtained control of the State machinery was thus not the only paradox apparent in this situation. There was also the paradox of an ideology of Arab unity of the extreme Left, which dominated both the party and the State apparatus, but which was used to promote a policy that worked against Arab unity. Hence the failure of fresh attempts at unity, such as the stillborn federation between Egypt, Iraq and Syria in the spring of 1963 or the later one between Egypt, Syria and Libya in April 1971. Hence also that implacable rivalry between Iraq and Syria which began in 1968 when the Iraqi Baathists recaptured power from a team of moderate unionists whom they had overthrown at the end of 1963.[11] The Iraqi Baathists, who claimed pan-Arab legitimacy, were represented by a team of civilians that had been thrown out of the party in Syria in 1966 and had found refuge in Iraq under the leadership of the party's founder, Michel Aflaq. This was an intolerable situation involving two 'brother enemies' grafted onto a dispute of considerable historical significance, Baghdad having been the seat of the Abbasids who had contributed to the downfall of the Umayyads of Damascus. This situation was additionally intolerable because nobody could distinguish between schism and orthodoxy any longer.

It is necessary here to recognize that as soon as the ideology or Arab unity became incorporated into political practice, it began to show its limitations. It was not easy for these young States, heirs to old civilizations, whose sovereignties had only recently been established in the international order, to abandon such a privilege, all the more precious after centuries of foreign domination. The experience of the short-lived Syrian-Egyptian union between 1958 and 1961 was traumatic for everybody. The cumbersome Egyptian bureaucracy had heavy-handedly tried to turn Syria into a province of Egypt under a United Arab Republic (UAR). But the Baath party was no cleverer in supporting the Syrian secession, mainly the work of conservative forces. Hence the exchange of facile accusations between Egypt and the Baath parties in Syria and Iraq, complicated by those that developed between the Left and the Right of the Baath party itself, the former accusing the latter of being responsible for the secession. The picture becomes even more complex when one learns that in

Syria the party's Right was composed mainly of urban civilians and its Left of those whose social origins were in the poorer peasantry; that between 1963 and 1966 these soldiers came to manipulate the party increasingly and that ever since the party had exercised almost exclusive control over the State.

In Iraq, while the civilian wing of the party, with the help of sympathetic army officers, was busy taking power in 1963, then losing it again a few months later only to get it back again in 1968, the internal struggles all revolved around two themes: unity with Egypt and internal social and economic radicalizations. The unionists were rather conservative and the radicals rather anti-union. As a backdrop to the scene, the Nasserite propaganda of the 'Voice of the Arabs' came over the powerful transmitting station broadcasting unitarian, radical and anti-Baath propaganda from Cairo. The survival of the government depended on avoiding the kind of ultra-Leftism that advocated unity of popular forces against the State apparatuses in the hands of 'reactionaries' and a kind of evolutionary socialization of the economy which would allow the people to appropriate its wealth. Thus, after 1961, Nasser's unitarian orthodoxy was continually challenged from the Right by Arab monarchies promoting Islam and on the Left by republics claiming to be popular but run by armies jealously guarding the new-found sovereignty of the States they had just inherited.

Egypt was powerless to avoid a repetition of what had already happened at the beginning of the Christian era, namely a continual outbreak of schisms in the Near Eastern and Middle Eastern provinces of the Arab Byzantium of the century. It was the same for North Africa, where the Moroccan monarchy, the People's Algerian Republic and the Tunisian Republic held very specific conceptions of Arab unity. Only Gadaffi later on wanted to be the synthesis between orthodoxy and the schisms, which made him not only pro-Nasser, and therefore in favour of Arab unity, but also ultra-Leftist and pan-Islamic.

In practice, the Arab Heads of State summits, inagurated in 1964 in an atmosphere of extreme cold war hostility between Arab regimes, undoubtedly set out to achieve minimal agreement, so as not to allow exceedingly explosive situations to degenerate to the extent of the initiative's passing from the hands of the leaders into those of the 'popular' forces, which would become uncontrollable. In the 1960s, in fact, the masses in the Arab metropolitan areas, roused by the official mass media and by the wide availability of the transistor radio, were highly politicized. This was seen in 1967 when Nasser offered and then withdrew his resignation, and again in 1970 when he died.

During the 1960s Arab military rulers had already become very touchy about matters concerning sovereignty, and increasingly so as they consolidated their power over the State. This is why, when it comes to it, Arab ultra-Leftism, which was in fact mainly Palestinian and Lebanese, had never really thrived in Egypt, Iraq and Syria. It was to be tried out only in Jordan and the Lebanon, the very countries where the military did not rule and where traditions of State control were weakest. The Palestinian movements were perhaps so pronouncedly ultra-Leftist because they did not possess a State. In any case, in Syria, Egypt and Iraq, and even in Algeria and Libya, Palestinian guerrillas could never mingle with the population, carry arms or play a direct political role as they did in Lebanon and in Jordan. Furthermore, at the time of the 'Black September' confrontations in Jordan between King Hussein's army and the Palestinian resistance movements, the Iraqi battalions, present on Jordanian soil to support the Kingdom in its confrontation with Israel, did not fire a single shot in aid of the Palestinians, in spite of their being so admired as the 'spearhead' and 'vanguard' of Arab revolutionary forces. Some Syrian tanks did cross the Jordanian frontier but had to pull back quickly in the absence of the air cover refused them by General Hafez al Assad, Minister of Defence and former air force boss, Some months later he removed the ultra-Left team from power once and for all, to the great relief of the other Arab States.

An aborted controversy: an army of partisans or regular armies?

The Arab States (with the probable exception of Algeria) have never believed that Palestine could be liberated by a people's war. After the 1967 defeat, Nasser's confidant and official spokesman, Hassanein Heikal, one of the leading figures of the Arab press, devoted numerous editorials in the big Cairo daily *al-Ahram* to demonstrating the futility of the Vietnamese model for the Arab—Israeli conflict. The Middle East does not have protective jungle, said Heikal, but deserts where units of partisans could find no refuge and would immediately be discovered by the enemy air force. Only properly equipped, regular armies with sophisticated military technology, affirmed Heikal, could confront the Israeli army, the superiority of which results from effective use of the most modern military technologies. The Polisario[12] invalidated this far too facile and utterly superficial reasoning with great panache some years later by successfully conducting heavy guerrilla action against the regular Moroccan army right in the middle of the Western Sahara. Before dying out under the influence of oil prosperity, guerrilla warfare in the Dhufar region on the border between South Yemen and the Oman sultanate produced further proof that the jungle was not a necessary condition for development of partisan war. The setbacks of guerrilla warfare in Latin America further show that it was not even a sufficient condition.

In reality, the controversy over the respective roles of the regular and partisan armies in the Arab–Israeli conflict was above all a quarrel of an internal nature in Arab society, and for this reason was never seen as basically a military problem. In so far as any kind of partisan war in the long run calls into question social values and structures, what was really at stake for Arab society was whether to preserve or destroy the existing social hierarchy. Furthermore, the emphasis on the need for the most sophisticated technology in order to confront the Israeli army successfully always enabled the Arab politico-military establishment to shift the blame for the Arab armies' helplessness onto the big industrialized countries. Already, in drawing lessons from the 1967 defeat, Nasser has emphasized the inferiority of the Arab armies' equipment compared with that of the Israeli army. From then on the under-equipment of the Arabs would be constantly referred to as a factor not only in their military, but also in their social and economic underdevelopment.

This was a very convenient argument, for its corollary was that responsibility for this state of affairs fell on the big Powers and not on Arab society. The United States over-equipped the Israeli army with the latest refinements of military technologically outdated material. After Nasser, Sadat would use and abuse the argument, even breaking with the Soviet Union, an act which suddenly gave powerful credibility to the Right-wing position in the controversy. Some years later, in their struggle for accelerated industrialization, the Algerians also made use of the myth of externally derived 'technological' underdevelopment as a shock argument in their claims against the capitalist world, one that could easily make the most vehemently Left-wing radicals move to the Right.

It was this argument which, pushed to its logical extreme at the political and economic level, legitimized the Arab countries' reconciliation with the United States. Since the latter always guaranteed Israel qualitative superiority over the Arab armies by delivering very high technology material, unlike the Soviets *vis-à-vis* the Arabs, the only door open to the Arab States was rapprochement with the United States. This should enable a mutual understanding to be reached which would negate the American policy of undue favouritism towards Israel and prejudice towards the Arab countries. Here too, Heikal's theories, authentically representing those of the caste of Egyptian officers in power, opened the way for a policy progressively put into practice after the 1967 defeat and actively followed since the Arab–Israeli war of 1973.

Nevertheless, despite its technological underdevelopment, the Egyptian army began the 1973 war by crossing the Suez Canal, a military feat very few believed it capable of. This alone ought to have been enough to re-open the controversy and to call the 'technology' myth in question. But it did nothing of the sort. Nobody was interested in the military aspect of the controversy; it was the socio-political aspect that was important, its cause long understood. In this respect, the social forces influential in the Arab world were no different from those that existed elsewhere, even in Maoist China, in disliking the idea of the 'popular masses' becoming an effective force, upsetting the established military order, organizing themselves into 'soviets' and leading a war of partisans which might sweep out imperialism, and with it its protégé Israel, as well as the reactionary Arab forces kept in being only by imperialism.

This ultra-Left thesis, so often brought up in talk, never found enough social support to enable its implications to be put into practice outside the romantic, revolutionary circles of the Palestinian Left, which was linked with the Western and Japanese extreme Left in operations more spectacular than politically effective. Thus, in this period, Nasserism could appear radical to the extreme Right conservative forces, but conservative in the ultra-Left debate.

The end of radicalism?

In any case, the end of the 1960s and beginning of the 1970s marked not only the eclipse of ultra-Leftism but also of the radicalism of the Nasserist and Marxist Left. In November 1970, after finding himself in a minority in the party bodies, where he was reproached especially for not having let the army intervene massively on the side of the Palestinians in Jordan, General Hafez al-Assad took power in Syria and got rid of the entire extreme-Left tendency in the party. The new Syrian leader rapidly adopted a moderate domestic and foreign policy which broke Syria's isolation (an isolation provoked by the State's ultra-Leftism between 1966 and 1970), both among the Arabs and internationally. In 1973 this led to Syria's negotiating with Henry Kissinger, signing a disengagement agreement with the Israelis and receiving President Nixon on an official visit.

Internally, and in a much more discreet manner than President Sadat in Egypt, General Assad relaxed some of the economic controls of the preceding period which had totally suffocated the private sector, in particular import controls, thus enabling the Syrian commercial class to prosper. This won him the not inconsiderable support of what remained of upper middle-class Damascus and especially of the small traders of the bazaars. External economic relations were likewise re-oriented towards the capitalist West. From the outset, the discreet and controlled shift towards greater economic freedom was accompanied by a no less controlled opening up on the political front, through the construction of a national front, which regrouped pro-Nasser and Communist party forces under the aegis of the Ba'ath party.

Elsewhere in the Arab world there was a general political shift towards the Right, sometimes occurring at a spectacular pace. It was thanks to the active complicity of President Sadat and the then vehemently anti-Marxist Colonel Gadaffi that in July 1971 a *coup d'état* fomented by Marxist officers in the Sudan was thwarted. A terrible repression followed in which all the leading figures of the Sudanese Communist party, one of the most active in the Arab world, were eliminated. By removing the civilians who themselves had seized power from the military with the help of a popular revolt in 1964, General Nimeiri, who had taken power in 1969, was able to consolidate his position. He was already very close to the Saudis. As for Gadaffi, who had overthrown the

Libyan monarchy in September 1969, his intervention on the side of Nimeiri and Sadat confirmed his reputation as actively anti-Soviet and anti-Marxist.[13] Sadat, for his part, effected a reconciliation with the Saudis as soon as he became Head of State. In May 1971, after weeding out all the pro-Soviet elements from the Egyptian political apparatus, he did sign, for whatever it was worth, a carefully worded friendship and co-operation treaty with the Soviet Union but about a year later expelled all Soviet military experts from Egypt.

Thus, at the beginning of the 1970s the Arab political landscape had changed considerably. Ultra-Leftism having more or less disappeared from Syria and Jordan, it was now Marxism that became the object of attack in Egypt, the Sudan and Libya. Iraq also was hard on its communists. Syria veered to the Right. Algeria, which had tried hard between 1967 and 1970 to radicalize the eastern Arabs, to push them into not accepting a cease-fire, to arm the Palestinians and to fight Arab reactions and feudalism, gave up at this point. Discouraged by the move to the Right which had begun with the Khartoum summit, the Algerians diverted all their attention to making a success of their accelerated industrial programme.

For the Arab military regimes, there began an era of surprising stability, since, at the beginning of the 1980s, the following leaders were all still in power. Hafez al-Assad in Syria, Gadaffi in Libya, Sadat in Egypt, Nimeiri in the Sudan and Saddam Hussein in Iraq. In Tunisia, Ben Salah, who had promoted a degree of socialization in farming programmes, fell into disgrace in 1969, and the pro-Western Bourguiba line was strengthened. In Algeria, President Boumedienne imposed himself as a man of order and sound economic ideas, in contrast to the disorganized populism of the still imprisoned Ben Bella.[14] The dynamics that had made Arab countries susceptible to military *coups d'état* with politically and ideologically significant overtones had unquestionably been broken. Apart from the Left-wing student movements active in Egypt until 1973, the Arab public opinion and urban mass movements that used to animate the games of musical chairs played by army officers in search of power had disappeared from the political scene.

The only anchorage on the Left in a world moving to the Right was a body of young Lebanese who worshipped the Palestinian Resistance and the Dhufar guerillas receiving support from the

South Yemen, which had attained independence in 1967 thanks to guerrilla action against the occupying British army. Here, at any rate, the extreme Left had triumphed since FLOSY, supported by Egypt, had been eliminated by the NLF,[16] a movement of radical Arab nationalist tendency which inclined more and more to the Left in the exercise of power. The NLF made the South Yemen into the Cuba of the Arab world, hemmed in by all the Arabian Peninsula countries reluctant to accept a Marxist People's Republic in the very heart of royalist and fundamentalist Islam.

As Khartoum had shown, oil had already erupted into Arab society and from then on became the one and only real tyrant, slowly but surely devouring it. It resurrected the old demons of religious fundamentalism that seemed to have disappeared for ever, destroyed the whole Arab revolutionary heritage, smothered what were already the most downtrodden classes and corrupted the intelligentsia once so enamoured of universalising radicalism and now merely a sounding board for the intellectual and ideological vagaries of oil-rich governments, divine-right monarchies or republican officers.

The inheritors of the historical period that had drawn to a close, that of the Nasser epic and of romantic ultra-Leftist dreams, were no more than mostly humourless caricatures of the lost heroes. They were to be found in the Lebanese National Movement, the armed Palestinian resistance movements reconstituted in Lebanon and among the leaders of the countries who proclaimed 'No Compromise' in the compromises with imperialism and Zionism symbolized by the Camp David Agreements. Besides, they no longer had any real hold on mass public opinion, for the game of charades had lost all conviction and Arab society was weary, too sick from oil, inflation and the various exchange speculations that oil engenders, to maintain any kind of political role. But could it perhaps also be that the heritage itself was rather slim? The Nasserist discourse died with its author. Ultra-Leftism died in 1968–9 in the jungles of Latin America, in the streets of Paris and in the senility of Mao Tse-tung. At breakneck speed, oil would henceforth widen the cultural gap that the Nasser discourse had tried to fill through self-education.

3 The rise of the tyranny of oil: 1945–73

Until the end of the 1960s, Arab society had known only the tyranny of poverty. In future it would have to accommodate itself to that of a type of wealth coming not out of an industrial revolution, the Promethean effort that societies make to escape the determinism of nature, but from amidst poverty and underdevelopment.

Though the discovery of oil in the Near and Middle East began at the beginning of this century, its exploitation on a significant scale goes back only to the 1940s, while its decisive importance to the economies of industrialized countries was only clearly revealed in the late sixties and early seventies. From then onwards, events moved at a breath-taking speed, like a runaway machine that nobody could stop. In the West the crisis provoked, though serious, was only an economic one, but in the East in the 1970s the flows of oil attained the scale of a river dangerously in spate and threatening to wash everything away.

This oil tyranny, new scourge of the Arabs, was, alas, born of the West, which had again fastened onto the East in an unequal relationship, though this time it was less easy to distinguish the master from the slave. For this reason, it is essential to carry out a preliminary investigation in the oil countries before attempting a diagnosis which will no doubt run up against accepted ideas and propaganda cliches.

Western failure of economic rationality

The 'energy crisis' can only be understood within the context of certain basic facts. The great Industrial Revolution of the West is appropriately symbolized by two great discoveries, the steam engine and electricity, which established the fundamental link between heat and energy, thus enabling machines to replace human labour. All the power and wealth of the contemporary

West stem from this relationship; and the West can unquestionably take credit for having established it in the wake of that avid
scientific curiosity that gripped it in the sixteenth century and that
has never ceased.

In the nineteenth century energy was produced from coal, of
which there was a plentiful supply in Western countries. In the
twentieth century, it is being produced from oil, which the Americans had already started to exploit in the second half of the
nineteenth century. Long before reaching adolescence, oil became
subjected to cartels, the first anti-monopoly law, aimed at carving
up the Rockefeller empire's oil interests being promulgated in
1890. This historical context made it easy, a century later, to get
the Arabs to carry the weight of the sins of the famous 'seven
sisters', the seven great oil companies of the Western cartel.[1]

In a rather facile and quite unjustified comparison, the thirteen
oil-exporting members of OPEC[2] have been considered by
Western opinion as equivalent to the famous 'seven sisters' cartel
which dominated the world oil market for fifty years, to the great
detriment of energy users. In reality, the partial or total nationalizations that took place during the 1970s merely gave the poverty-
stricken oil countries the legal opportunity to acquire sovereign
control over their wells. But this did not at all give them control
over the world energy market, much less turn them into a cartel;
it made them solely the inheritors of the colossal historical errors
of the 'seven sisters' and, more generally, of the Western economies of which the latter were merely a product. Oil does not,
however, involve only extraction, it has also to be researched,
drilled, transported, marketed, refined and delivered. Even after
the nationalizations, the Arab oil countries, along with the other
OPEC countries, exercised direct control only over the rate of
extraction. They never managed to coordinate the different levels
of production and in fact did not even try to do so. State sovereignty was at stake, a sensitive subject.

For drilling, research, transport and marketing, the OPEC
countries are entirely dependent on the oil companies of the
industrialized countries, whose supremacy remains unquestioned
and, in fact, uncontested even by the producing countries themselves. To transfer the term 'cartel', which refers historically to
the 'seven sisters', onto OPEC, is thus a facile abuse of language,
which evidently has the great advantage of shifting the blame for
all the economic misfortunes of the industrialized countries onto

the Arabs. How could the former fail to take advantage of it?

Nevertheless, the West's energy record is damning, showing not only pillage of the East's most precious resource, but also waste and bad management in the industrialized countries. Like coal, oil is a non-renewable energy-producing substance and its waste is therefore an economic crime with inevitable long-term consequences. This became abundantly clear during the 1970s. Certainly, within the more general framework of an increase in the Third World's economic claims, along with the partial and temporary cessation of supplies accompanying the great events of the Near and Middle East in 1973 and 1979, a certain amount of militancy in the OPEC countries did accelerate the exposure of imbalances in the world energy market. But these imbalances would have inevitably appeared, for, whereas production fell during the 1960s, particularly in the United States, the rate of increase of oil consumption in Western countries mounted disproportionately.

The tragedy is that a too cheap oil policy had led European countries into closing numerous coal-mines as financially unprofitable. At an extraction cost of 10 American cents a barrel, Middle Eastern oil put other sources of energy out of competition. At an average selling price of 2 dollars a barrel between 1945 and 1970, the oil companies also made spectacular profits. In its euphoria, the West gave no thought to the future. The Third World, and particularly the Middle East, seemed an enormous reservoir of energy resources. Nobody bothered to look into the future.

It was not until the end of the 1960s that a group of important people in the West finally sent out a cry of alarm over the tensions that would develop in the world economy as a result of excessive and wasteful economic growth in the West despite finite resources.[3] It was, however, too late, for the Western economies had been overheated to such an extent that, by the beginning of the 1970s major inflationist pressures were already operating in the industrialized countries and the price of raw materials had rocketed. The partial oil embargo imposed by the Arab oil-exporting countries on the occasion of the fourth Arab–Israeli war in October 1973, caused the oil market, already unbalanced by several years of too high demand, to explode.[4]

By unilaterally fixing the price per barrel successively at 5.11 dollars on 16 October 1973, then at 11.65 dollars on 23 December 1973, the OPEC countries did no more than re-establish true

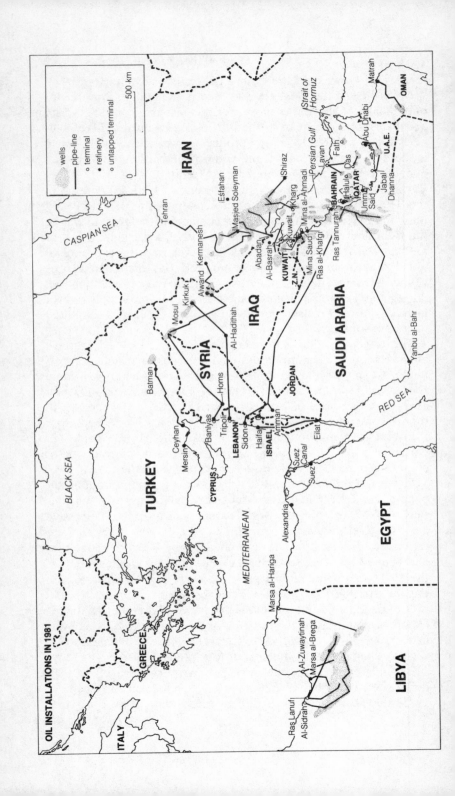

OIL INSTALLATIONS IN 1981

The rise of the tyranny of oil: 1945–73

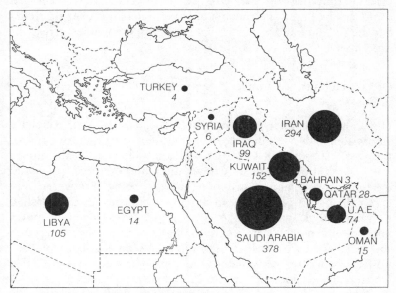

OIL PRODUCTION IN 1973 (millions of metric tons)

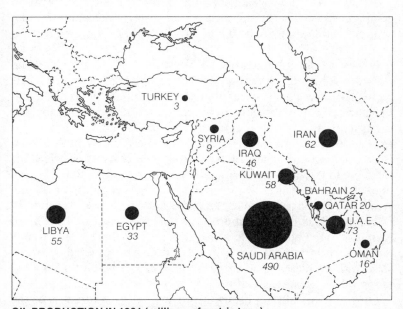

OIL PRODUCTION IN 1981 (millions of metric tons)

prices in the world energy sector. They would never have managed to do this had there not been a growing imbalance over the years between supply and demand, which the oil companies' irresponsible managements had concealed.

OPEC: militant trade union or barometer of the world energy market?

OPEC had until then been only an association of poor countries whose demands were hardly of much interest to the powerful of this world. Created in 1960 at Venezuela's instigation, the aim of the Organization was to slow down the fall in oil prices provoked by the growing abundance of resources being discovered and exploited by oil companies in member countries. It also wished to improve yields from the modest oil taxes member States imposed on company profits. In the absence of a concerted policy to limit production, which has still not seen the light of day, OPEC's activities remained futile until the end of the 1960s. During that period the organization was rather like a group of small provincial *rentiers* trying to protect their meagre purchasing power against the dynamism and power of the Western oil companies. The market had not yet been turned around and the economic militancy of the Third World had not yet experienced its new take-off.

It was actually the Arab–Israeli war of 1967 that opened the way to a complete inversion of the world's energy situation. This happened once again on familiar territory along the Suez Canal, the ancient colonial artery between East and West already the catalyst for Egypt's awakening in the 1950s, and through Egypt for that of oppressed countries in Africa and Asia. With the Canal closed on account of Israeli occupation, the costs of oil transport were the first to rise. In 1969, and then again in 1970, Syria, closed one of the two huge oil pipelines, the one running from Saudi Arabia through Jordanian and Syrian territory to Saida in Lebanon.[5] This meant a shortfall in the flow towards Europe of 25 million tons per year, in a market in which there were already tensions. Prices went up and up and Syria obtained a whole succession of increases in charges for transporting oil through her territory. To this extent ultra-Leftism was certainly paying.

Other factors at play brought ever-increasing awareness of the ravages to which these exploited countries, rich in energy but poor in economic capacity, were being subjected. In Libya, where Gadaffi had come to power in 1970, a genuine oil policy was swiftly adopted that, from the start, forced foreign companies to reduce their production volumes, which had in fact been detrimental to the Libyan oil deposits. Further, Gadaffi nationalized internal distribution and successfully increased both tax yields and prices. He achieved this without too much difficulty, for oil production in Libya was not dominated by the cartel companies, but by newcomers to the Western oil world, the 'independents', mainly Italian and French, and some American. Thus a new movement was set in motion towards a clearly needed better conservation and towards nationalization. This had been consigned to oblivion ever since the 1951 attempt of De Mossadegh, the leading Iranian bourgeois-nationalist, to take control of production in Iran, had provoked the CIA's direct intervention to re-establish the *status quo*, i.e. the continued pillaging of Iran's resources.

Among these first fruits of oil emancipation, one should also mention the measure decreed by General Kassem in Iraq in 1961 to recover control of the vast unexploited oil concessions. This led to Iraq's being put into quarrantine by the producing companies, which had for a long time lacked interest in developing its resources. This quarantine was intended as a warning for underdeveloped oil countries irresolutely desiring to acquire better control of their natural resources.

The two oil stars: Boumedienne and the Shah of Iran

However, it was to Iran and Algeria, at the two extremities of the Near and Middle East, that the OPEC owed the breath of fresh air which enabled it to sense the inversion in the market trend at a very early stage and draw the maximum benefit from it. Both the Algerian Caesar, President Boumedienne, and the Iranian (disguised as a monarch, for he was merely the son of an officer who had usurped the throne of the Qajars*) had dreams of grandeur and of accelerated modernization. An active, positive complicity linked the two regimes, which, in a close dialogue, were to play out not only the oil game but the whole movement for the reform of the international economic order. What they really wanted was to become more quickly integrated into the

*Last Qajar in 1922: Reza Shah proclaimed 1925

Western prosperity networks, by accelerated modernization of their people, the overwhelming majority of whom were still peasants.

The Shah in addition dreamt of rebuilding the Empire of Cyrus[6] in all its glory and replacing shrinking British power and the enfeebled West in general as master and guardian of the Near East, strategic international crossroads and great reservoir of energy resources on which the future of the world depended. Though politically more modest, Boumedienne was as obsessed as the Shah with modernism, technology and industrialization. As a man of order and planned action, he rejected the fiery, bubbling populism of Ben Bella. He aimed to channel and organize effectively the mounting claims of Third World countries against their former colonial masters. The non-alignment movement undoubtedly owed to him all its economic programmes, which he fought for and which progressively made their way in the international order.

It was the Arab–Israeli war of October 1973 that enabled these two men to show their true mettle and, in conjunction with Saudi Arabia, the third member of this oil *troika*, for a moment to hold the future of the Near and Middle East in their hands.[7]

At the beginning of the 1970s, the Shah of Iran and President Boumedienne both understood perfectly well that the only way they could accomplish their dream of accelerated modernization was through oil, or, more precisely, through the financial resources oil provided. The distinction is significant. It shows that the logic of underdevelopment is not easily shaken off. In fact, although these two men were acutely aware of the importance of oil for providing energy to the West's industrial machine, they envisaged its utilization as a local instrument for modernization in purely financial terms. This error in perspective is specifically one of underdeveloped and poverty-stricken regions, where money alone seems important because it enables the symbols of dignity and power to be simply bought from the world's rich. It is for this reason that OPEC, prisoner of this financial logic, has been mainly concerned with maximizing the revenues of its member States. Its outstanding achievement in this respect is due as much to the militancy of some of its members as to the new economic realities of the world energy market which, thanks to the dramatic political events of the Near East, had come to the fore. Kept abnormally low for twenty years without development of other sources of equally cheap energy, oil prices inevitably took off at the first signs of shortage.

In tackling oil prices, the OPEC therefore unquestionably defended a just cause, even if, like a bad loser grinding his teeth, the West retaliated with an unbridled propaganda, which struck especially at the Arabs, always easy victims. The Shah, so favourable to the West politically, was usually exempted from its highly racist campaign. Yet when the carpet was pulled out from under his feet in Iran, and the West disdainfully turned its back on him, it is not at all certain that there was no element of retaliation in the domain of oil. It was actually in Teheran that, in February 1971, the cartel of oil companies was forced to give way to OPEC. The Teheran agreements ratified a price rise of 33 cents per barrel, an increase in oil taxation, and clauses for inflation-linked price adjustments for producers in the Persian Gulf. An agreement in Tripoli a month later extended these same advantages to Mediterranean producers. It was again in Teheran in December 1973 that the OPEC doubled the price of oil from 5.11 dollars to 11.65 dollars a barrel. In February 1971 Algeria took control of the French oil companies operating in its territory. In June 1972, Iraq, in its turn, nationalized the British oil interests predominant there, while leaving untouched those of France, with whom a more co-operative relationship was being sought.

Freeing of prices was thus accompanied by recovery of juridical sovereignty. Economic and legal reality were finally brought together. Soon the Gulf Emirates and the Saudi monarchy would have to follow in OPEC's footsteps and negotiate the gradual buying back of assets from the oil companies operating in their territories. Regarding both prices and sovereignty, it was Saudi Arabia that dragged its feet the most, and it was not until 1979 that it finally bought out the consortium of companies operating in its territory. The oil giant's feet may be of clay, but all said and done it was its action that proved decisive in that part of the world. This is what we must now consider.

The crescent and the pipeline

Arabia's history over the last fourteen centuries is marked by two great events: the appearance in Mecca of the last monotheist prophet, Mohammad, at the end of the sixth century and the discovery of colossal oil deposits in the twentieth century.

Between the two, there is an almost total historical vacuum, for soon after the death of the founder of Islam the focus of Arab history moved away from the peninsula first to Damascus, then to Baghdad, and then proliferated in Islamic kingdoms along an enormous crescent from Castile in Spain to the very extremity of the Indian peninsula.

The epic of the Wahhabis, creators of the Saudi monarchy, began at the end of the eighteenth century. But if the story of this group of Bedouin tribes in the throes of religious fervour had not reached a high point just when the Americans were discovering fabulous oil riches on the same Arabian soil, theirs would have remained a local historical development of interest only to specialists. At a stroke these Bedouins, still living in the time of the Prophet, acquired an international status without equivalent in history, but had also to endure the most violent socio-cultural adjustments imaginable. Had oil been as important to the triumphant economy of the West in the eighteenth and nineteenth centuries, the tribes of Arabia would in all likelihood have suffered the same fate as those of America.

The Wahhabis were actually lucky to have put the final touches to building their kingdom before the West transformed their territory into an immense petrol pump. They thus benefited from the powerful Third World decolonization movement, which in the 1950s dissuaded former colonizers from embarking on new conquests. They were lucky to have established legal sovereignty for the control and social management of an under-populated desert kingdom, under the tremendous shock of confrontation between the modern world of oil and traditional religious fundamentalism, constituted an immense, if not hopeless, task without it. It would be inappropriate to make any judgements about the Kingdom of Saudi Arabia, or the other oil Emirates of the Peninsula, without taking this fundamental element into account.

Moreover, the Wahhabis have always fascinated the West. Material interests apart, Islam and the Bedouin way of life have exercised a dual cultural influence over that element in the Western mind that is sick from industrialism and technical progress. What more attractive vision then than Wahhabism, an austere form of Islam stripped of any borrowings of piety from other religions and punctuated only by Koranic prayer, to the exclusion of all other forms of devotion? It would be difficult to imagine anything more marvellously ascetic than the Bedouin life so splendid in its frugality. Viewed from Paris, London or New York, world capitals of futility, waste and insolent wealth, the military and religious feats of the Wahhabis in those desert silences or the engaging simplicity and chivalrous spirit of the Hashemites, guardians of Mecca and direct descendants of the Prophet, take on an irresistible fascination. European literature bears illustrious witness, for example, T.E. Lawrence's *The Seven Pillars of Wisdom* and Benoist-Mechin's trilogy.[8] In taking power later on, Ayatollah Ruholla Khomeini was to profit greatly from this fund of sympathy which a rudderless West in search of spirituality and exoticism felt for those who, in remote and indistinct Asian spaces, claimed a divine afflatus as guides of a return to a pristine source.

These throw-back movements constantly recur in the history of people and of civilizations. With all due respect to lovers of exoticism and to zealots, Islam is not alone in its periodic quests for purity. Christian and Jewish history is strewn with rigorist and fundamentalist movements which, on behalf of the divine, seek to turn men, as it were, into an identical and immobile series of columns in a sacred temple. From the mystical to the political is but one step: this is a point that Peguy has already emphasized, for the people of the West have also experienced periods of traditionalist reaction and of religious or national exaltation which brought disruption and conflict into their lives.

Wahhabism was actually the first of the four great fundamentalist movements that shook Islam after the eighteenth century, in the face of the increasing pressure of Western Christian culture as the conquering Europe of the Renaissance and the Industrial Revolution spread to all four corners of the globe. Between Wahhabism and the Khomeinist reaction in Iran, two important nineteenth-century African-Arab Islamic movements should be taken into account, Mahdism[9] in the Sudan and the Senussi sect[10] in Libya. Each was both religious and nationalist, religious in their quest for the pristine purity of Islam, reduced its Koranic core and thus cleared of all later jurisprudential, doctrinal and philosophical additions, and nationalist in opposition to European colonial penetration in Africa. Thus, in 1885 the Mahdis besieged and then occupied Khartoum, killing General Gordon, Commander-in-Chief of the Anglo-Egyptian forces charged with restoring order in Sudan. The Senussi movement, for its part, penetrated deeply into Black Africa and actively opposed French colonial penetration, and the occupation of Libya by Italy.

The rise of the Wahhabis was made possible through an alliance between military force and religion. Muhammad Ibn Abdal Wahhab (1703–92) was a preacher who sought to strengthen and purify Sunni orthodoxy. The Ottoman Empire, guardian of that orthodoxy, was already in decline, Shiite Persia was consolidating its authority. Muhammad Ibn Saud was Emir of Dariyah in the Najd, in the heart of the Arabian Peninsula; and in 1740 he formed an alliance with Muhammad Ibn Abdel Wahhab in order to spread the latter's teachings. It was above all the Emir's son Abdel Aziz who led the conquest and who in 1802 reached Karbala, the most important of the Shi'a holy places in Iraq after conquering Riyadh in 1773 and unifying the Najd in 1786. Abdel Aziz's son, Saud, continued his father's work and in 1805 conquered Islam's two most important holy places, Mecca and Medina. In 1810, he reached the gates of Syria. This first Wahhabi kingdom was destroyed by Muhammad Ali, Viceroy of Egypt, and his son Ibrahim on behalf of the Ottoman Sultan. In successive campaigns, Egyptian armies reconquered the Najd and the Hijaz and in 1818 took Dariyah, starting point of the Wahhabi conquest. Saud's son, King Abdullah, was taken to Istanbul and beheaded.

A second Wahhabi kingdom, soon formed by a younger branch of the Saud family, though without the extent and power of its predecessor, disappeared in 1884. However, in 1901 the Wahhabi epic was resumed, thanks to the strong personality of Emir Abdal Aziz (1880–1953), who in stages reconquered the Najd and the Hijaz, whence he drove out the Hazhemites, custodians of Mecca and whose head, Sherif Hussein, hoped, with the help of the British, to rebuild a great Arab kingdom on the ruins of the Ottoman Empire. In 1928, the existence of the Kingdom of Saudi Arabia was conclusively established. International recognition came in 1945 at the meeting on an American warship in the Red Sea between the Saudi King and the American President, Roosevelt, who was on his way back from the Yalta Conference. During this meeting Roosevelt obtained a concession of 1.5 million km^2 for the consortium of American oil companies operating in Saudi Arabia.[11] From then on Saudi Arabia remained solidly within the American camp.

Faisal of Arabia

King Abdel Aziz died in 1953 and was succeeded by his son Saud. In 1964 Saud was obliged to yield his throne to his brother Faisal, his administration having shown itself disastrous for the kingdom, especially in the financial sphere where, despite increased oil production, royal chaos had constantly led the State to the brink of bankruptcy. With Faisal's accession to the throne, Saudi Arabia entered an amazing era. It was almost as if this ascetic, with his pained emaciated face, had been specially chosen by God to make the kingdom in his reign that regional super-power on which world peace rested. Faisal was the complete antithesis of the 'Arab oil sheikh' who whittles away millions on roulette in the casinos of Cannes or Nice and owns a harem of wives for whom he buys entire shop windows full of jewellery in the Place Vendôme in Paris. This strictly monogamous man led an exemplary life of austerity and conserved the simplicity of a true aristocrat. His preoccupation with Islam was as much by personal conviction and piety as by necessities of State. He thus became the great catalyst for the holy alliance of religion and oil, strange pact the iron hand of which came increasingly to govern a part of the world so unstable in all respects. Faisal orchestrated the parallel rise of religious and oil power so well that even the coldest and most secular of intellects in the Arab world could not help but be swayed.

It should also be mentioned that the new Saudi monarch, at first overshadowed by the rise of Nasserism, which coincided precisely with his brother's colourless and incompetent administration, showed his true worth at the Khartoum summit. Faisal was opposed to Nasser, but also, later, to Sadat. A man of few words, he never made sensational speeches and always faced triumph with modesty and adversity with dignity. His language, like his political action, was never hurried, but assured and thus majestic in its slowness. He rejected modern ideological discourse, for his values were those of the sacred heritage of which he was the guardian, through Mecca and Medina, the two great holy cities of Islam and jewels of his kingdom. As if to reward and to show their favour to that unwavering believer, the skies rained on him fortune and power in unceasing abundance.

The kingdom's oil revenues, of the order of half a billion dollars at Faisal's accession in 1964, rose to over 1.1 billion in 1970 and

27.8 billion in 1974. It was thus under the reign of this pious king that Saudi Arabia's financial resources increased 55.6 times. These figures remain modest in comparison with the financial strength of Western countries: in 1974 the Bank of America's balance was 57.5 billion dollars, and German exports in 1974 of the order of 90 billion dollars. But in relation to the world of poverty to which the Arabs belong, Saudi Arabia's 27.8 billion dollars in 1974 represented almost three times the national income of the 37 million Egyptians for a Saudi population which was estimated at between 4 and 6 million.

It is therefore not surprising that at the beginning of the 1970s the Saudi phenomenon so powerfully affected the Arab imagination. For this kingdom of orthodox believers, so disparaged in the 1960s by the socialist and secular thrust of Arab nationalism, had become an international power wooed by the mighty of this world just when the heroes of the radical and ultra-Left Arab adventure were on the way out, perhaps, like Nasser, with a certain panache, but usually in the ridicule associated with cabals of officers trying to bring about revolutions in lands to which Providence continued to deny resources. The next step was to think that God rewards his own and punishes the wicked. Many did think so, even among those who did not profit directly from the oil manna, and who were not necessarily religious. This is not a wholly naive position if one considers that a large part of Western opinion, Christian, Jewish, and sometimes even secular, sees divine approval in the story of Israel and its military successes. Average opinion, whether East or West, cannot be expected to undertake exhaustive analyses or to attain the strict detachment possible to an outside observer. With Nasser gone, Faisal became the new hero of the Arab world. He had all the qualities for it, especially since, man of few but grave words that he was, he declared for all to hear that his most cherished wish was to pray in a liberated Jerusalem. And then, in no time, the problem regarded as one of infringed rights of Arab national existence, especially for the Palestinians, took on a religious hue.

Islamic solidarity against communism and Arab nationalism

This reorientation is part of the logic of the Saudi system. Since the 1950s, and with the active encouragement of the United States, the favoured ally, Saudi Arabia, had done its best to contain the rise of Jacobin Arab nationalism and to promote Islamic solidarity at the international level. For this it relied on the support of two other political regimes whose legitimacy rested entirely on religion: on the one side, Pakistan, whose secession from India was justified exclusively on the grounds of regrouping Indian Muslims in a State guaranteeing an Islam-based socio-political system; and on the other, Morocco, an old monarchy with religious legitimacy, since the reigning dynasty claimed direct descent from the Prophet. This Islamic 'Commonwealth' was in fact primarily an anti-communist, pro-Western grouping. They were quite open about this because, for these Heads of State, who had to be good Muslims, the Soviet Union was the spearhead of an atheistic materialism quite contrary to the very spirit of their religion, whereas the Western countries, on the other hand, which were fighting the spread of Marxism, preserved at least a modicum of religion.

It is easy to imagine the new boost that oil gave this movement of Islamic 'solidarity', which had up until then been marking time during the triumph of Nasser and President Achmad Sukarno's[12] militant Third Worldism, to speak only of these two important political leaders ruling over predominantly Muslim countries. This boost was perfectly timed, for in 1966 Sukarno, the other leading light of non-alignment and pro-socialist radicalism, who had been governing Indonesia, the most highly populated Muslim country in the world, was thrown out of power. Nasser was in retreat and was to die not long after.

It was thus at the end of the 1960s that this movement became institutionalized into the international order. A conference of world-wide Islamic organizations had already been held in Mecca in 1968. In 1969, the fire at the al-Aksa mosque in Jerusalem provided the pretext for convening the first Summit Conference of Islamic Heads of State in Rabat which, despite opposition from secular and radical Islamic countries to institutionalizing the conference in such a way, decided to set up a permanent Secretariat. By then the wind had changed, especially since 1970 when, on Nasser's death, Sadat took firm steps towards a reconciliation with Saudi Arabia and Iran and put on a show of Islamic solidarity for their benefit. The 'Islamic Commonwealth' was thus well founded, with countries politically close to the West as its pillars. Third Worldist secular radicalism was on the way out and the influence of the Soviet Union declined rapidly. Soon, in 1973, at Saudi Arabia's initiative, an Islamic Development Bank with 1.2 billion dollars[13] of capital was created in Jiddah. Its activities were aimed at consolidating Islamic solidarity by distribution of funds in addition to the bilateral assistance that Saudi Arabia was generously granting Islamic countries effectively fighting Soviet influence. At last the West had at its disposal in the East a protective shield for its oil interests on the one hand and for its strategic global interests on the other. At the beginning of the 1970s, it did not, however, suspect that the Islam of oil would sow the seeds of very serious social upheaval that, some years later, would cast doubt on all the efforts accomplished to tip the Arab Near East permanently into the Western sphere of interests.

At the time, the operation seemed wholly successful. Faisal had taken over from Nasser as the charismatic figure of the Arab world. In 1969, another Western stronghold, Rabat, hosted the first Islamic summit, at which radicalism and ultra-Leftism were hardly considered good form and where the Soviet Union's friends were in the minority. Local axes around which oil riches worked wonders were drawn up. Saudi Arabia, Morocco and Egypt formed a dynamic *troika*. At Rabat secret contacts were made between the Egyptians and Israelis in 1977.[14] Iran, Pakistan, Jordan and Oman formed another important quadrille, for Pakistani and Jordanian soldiers and Iranian pilots were trying to end the Dhofar rebellion on the border between Oman and South Yemen. This task was accomplished in 1975. Jordan, for its part, needed support in its attempt to become a viable alternative to the PLO, in which extremely radical trends continued to thrive; hence King Hussein's plan in 1972 for a United Arab Kingdom which would unite the two banks of the Jordan under his sovereignty.

Despite a certain amount of antipathy between the Iran of the Shah and the Arabia of Faisal, both aspiring to be the dominant regional power, the *troika* and the quadrille co-operated and co-ordinated their actions. There were thrones to protect in a world of poverty where the oil manna was very unevenly shared. But this community of interests did not prevent the surfacing of hidden rivalries, especially since an important historical and religious dispute existed between the Persians and the Arabs, which was to trigger hostilities between Iraq and Iran in September 1981. Faisal's 'Arabism' was thus also a means of confronting the pretensions of the Iranian monarch to dominate the Gulf and whose army in 1974 had occupied some small islands under Arab sovereignty. Faisal in fact accomplished the Wahhabi dream of becoming the centre of gravity and arbiter of the Arab world.

The psychology of a friendship

Increasing oil resources, and the good working order of the inter-Arab 'social security' system set up at the Khartoum summit, ensured Saudi Arabia a position of prestige in Arab, Islamic and oil terms. After taking power, Faisal reformed the State administration, separated its budget from that of the royal family, established fixed civil lists for five thousand members, set up a central bank directed by a Pakistani delegated by the International Monetary Fund (IMF), and speeded up a campaign for literacy and education. Unlike his predecessors, Faisal was resolutely modernist. He allowed women access to education by setting up a separate school system and accepted all instruments of economic and social progress, even for example television, despite serious opposition from ultra-reactionary circles.[15]

In the task of great modernizer, he was assisted at all levels by the United States, for which the Saudi royal family has maintained unfailing esteem. He sent an enormous contingent of the country's elite to the United States for advanced studies. This privileged relationship does not stem only from the activities of the consortium of oil companies operating in Saudi Arabia which provide the country with an immense nucleus of modernization and prosperity. It rests also on active and mutual sympathy. In those deserts the Americans relive their epic of conquering vast expanses, but more peacefully and without any genocide of Indians. The Saudis seem at ease with these transatlantic Europeans, without great historical, cultural or social traditions other than, as in their own case, the adventure of conquering a continent on horseback.

As descendants respectively of 'cowboys' and of '*Ikhwan*'[16] Wahhabis, Americans and Saudis have no trouble in feeling an affinity for one another,[17] sharing as they do the same love of religious puritanism and progress, the same dynamism and the same appetite for arbitrating things at international level. But above all, they share the same antipathy for atheistic communism and for Soviet expansionism. Moreover, with time and age, Faisal developed a bizarre phobia against the Soviet Union. He had been there in 1932 as Minister of Foreign Affairs, but despite this remained implacable for the whole of his life, refusing to establish diplomatic relations with the USSR and, consequently, depriving his kingdom of an important element of balance in its international relations.

Furthermore, he was obsessed by an obscure theory, which he always explained to visitors in utter seriousness: Zionism was only a product of communism, and communism itself only a vast plot by international Jewry to destroy morale and morality in order better to dominate the world. The struggle against Zionism and the State of Israel therefore necessarily involved struggle against the Soviet Union and all forces associated with Marxism. The factor of constriction and the cultural obliquity of which he was a victim were serious shortcomings for a Head of State. This does not in any way call in question any traditional aspects of Islam or of Arabness, for the version so dear to him was a direct import from the great anti-Semitic traditions of the West, from the famous 'Protocols of the Elders of Zion',[18] product of Christian obscurantism of the late eighteenth century which held the Jews responsible for the French Revolution as well as for secular, and thus corrupting, attitudes.

Islam has never known these excesses, for although the Jews of Arabia did put up some opposition to the prophet Muhammad in the seventh century, they were never held guilty of deicide, as they were by the Christians. The 'Protocols of the Elders of Zion' are thus a twentieth-century cultural import from the West. That the creation of Israel and the Palestinian tragedy it provoked should create fertile ground in the East for receiving Western anti-Semitism is hardly surprising. East and West meet up again here in a shared obscurantism, of which the Near East is a victim, for it creates a political short-sightedness leading to errors in decision-making. In any case, Faisal's kind of anti-Semitism was highly beneficial to the United States, which did not have to worry about a possible Soviet irruption into the Arabian Peninsula so long as the Saudi monarchy was there. Furthermore, the Saudis always regarded the United States' support for the State of Israel as a pardonable error attributable to the imaginary decisions by ruling bodies in American society. Faisal was not the only one to make this serious error of judgement. Many influential Arabs, who are not necessarily anti-Semitic, believe United States policy in the Near East to be against its own best interests because a too-powerful Jewish 'Lobby' has been able to dictate to the American administration – political naivety arising from boundless admiration for American power and its economic and technological achievements.

There is no question that many Arabs, and not only Saudis, are consciously or otherwise favourably disposed to the United States. Of the Western powers, it is the only one (except Germany, which is just as much admired) not to have exercised any direct colonial rule in the Arab countries. In those oil countries where its influence has prevailed, as well as in countries like the Lebanon, Jordan and Morocco, prosperity and relative political stability have reigned. On the other hand, Egypt, Syria, Iran, the Sudan and the two Yemens, where socialism has had its innings, have been wracked by successive *coups d'état* and by revolutions and counter-revolutions that did nothing for poverty, much less for the humiliation of defeat by the Israeli enemy. It made no difference that Russian military supplies had enabled the Egyptian army to cross the Suez Canal in 1973 and that Soviet technology had assured Iraq and, to a lesser extent, Syria, unprecedented increase in oil production: anti-Soviet prejudice went on increasing in the Arab world. The wave of Islamic austerity which Saudi Arabia imposed at the end of the 1960s, along with its increasing supremacy in the region, brought the surge of anti-Sovietism to a climax in the Arab world, so that even President Gadaffi started hunting down atheistic Marxism.[19]

Religious fundamentalism and pro-colonialism put to good use

Psychologically, the Saudis have fewer complexes than the other Arabs in their relationship with the West, headed by the United States. Their territory has never been subjected to Western colonialism, in the course of their history, the Wahhabis have had to face Turkish occupying forces and Egyptian armies but never those of European powers, contenting themselves with the edges of the Arabian Peninsula, notably Aden and the famous Pirate Coast. Thus, everything worked to reinforce the preferential ties between the American giant and the Saudi kingdom on the way to becoming itself an oil giant.

Besides, the Saudi leaders were perfectly aware that to assure the stability of their power, based on an island of oil in a sea of poverty and surrounded by international cupidities, two major ingredients were essential: the consolidation of religious legitimacy on which their throne rested and the active goodwill of the most powerful of the Western powers. These were the two permanent axes of the kingdom's policies. For this reason, the increasing Saudi share in the official subsidies paid to other Arab countries, as well as in the aid to other Islamic countries, was adjusted according to the degree of anti-Sovietism deployed by the beneficiaries of its generosity. For like reason, all over the Arab and Islamic world, officially or unofficially according to the situation, the Saudis generously financed fundamentalist religious movements, the building of mosques, Islamic charitable organizations, newspapers or magazines with fundamentalist religious tendencies, and schools or community clinics administered by religious associations.

The revival of Islam in Eastern countries, which so fascinates the West, is thus, in many respects, a Western product, for the kingdom's oil wealth was really made possible entirely by the United States. The Iranian revolution may still prove that this is not entirely the case but even then only to the extent that it is not itself a development regulated by oil. It is still not clear whether the revival of Islamic fundamentalism and rejection of modernism are anything other than an enormous malaise brought on by poorly assimilated and badly shared-out oil wealth clogging up the scrawny frames of these societies, still historically deprived of real industrialization.

In any case, the Saudi leaders have proved that their policy of alliance between modernism and religion has so far conserved their throne, whereas the Shah with his solely modern nationalist policy lost his. It is clearly too early to judge the final results of this apparently contradictory blend of modernism and religious orthodoxy. The way in which a group of anti-modernizing fundamentalists captured the main mosque in Mecca at the end of 1979 is perhaps an indication that the Saudi leadership is also threatened.[20] The Wahhabis present modernizing religious puritanism could in fact be easily overtaken either on the Right by Khomeini's Iran or on the Left by Gadaffi's fundamentalist, yet revolutionary socialist Libya. All the more reason why Saudi Arabia should want to keep well within the American orbit.

Since King Faisal's father founded the third kingdom, Saudi Arabia has never refused the United States anything it desired. It depends on the United States for political and military security and owes its oil wealth to it; and so naturally the accelerated modernization of the kingdom has been entrusted to it. At the beginning of the sixties, this underpopulated country composed mainly of illiterate Bedouins was hardly in a position to provide the necessary managerial cadres. Obviously, the whole of the West profits from such a policy, for the rate of oil production is faithfully adjusted to the needs of the industrialized countries – to the detriment, moreover, of good conservation of the deposits. Capital surpluses are wisely converted into American Treasury bills on a massive scale, or, if need be, into Japanese, German, French and Italian bonds. Saudi development plans are drawn up by American university professors; Saudi Airways is run by Pan American; and a private American company has been engaged to recruit GIs to guard the oil wells, etc.

In many ways, all this might seem aberrant, but it does nevertheless stem from the logic of the Saudi monarchy's socio-political structures in the particular historical and geopolitical context in which they operate in the second half of the twentieth century. The main contradiction in Saudi policy is obviously its clear and unequivocal 'yes' to the West, but refusal to accept Israel. Doctrinally, this is somewhat mitigated by the ideological haziness described earlier which holds the Soviet Union responsible for Israel's existence. But it makes itself felt strongly, at the political level, impelling the Saudi monarchy to do all it can behind the scenes to settle the Palestinian question, without however undermining its legitimacy as an Arab and Islamic force. What it really wants then is a Palestinian State and Jerusalem, Islam's third Holy Place, back in Arab hands. It is well aware that an Arab world faced with the permanence of Israeli occupation is in constant danger of radicalization from frustrated Palestinian aspirations, championed by a Soviet armed, revolution-bent PLO, not to mention from the weakness of all the regimes it has salvaged since the Khartoum summit. If no cure can be found for the running sore of the Arab–Israeli conflict, all its recent political achievements at both Arab and international level will be threatened. It was under Saudi leadership and in Saudi Arabia's interests that Henry Kissinger and Sadat tried so hard to reach a settlement in the 1970s.

Everything nearly succeeded at that time. The 1973 war, the big oil panic in the West that followed, the eruption of the Palestinians into the United Nations, the setting up of a vast North-South dialogue to settle the problem of rich and poor, the exploiters and exploited of this world: all events which made it possible to believe in the mid-1970s that the Arab–Israeli conflict was on the way to gradual solution and that at last everybody could join the grand celebrations of Tyrant Oil.

History is not as capricious as it may sometimes seem, when it appears to recoil, to obfuscate its meanings, to defy prediction, but this is only when man demands from it the solution of insoluble problems or at any rate of those whose terms have been wrongly posed. The 1973 war and its consequent events actually created still further problems and opened the way to even more ambiguities. The still bleeding wound it inflicted on Lebanon, the most sensitive point in the Near East, is proof enough. The tearing apart of Lebanon created more victims between 1974 and 1976 than the total of all the Arab–Israeli wars since 1948. Before arriving at this point however it is necessary to consider the war of October 1973, a time separating two epochs, a confluence where all the contradictory currents that shake the Near East came together.

4 One war, two epochs: October 1973

On the brink of the abyss

Palestine in danger of disappearing

Seen in retrospect with a certain clarity changes are much less distinct than when they first begin to influence events; moreover the protagonists of history are not always fully conscious of the motives behind their decisions and of the real effects of their actions. By the same token, events themselves in their exterior facets may not reflect their own inner reality at a given time, and thus escape from political awareness. This is exactly what happened in the Arab Near East at the beginning of the 1970s. The general impression there of stagnation and sterile repetition was particularly accurate in the case of the Arab–Israeli conflict and of inter-Arab relations, the Arab world's two most painful failures in the twentieth century. Helplessness against Israel and failure in unity doubly nailed down Arab society. And at the beginning of the decade, there seemed no way of release.

On the first count, Israel, anchored in its intransigence, was quietly digesting its large conquests of 1967. The powerless Arabs felt as if they were reliving the nightmare of the first conquest of Palestine in 1948–9, or were, rather, the humiliated witnesses of a second that put the finishing touches to the first. The Arab defeat in 1948 had already enabled Israel to claim far more territory than accorded to it by the international community through the United Nations Partition Plan, voted in 1947 in a dubious atmosphere of extreme United States pressure on the small client states.[1] The subsequently established armistice lines were, in time, transformed into the recognized frontiers referred to in all the documents pertaining to the 1967 war calling for Israel's return to pre–5 June 1967 frontiers, the date of the outbreak of military operations.

The Arabs were therefore acutely conscious that the more time that passed, the greater the likelihood that the cease-fire lines established at the end of the June 1967 war would become permanent frontiers. Besides, Israel had already annexed the Arab part of Jerusalem and declared it would never evacuate the Golan Heights taken from Syria or return Sharm el-Sheikh in Sinai, while strips of the West Bank of Jordan, so charged with biblical history, would at most be returned to Jordan, trusted United States client, and not to the Palestinians. Following up words with deeds, the Israelis did everything to encourage Jewish colonies to settle on the conquered territories, to prevent the return of Arabs who had fled during the violence of military operations and to pressurize those who had stayed into emigrating.

Despite all Nasser's efforts, the war of attrition on the Suez Canal had brought no results and after the summer of 1970 a cease-fire prevailed there. The Syrian front also remained perfectly quiet after the end of hostilities in 1967. Gunnar Jarring's attempts to mediate under United Nations auspices were dragging themselves out pitifully, without any illusions on the part of the Arabs, for they well remembered Count Folke Bernadotte, assassinated in Jerusalem by Jewish terrorists in 1948. He had been United Nations mediator and, it seemed, too sympathetic to the injustices done to the Palestinians. In 1972, the goodwill mission of President Senghor of Senegal hardly gave any better results. The great hopes raised by the development of Palestinian armed resistance foundered in the 'Black September' tragedy in Amman, when the resistance movement's 'revolutionary' excesses led to King Hussein's forceful and successful clampdown. This confined Palestinian operations to Lebanon, the only territory that still remained open to resistance action.

The enthusiastic support of a substantial part of its population to the Palestinians obliged the Lebanese government to grant them the right to carry arms and undertake operations against Israel from certain regions of South Lebanon.[2] The small Lebanese army had neither the will nor the capacity to resist massive reprisals by the powerful Israeli army and accordingly kept itself entirely aloof from the operations taking place on its territory. In the absence of a concerted Arab policy of counter-reprisals, operations based in Lebanon were of no military consequence. Yet it was obvious that in the long run Lebanon would be unable to survive Palestinian excesses and Israeli batterings.

For the Palestinians, however, this was the only way of continuing to affirm their existence.

Major anti-Israeli terrorist operations were also carried out overseas, particularly the hijacking of aircraft and attacks on Israeli presence, such as the terrible Munich operations during the Olympic Games of September 1972, which made such a profound impression on the world. Still Arab opinion realized that Palestinian raids on Israel solely from isolated and vulnerable Lebanon, as well as such spectacular operations, however much they might bear witness to a regained Palestinian identity, could well have negative repercussions in the long run, even if the first spontaneous, emotional reaction (particularly among the young) was of unquestioning support for these manifestations of Palestinian existence.

President Sadat became more and more unconvincing with his announcements, first in 1971, and then in 1972, that the year would be decisive because he was going to start hostilities if Israel made no concessions.[3] Not only did he do nothing, but in 1972 dismissed 18,000 Soviet military experts,[4] sure indication that the Egyptian army did not intend to launch an offensive in the near future. The Syrian President, Hafez al-Assad, on the other hand, adopted a moderate position so that his country's years of ultra-Leftism, which had been responsible for Syria's Arab and international isolation, might be forgotten. Iraq, where the Ba'ath party was consolidating its power, could afford to speak out loud and reject the Security Council's famous Resolution 242,[5] for it had no common frontier with Israel, and who could forget that, during the events of September 1970, Iraqi troops present in Jordan had given no support to the Palestinian resistance? Libya had also begun to make loud international noises but President Gadaffi seemed more concerned to consolidate his position inside Libya by playing the new zealot of Arab unity than with worrying about Palestine.

The prevailing impression during 1971–2 was that the Arab countries were desperately seeking peace; that revolutionary romantic ultra-Leftism was living through the last stages of extremism in the shape of Palestinian operations from Lebanon and overseas; that though the Arab Near East had imperceptibly drawn closer to the West the latter held off because of inability to exercise sufficient pressure on Israel to ensure return of the occupied territories to their rightful owners. As had happened in the 1950s, after the first conquest of Palestine, all seemed to be going round and round in circles. This stagnation was clearly very dangerous for the legitimacy and, consequently, the stability of the Arab regimes and especially so since none of the attempts to bring about inter-Arab unity really got off the ground.

The thousand and one deaths of Arab unity

The fiery 27-year-old Libyan officer, Moamer al-Gadaffi, who overthrew the Senussi monarchy in 1969, sought legitimacy for himself by promoting and concretizing Arab unity. With Nasser gone, Gadaffi was convinced that he was the spiritual heir. His dynamic efforts resulted in a Federation of Arab Republics comprising Egypt, Syria and Libya being proclaimed in Benghazi in Libya in the spring of 1971 and receiving massive support in a referendum in the three countries by the end of summer. Gadaffi tried in vain to include Sudan in this ephemeral federation, but since the latter was trying to end a state of quasi-secession in the South Sudan, where the majority was non-Muslim and non-Arabic-speaking, it turned a deaf ear to a proposal that might have jeopardized all its efforts.

After the total collapse of the Federation, Libya then tried bilateral unity with Egypt but with no more success (August 1972). It should be mentioned that President Gadaffi was yet another illustration of the lack of phase existing not only between Arab and Western society, but between Egyptian society and the new Libyan society he embodied. The Libyan Head of State was, in fact, a direct product of Bedouin society, his cultural horizon limited to a simplified form of ethnicity composed of a mixture of Arab and puritanically Islamic sentiment. His only contacts with the modern world were derived from his military training but because of his youth these were unseasoned by experience. It was only oil wealth that gave his ardour the means to implement policies which neither the structures of Libyan society, nor his own cultural horizons or political experience would normally have allowed.

As an ancient society urbanized for millennia and on its way to political stability after the years of upheaval under Nasser, Egypt had no interest in an alliance with this young Arab of poor Bedouin stock, who had suddenly appeared with his oil to play the *nouveau riche* of Arab politics. For Egypt, the Wahhabis of

Saudi Arabia were partners of another calibre altogether, with a patent of nobility acquired over a long period. The new Libyan President's unionist attempts coincided exactly with the great reconciliation between Sadat and Faisal, between post-Nasser Egypt finding its feet again in the Near East and Saudi Arabia succeeding at last in a solid Pan-Arab breakthrough. Gadaffi's period Nasserism and Islamic puritanism, 170 years behind that of the Wahhabis, had hardly any appeal to the new political class of the Sadat era. And the summit of horror for the deputies of the Egyptian National Assembly may well have been Gadaffi's lecture to them in public session setting out his views on the position of women in Arab society.

Why then, one might ask, did Egypt lend itself to this farce of a new federation? In spite of the change of direction Sadat was leading the country towards, it was still in the last throes of Nasserism; Sadat, newly in power, could not afford to neglect the element of legitimacy that his nuisance of a neighbour was dangling over his head. There was, in addition, the financial aspect of Libyan oil wealth for a population of barely 2 million, against Egypt's mass of 36 million, with one of the lowest national incomes in the world. So in the autumn of 1971 they went ahead with the attempt and federated bodies were set up. But it came to a rapid end as soon as the question arose of unifying the two armies, the Libyan President wanting to play a major role which the Egyptian army evidently could not accept. Similarly, when it came to unifying banking and financial institutions, Gadaffi could not allow the Egyptians to get at the exchange reserves and oil revenues which were the sole source of his power. Both Presidents, however, could claim that they had tried to realize the dream of unity and were, therefore, honouring the political ideal until then prevailing in Arab political society.

In fact this was just another failure to add to the others: the three years of a Syrian-Egyptian union (1958–61) that backfired; an ephemeral federation between Egypt, Iraq and Syria in 1963; not to speak of the lack-lustre Presidential Council established in May 1964 to promote Iraqi-Egyptian unity. It thus succeeded in discrediting the very idea of unity in the eyes of public opinion, and, more seriously, depoliticized Arab society, which from then on began to realize that its political leaders were actors before they were statesmen. By now the people had come to see the ideal of unity as no more than a pretext for spectacular political gestures by autocrats seeking popular acclaim and legitimacy, while in practice only uncompromising political sovereignty intolerant of any limit dominated the scene. Besides, there were many to think that it was better that way, for if Arab unity meant having to put up simultaneously with underdevelopment, cultural discordances/dissonances and the fantasies of the military castes in power, it would be better to abandon it altogether.

The seizure of power by the Ba'athists in Iraq in 1968 did more to open a new era of rivalry between Syria and Iraq, two countries whose geographical situation ought to have favoured a natural unity, than to bring about unification. The Iraqi Ba'ath in fact claimed its legitimacy from the party's two founders (Michel Aflaq and Salah Bitar) who had been ousted from Syria in 1966 and with whom the Assad regime had no wish to become reconciled. Syria's entry into a federation with Egypt and Libya, still symbolized by Nasserist legitimacy, could well have been seen as an insurance against local public opinion unquestionably in favour of party unity in Syria and Iraq, but which nonetheless was nostalgic for Nasserism. This sterile political game, which we have already seen at work in the 1960s, increased Arab bitterness and, all said and done, undermined the legitimacy of the Arab political elites, which in turn often felt obliged to try and carry out ever more spectacular gestures even if lacking any prospect of success. This was to happen later in the shape of the abortive attempts at union between Libya and Tunisia in 1974 and between Syria and Libya in 1980. Likewise in 1972, when, in an attempt to assure himself of Palestinian support, Sadat broke with Jordan, which was trying, through its plan to bring the two banks of the Jordan together in a United Arab Kingdom, to recover the initiative from the hands of the PLO.

The genesis of a decision: to dismantle the Khartoum summit

Totally powerless against Israel, and with Arab aspirations for unity reduced to political games played solely for the survival of regimes rather than for any progress of society, there was no doubt that on the threshold of the 1970s the Near East was on the verge of breaking apart. The logic of a total alignment with the West, a powerful driving force behind Arab political behaviour, had come up against Israeli intransigence. As in 1948, Israel refused to implement the United Nations Resolutions, particularly those concerning the return of the Palestinian refugees expelled in 1948 and 1967, and above all the famous Security Council Resolution 242 of November 1967, already accepted by Nasser, condemning the acquisition of territory by force. This Resolution risked becoming ineffective with the passage of time and thus suffering the same fate as the 1947 Partition Plan, and thereby endorsing the new Israeli conquests, which this time had extended beyond the frontiers of Palestine itself. The big Western powers, however, seemed unaware of the gravity of the situation.

Western attention was focused mainly on the Vietnam war, the anti-Establishment student movements and the rise of terrorism, particularly in Germany and Italy. There was nothing in the Near East to threaten their oil supplies, guarded vigilantly by the Saudi monarchy and the Shah of Iran, whose thrones depended on Western goodwill. Too bad for Egypt which must suffer for so many misdeeds since the nationalization of the Suez Canal. As for Syria, Western chancelleries had long given up trying to understand its *coups d'etat* and international policy. Even if it seemed clear that General Assad had taken a turn to the Right, nobody could say how long his rule would last.

The United States was well aware that this powerlessness against Israel did serious harm to the Soviet Union, whose support for the Arab cause had hardly contributed even an inch of progress. This upset Sadat, as the expulsion of Soviet military experts from Egypt in 1972 confirmed. The only course left open was to wait for the fruit to ripen so that it could drop into the lap of the United States. It was the Kissinger policy that triumphed over the pro-Arab 'lobbies' in the United States, especially the oil companies, which were both very close to the Saudi monarchy and influential with the State Department. In another sphere, that of the established order in Western countries, the ties between the European extreme Left and certain Palestine resistance movements justified Israeli insistence on treating the Palestinians as terrorists and its refusal to negotiate with anyone except pro-Western Jordan.

In fact the Arabs seemed so ridiculously weak and disunited in the face of the all-powerful Israeli army that no one imagined a war could break out. All the more so not only because of the serious deterioration in Soviet-Arab relations, but also because of the very firm position taken by the Soviet Union, which, in the middle of working out a policy of peaceful coexistence with the

United States, seemed totally averse to a new war in the Near East. A new Arab defeat might very well cost it what little remained of its influence in the region.

Actually, the Soviet Union knew that Egypt intended to throw caution to the winds because the regime was tottering. In order not to lose permanently a country in which it had 'invested' so much, it delivered important military equipment after the expulsion of its experts in July 1972. Here too there was hardly a choice. Refusal to support Egypt's opening of a military front would have earned the Soviet Union final condemnation by the Arabs and the loss of the benefits of the enormous efforts it had been making in the Near East for twenty years. Even a very limited military success by Arab armies could only improve its dangerously eroded influence. Sadat too had little choice. Despite an active antipathy for the Soviet Union, he realized that hostilities with Israel would not get very far without the active military co-operation of the USSR. Hence the last episode, before and during the October war, of Soviet-Egyptian co-operation which in reality sounded the death knell of Russian presence in Egypt and by the same token of the legacy of Nasser.

Sadat's policy succeeded in excluding the Soviet Union from the search for peace in the Near East and allowed a massive American presence to return to Egypt, notably by providing military facilities. The Egyptian President thus achieved the far from trivial political feat of using Soviet arms for the last time (but this time successfully) for the purposes of a definite alignment with the capitalist West. In this respect, he was pursuing the great dream of all Egyptian sovereigns since Muhammad Ali, including Nasser, of seeing the Near East firmly attached to the West. It is not certain that the tactics employed were adequate, for if the end is to justify the means, especially in politics, a nation must display at least minimal consistency in the broad lines of its foreign policy if it is to retain its credibility. Furthermore, one should never expect to get away with holding a great power up to ridicule. Before Sadat, Nasser had learnt this to his cost. But, as we have already noted, the two men were much too much alike and Sadat could not therefore draw lessons from his predecessor's unhappy experiences.

The outbreak of war in October 1973, involving perfectly co-ordinated action between Egypt and Syria, thus took Israel and the United States by surprise. The latter, however, were not too greatly displeased. The prevailing Kissinger-type realism enabled it to see that the deadlock was at last going to be broken, all the more so as, to everyone's amazement, it was the Israelis who were taken unawares and the Arabs who were in full control of their movements. There was thus hope of ending Israeli intransigence so far secure in the unshakeable belief in its own total military superiority. For early in October 1973, the unbelievable really happened. A perfectly disciplined, logistically confident Egyptian army crossed the Suez Canal, considered a practically insurmountable natural obstacle, in the space of a few hours, installed itself comfortably on the other bank, occupied Israel's famous Maginot line, the Bar-Lev line, without encountering any opposition, and then with disconcerting ease routed timid enemy counter-attacks. The Syrian army for its part broke through all Israeli security dispositions on the Golan Heights and prepared to hurl itself down those steep slopes to sweep onto Galilee, occupied in 1948 but still peopled by a majority of Arabs. It was like a dream in which the 1967 war had been turned back to front, with the Israelis in the role of Arabs and the Arabs as Israelis. Had the wave of some magic wand changed the face of the Near East? Or indeed had things been happening there which the outward appearance of those repetitive events that have been described concealed from even the most perspicacious of observers?

Many believed that the October war had been planned in CIA computers to permit Egypt's honourable and permanent return to the Western fold, and to knock a bit of sense into Israel while consolidating the latter's position by obtaining for it recognition by the Arab countries. If the personality of Dr Kissinger – obscure German-Jewish professor of political science who in a few short years had hoisted himself to the summit of international power – is taken into account, the hypothesis acquires an additional dimension. But it is clearly absurd, even if Kissinger's Jewishness gave free rein to the propensity of anti-Semites to imagine international conspiracy. It was, besides, a pathetic enough spectacle to see the Secretary of State of the world's greatest power exhausting himself some months later in innumerable shuttles between Jerusalem, Damascus and Cairo to obtain an agreement for disengagement of the troops and then on 1 September 1975 for non-belligerence between Egypt and Israel. On one occasion, leaving Jerusalem when all seemed lost, Kissinger was even seen with tears in his eyes.

There is no doubt whatsoever that the decision to launch the October 1973 war was that of President Sadat, a courageous decision taken against the advice of many Egyptian officers who believed that an attempt to cross the Canal was unlikely to succeed. The decision was in fact the very logical conclusion to the deadlock in which the Arabs found themselves. When the economic pressures involved are taken into account, it is hardly surprising that the decision was Egypt's, Syria merely following. Syria was under-populated, with balances of resources and under-exploitation of its agricultural potential. Egypt was over-populated and without notable resources outside its limited and over-exploited agricultural land. The Suez Canal closed, tourist trade halted, Sinai oil wells occupied, half a million men under the colours, a million refugees from the Canal zone in Cairo: so many factors bringing the economy to its knees, despite subsidies from Arab oil countries, which barely compensated for the loss of revenue from the closure of the Canal alone.

Sadat was not alone in his historic decision. Besides being in total co-ordination with Syria, he had the full support of Saudi Arabia, which also wanted the situation eased at any price, and the active sympathy of the Algerian President. In this, Boumedienne was faithful to the ideals of the Algerian war of liberation but, fanatic that he was for rapid modernization, tried like Faisal to remove political obstacles hampering relations with the capitalist West, symbol of industrial progress and prosperity. Shortly after the military disengagement between Egypt and Israel, Algeria re-established diplomatic relations with the United States, which had been broken immediately after the Arab–Israeli war of 1967.

The decision to resume hostilities with Israel was in reality in keeping with the situation created at the Khartoum summit, which, as described earlier, put the Arab countries in the false situation of accepting the West but refusing Israel. Since 1967 the Arab world had suffered from the deadlock, of which its leaders became increasingly aware. The idea of normalizing the existence of Israel had gained ground within the community of Near Eastern countries since 1967. But accepting Israel implied first recovering the territories conquered in 1967. To recover them meant getting the West to change position. To get the West, insensitive to the tragedy of the Arab political elite, to do that a dramatic crisis had to be created. And that precisely required armed conflict which would obviously involve the Soviet Union – the infallible red rag to the American bull. It is only these factors which enable the significance of the October war and the military developments to be properly grasped.

The semiology of a war and of an embargo

In the continuity of Arab politics (several of whose fundamentals have already been set forth) this context was new in form but not in substance. In 1967, in the build-up to the crisis leading to the opening of hostilities by Israel, Nasser raised his bids in the hope of better negotiating an overall peaceful settlement of the Arab–Israeli dispute. Closing the Straits of Tiran to Israeli shipping and demanding the withdrawal of the United Nations peace-keeping force from Sinai were spectacular gestures, but also signals sufficiently clear to political semiologists. All the more so, as on 28 May 1967, a few days before Israel's lightning attack, at the same press conference at which he had threatened Israel with destruction in the event of aggression on its part, Nasser, affirming that under no circumstances would Egypt be the first to open hostilities, proposed reactivation of the mixed Israeli-Egyptian armistice commission as well as global negotiations with the good offices of the big powers to find a solution to the Palestine problem. In turning to his own political advantage the crisis that Syria's ultra-Leftism provoked with Israel in the spring of 1967, the Egyptian president already sought a solution to the Arab–Israeli problem as a whole, in deadlock since 1949. At that time the problem concerned only the Palestinian refugees, for Israel had not yet conquered the territories of any Arab country other than Palestine.

Among the Western powers, however, only de Gaulle, in France, understood the significance of Egyptian policy. In the United States, President Johnson and his placid Secretary of State, Dean Rusk, hardly possessed the same high astuteness as the Nixon-Kissinger team in 1973. But more than anyone Nasser was the *bête-noire* of the West. The big 'international' newspapers solidly in favour of Israel went all out against the Egyptian president, whom they saw as the hated symbol of the Third World's economic anti-colonialism. The atmosphere of hostility against Arabs in general thus built up in the West as a whole hardly encouraged the governments to intervene in any positive manner.

It was as if all the resentment that the rich and powerful West felt against the revolt of the oppressed was crystallized in the Arab Near East, where good and evil were at last confronting one another so that 'Justice' could triumph.

What a marvellous triumph the victory of the little David against the giant Goliath was for the West, so deeply and naively hypocritical in this matter. What a hotch-potch of error and confusion in those days of 1967 when the West and its ambiguous, narcissistic reflection, Israel, savoured the Arab humiliation! It is pointless now to dwell on this inglorious aspect of the Western 'psyche', in no way outdone by the darkest mysteries of Oriental 'soul'. It is enough to recall how General de Gaulle was vilified in Paris[6] for his discordant note in the enormous physical and psychic beating the Arabs were undergoing and his adoption of a political line distinguishing him from other Western leaders. But we may take the opportunity to reaffirm that morality and politics are not necessarily contradictory, for to this day France continues to reap substantial dividends from de Gaulle's Near Eastern policy.

By 1973 nothing very much had changed. It was simply that the Arab–Israeli conflict was both more bitter and more far-reaching. The former because resentments had built up and the Palestinians, until 1967 hermetically sealed in their refugee camps, had escaped and were violently expressing themselves, not only among the Arabs and the Israelis, but also in Europe. The latter because in 1967, Israel, no longer content with completing the conquest of Palestine, had occupied an enormous chunk of Egypt, and a small but strategically very important region in Syria. Having learnt from their 1967 experience, this time the Arabs carefully prepared the new face that they intended to present to the West, as much military as political. To begin with, there was of course the expulsion of Russian experts from Egypt, but also Hafez al-Assad's turn to the Right in Syria, the hunt for communists all over the Arab world and the rally of all around the two great Arab pillars of the West, the monarchies of Saudi Arabia and Morocco. At the fourth conference of Non-Aligned countries in Algiers in September 1973, President Gadaffi made himself the spokesman of Arab dissatisfaction with the Soviet Union and virulently attacked pro-Soviet countries, particularly Cuba.

The Arab mass media, whose incredible stupidity and bragging in 1967 had been so helpful to Israeli propaganda, were quite different in style now that they had purged themselves of monotonous incantations against imperialism. To this was added solid groundwork in explaining the Palestinian cause to Western opinion, with supporting facts and figures. Beirut became a big information centre for the Palestinian cause, which was visited diligently by the international press. This role, so vital in any war of national liberation in which information is as important as arms, was to cost it dear.

Militarily, the Egyptian army's conduct of operations left no doubt about the limited nature of the war it was undertaking. It was to cross the Canal and not to move from the east bank whatever the cost. During the operations and despite massive aid from the Soviets, who mounted a non-stop airlift between Egypt and Syria, there was no pro-Soviet declaration of friendship and no warm welcome when, in the middle of the war, Alexei Kosygin spent three days in Cairo.

Lastly, the new weapon: oil, made by the West into an abuse that it could no longer do without, like morphine, and had to have in absurd and monstrous quantities. Oil prices began to rise in 1970, but even in their hour of greatest distress, in 1967, the Arabs had not dared to withhold it, crushed though they were by the hostile indifference of the West. Here again the gestures were unmistakable, but were nevertheless misunderstood; the West's power was being touched in its most sensitive place, again unleashing torrents of anger. Who can be sure that Faisal the majestic, architect of the oil operations that accompanied the war, did not pay dearly for his 'impertinence' towards the West with his own life in 1975? Yet the meaning of the 1973 embargo was crystal clear. The West was meant to understand without too much dislocation – in fact just what occurred. The timid restrictions on the use of cars at weekends in some European countries during the winter of 1973 did not really do much harm; the queues at gas stations in some American States were due more to the peculiarities and muddles of different American oil laws than to serious breakdowns in supply.

Saudi Arabia had actually made it clear to the consortium of oil companies operating on its territory that they should be ready to face difficult circumstances as a result of Israeli stubbornness. As from May 1973 Aramco had considerably increased Saudi production, so that the reduction due to the embargo merely restored it to its normal rate of increase, which was in any case very high. Thus, while Saudi production dropped by 19.5 per cent between the third and fourth quarter of 1973, it had increased by 36.4 per cent during the first nine months of 1973 compared to the same period in 1972.[7]

The Arab oil-exporting countries[8] decided to go ahead with the embargo only on 17 October, in Kuwait, eleven days after the start of hostilities. The date is important because it shows that the dangerous decision was taken only when there was no longer any doubt about the extent of the airlift the United States was providing to Israel from 14 October, far in excess of that the Russians were providing to the Arabs. Thanks to the American airlift, the Israelis were able to retake the offensive, cross over to the west bank of the Canal, reoccupy the Golan Heights and there extend their former occupation zone. The decision taken in Kuwait was thus clearly aimed at punishing the Americans for their partiality. The embargo was, nevertheless, limited in extent, amounting to progressive reduction of production by only 5 per cent a month until a way out of the conflict had been found and a beginning made in implementation.[9] Friendly countries supporting the Arab cause were not included in the embargo, for example in Europe, France and Spain; and elsewhere many Third World countries, particularly Islamic and African ones. On 18 November the reduction was suspended for the month of December so far as the EEC was concerned, because at the beginning of the month it had adopted a more balanced attitude towards the solution to the conflict. In December, the embargo was re-imposed in principle, but with Japan included in the list of friendly countries, and a reluctant Algeria protesting that all deliveries should be restored to Europe which was not really hostile to the Arab cause.

In point of fact, the embargo could hardly qualify as serious, for it was partial and did not even apply to all Western countries. Further, since the marketing and distribution of their oil were in Western hands, in particular those of the big oil companies, the Arab exporting countries had no way of controlling enforcement. Tankers were often told their destination when well out at sea. Very big non-Arab producers like Iran, Nigeria, Indonesia and Venezuela continued to export normally. The Iraqis, supposed pillars of Arab intransigence, did not reduce their production and did not even bother to attend the meeting in Kuwait on 17 October at which the embargo was decided. Having already nationalized their oil in 1972, they argued that, in their opinion, nationalization was damaging imperialist interests more than any embargo.

It is therefore hardly surprising that the export level for oil-exporting countries as a whole shows the same rate of growth for 1973 as for 1972, that is the extremely high rate of 9.5 per cent. It was clearly the companies that benefited from the shortage and the rise in prices, which assured them super-profits on an unhoped-for scale. But also the American government, whose absurd oil policy had made the United States dependent on imports, and which was now actively seeking the right moment to persuade Congress to abolish legislation harmful to the development of domestic energy potential.

Although the embargo had not been officially lifted, from the beginning of 1974 supplies on the whole seemed back to normal. To dispel misunderstandings, and because the West was still ranting and raving over the sudden price adjustments caused by this modest and ineffective embargo, in January 1974 the two big oil names in the Arab world, Bel Eid Abdessalam, Algerian Minister of Oil and Industry, and Ahmad Zaki Yamani, Saudi Minister of Oil, together undertook a grand tour of Japan and the Western world to explain the Arab position.

Unwarranted interference: oil price chaos

Already in Vienna at the beginning of October 1973 the OPEC countries had failed to reach an agreement with the oil companies over adjusting oil prices to inflation, which in the industrialized countries, principal suppliers of the oil-exporting countries, was going up by the minute. On 16 October, the day before the embargo decision, and also in Kuwait, the five Arab producers of the Gulf and Iran decided to increase the price per barrel by 70 per cent, which brought it up from 3 to 5.11 dollars. They were doing no more than bringing their prices into line with those already charged by Algeria, Venezuela and Indonesia. This shows that, despite the coincidence of the dates, decisions about oil prices were separate from those concerning the embargo. In fact two completely different dynamics were at play. Some weeks later all the OPEC countries met again in Tehran on 23 December under the leadership of the Shah, and decided to double the price per barrel to 11.65 dollars. It had been under the Shah's auspices that the considerable price rise under the famous 1971 agreements had taken place.[10] The companies, on their part, now did a bit of pushing, since they were paying up to 17 dollars a barrel and were prepared to go higher.[11]

In reality, the market merely adjusted itself after years of cheap oil. All that was past history now hardly worth mentioning. But the political significance of the embargo, which the Arab countries had set up so well, collapsed in horror at the prospect of chaos in the market. Propaganda-wise, it was easy from then on to make the Arabs responsible not only for the energy crisis but also for the recession overtaking the economies of industrialized countries and for the general balance of payments deficits of energy-importing countries. Under pressure to modify their stand, the Israelis unceasingly clamoured to one and all that the West had abandoned courageous little 'David' for a few barrels of Arab oil. In the industrialized countries the mass media worked themselves up against oil producers and especially the Arabs. Kissinger headed an anti-OPEC crusade to which he sought to recruit all Western countries and which led to the formation of the International Energy Agency (IEA), Western counterpart to the OPEC. France alone opposed it and moreover refused to join the IEA. But the damage had been done; the chaos in oil, for which the West was primarily responsible, monopolized Arab attention from then on and diverted energy from the Arab–Israeli conflict. Sadat's road to a separate peace with Israel, which he took alone amidst the jeers of the other Arab leaders, was already open at the end of 1974. This is a point to which it will be necessary to return in greater detail.

In the meanwhile, let us finish the story of this embargo which turned into something quite different from what had been so carefully and prudently set up, and which was to have a profound effect on political developments in Near Eastern countries. In point of fact, the embargo very quickly burnt the fingers of its planners. All their caution was no help against the horror the rising spiral of oil prices engendered not only in the West but also in Third World countries, which saw their oil import bills mounting dangerously. Accordingly, the authors of the embargo, who had incidentally alleviated its practical effect almost immediately, rapidly tried to find some way of lifting it officially. It was over this that Kissinger became so active in the disengagement negotiations from the beginning of January 1974, in his famous shuttling between Jerusalem, Damascus and Cairo. At the same time, however, the Secretary of State was hatching a plan for a Western counter-attack against OPEC. The Americans made sure that the military noises being made in the United States were heard abroad, for example, special training of troops for rapid intervention, thinly veiled threats of military intervention in the Arab-Persian Gulf.

The two principal pro-American forces in the Near and Middle East, Egypt and Saudi Arabia, were disturbed by these developments which were turning their whole political strategy upside down. To alienate the West because of a phony embargo was absurd since their main objective was to settle the Arab–Israeli dispute so that the cultural and economic integration of the Near East with the capitalist West could be established on a firm basis. The hostility of the American protector would undermine the very socio-economic foundations of the Saudi monarchy and push Egypt, which had hoped once and for all to shake off the Russian alliance, back into the arms of the Soviet Union. From December, President Sadat had made it known to the Americans that he was doing his best to get the embargo lifted and, to this end, throughout January, did not cease to exert all kinds of pressure on the oil countries.

The lifting was only announced officially on 18 March at a meeting of Arab oil-exporting countries held in Vienna. This came after the Egyptian-Israeli military disengagement agreement was signed on 18 January 1974, but before the Syrian-Israeli disengagement, which took place only on 31 May 1974. Syria was thus abandoned in midstream. This it would find difficult to forget, especially since it had tried by every means to prevent this gesture towards the West, which, although purely symbolic effectively disrupted Arab solidarity. The tyranny of oil had already turned into a political catastrophe for the Arabs and in a few years would soon become an economic and social canker eating away dangerously the foundations of Arab society. Even within the OPEC, and more generally in the relations between the rich, industrialized countries and the Third World, nothing would ever be the same again.

Saudi Arabia was virtually traumatized by Western hostility at the quadrupling of oil prices, for which public opinion blamed the embargo and the Arabs. From then on, OPEC as in all important international negotiations, adopted a line exclusively favourable to the interests of the West. Because of its new oil and financial power, especially since the quadrupling of prices, its attitude considerably weakened the efforts of Algeria and President Boumedienne. In an attempt to move beyond the shock provoked by the oil chaos of the last months of 1973, Boumedienne had tried to improve the encounter with the West by raising and generalizing the debate towards a reform of the international economic order that would allow the Third World to participate on an equal footing in the prosperity and technical progress of the industrialized world.

Thus, the Suez Canal, object of the third Arab–Israeli war, was again to set off economic events significant for the twentieth century. It had played this role in the nineteenth, having been largely responsible for Egypt's occupation by Great Britain and, therefore, for the direct subjection of the Near East shortly afterwards by the European powers. In 1956, nationalization of the Canal had served as a symbol to mobilize support for the Third World's first wave of economic liberation. It faithfully played its role once again in 1973, when Egypt, economically on its knees since the 1967 war, decided to free it from Israeli occupation, so that, opened again, it could put the country back into the circuit of international commerce. The Arab oil embargo, more political than economic, instituted on 17 October was designed to help Egypt keep the east bank, which, contrary to all expectations, it had reconquered from the Israelis and was in danger of losing again through a massively American-armed Israeli counter-offensive on the west bank.

The action in the domain of oil that accompanied the freeing of the Canal activated the second wave of the Third World's economic liberation. But there was as much ambiguity now as during the 1960s. The tyranny of oil in the 1970s could have worked in favour of extreme Right fundamentalism, just as Nass-erist Caesarism in the 1960s had given an impetus to ultra-Left radicalism, which helped to give the forces of the Right a rallying point. The war of October 1973 was essentially a Right-wards tending war. Its origins and the motivations of its Arab protagon-ists clearly proved this, even if it still took place in the shadow of political symbols that belonged to the preceding period and with sociological constants traced out in the course of Egyptian history.

For all that, the ideological coloration of events is perhaps less important than the historical constants of societies, which limit the significance of ideological signals without necessarily invalidating them. This applies even more to Third World societies, where modern political language is still weakly organized and where it is often employed with a volubility all the greater in that it serves the purpose of masking the permanence of old structures of constraint. Besides, everywhere in the world oppression is possible under the guise of 'Left-wing' change or 'Right-wing' stability. Sadat, the great polarizer of contradictions, moved Right-wards in his crossing of the Canal yet in a Left-ward sense accomplished a gesture of great historical significance. The Arab partners, Syria engaged in the battle, or Saudi Arabia and Algeria actively supporting it, also simultaneously contain within themselves all the colours of the ideological kaleidoscope. This makes the 1973 war ambiguous at all levels, both at that of the international events it triggered off, as well as that of its own military and political development.

The military operations: first victory or last defeat

The next generation of historians will be able to say whether the October 1973 war was the first of the Arabs' victories against the Israelis or the last of their defeats. With its successful military feats and politically spectacular spin-offs, it is still difficult to apprehend the full effect of the war and the range of events it unleashed. Numerous controversies surround the various reports on the progress of the war, not only between the Israelis and Arabs, but also within each of the two camps in which there is lively debate over the causes of success or of reverses. The actual operations show clearly that the Egyptian and Syrian armies were wholly successful in their offensives, against both natural obstacles and defences considered impregnable.

For reasons already cited, by initially ruling out the opening of hostilities at the first signs of mobilization in the Syrian and Egyptian armies, the Israeli government realized only forty-eight hours in advance that the risk of war well and truly existed. Unlike in 1967, they decided against a preventive air strike because their most important ally and main armaments supplier, the United States, seemed against it and because the generals did not believe the Egyptian army could cross the Canal so quickly. They therefore considered that they had enough time to hold on until mobilization of their reservists was complete, not perhaps realizing sufficiently just how effective were the anti-aircraft missiles used by the Egyptians and Syrians, which paralysed their air force in the first days of the war. The Israeli government thus quite deliberately decided against a preventive attack, which might alienate the Western opinion that until then had supported it so well in its intransigence over the occupied territories. For the Israelis, the war was going to open the door to new territorial conquests and enable them to confirm the annexation of such of the territories taken in 1967 they had definitely decided to keep.

But subsequent military operations also showed without any possible doubt that once recovered from the shock the Israeli army would regain its operational initiative. It pushed beyond the cease-fire lines of 1967, threatening Damascus and Cairo from even closer than during the June 1967 war. The danger was all the greater because, as in all the preceding wars, the Israelis ignored the cease-fire declared by the United Nations Security Council on 22 October and repeated on the 23rd and continued to occupy new territories. Then followed a spectacular escalation in the confrontation between the Soviet Union and the United States. To what looked like preparations for Soviet armed intervention to enforce the cease-fire, the Americans responded by putting their entire strategic air command (SAC) on a third-degree nuclear alert[12] on the night of 24/5 October. The reality was that in response to Israel's failure to respect the cease-fire, the Russians, supported at the United Nations by the non-aligned countries, proposed a Soviet-American force to separate the combatants. Nixon and Kissinger, whose whole Near Eastern policy centred on getting the Soviet Union out of this strategic oil region, would not hear of a project that would sanction their presence. Yet even Sadat, who shared the Nixon government's anti-Russian obsession, supported the project. It was true that the Israeli army was approaching the suburbs of the important town of Suez on the west bank of the Canal, thus succeeding in encircling the Egyptian Third Army, which had spent several victorious days on the east bank.

After the lightning victory of the first few days and the extraordinary military and technical feat not only of crossing the Canal, but of doing it so quickly, the Egyptian army suffered astonishing reverses. In only twenty-four hours, beginning on 6 October, 100,000 men, 1000 tanks and 13,500 vehicles had crossed over to the other bank, under the very nose of the Israeli defences, which collapsed like a house of cards, showing the whole world that the notion of a secure frontier, so prized by the Israelis, was an illusion. The Egyptian setbacks after the victorious crossing of the Canal can nevertheless be explained partly by the nature of Egypt's political objectives in the war and partly in terms of certain traditional problems of the Egyptian army. For the objectives of the war, namely to cross the Canal and stay there, were very limited but were nonetheless seen as a formidable military under-taking, especially since the Egyptians hardly suspected the weak-ness they actually discovered in the Israeli defences.

Once the crossing had taken place without incident, and the first Israeli counter-offensives had been successfully pushed back, the Egyptian army had no contingency plan. It merely waited for the cease-fire, ready to turn to the diplomatic and political game, and did not develop its advantage by trying to reach the famous Mitla and Giddi passes, about 50 kilometres from the Canal and of fundamental strategic importance to the military domination of Sinai. When on 14 October the Egyptian army eventually tried to advance, ostensibly to relieve pressure on the Syrian army in retreat on the Golan front, it was too late. The American airlift was operating on a grand scale and the Israeli arsenals had been re-supplied following the heavy losses of the first few days. The Egyptian offensive failed. On the night of 15–16 October, the Israeli army infiltrated the Deversoir area of the west bank. It apparently took several days for the Egyptian command to realize just how irreversible the Israeli offensive was.

Having been very intensively trained by the Russians in a war of position, the Egyptian army could not actually keep up with a war of movement, in which the Israeli enemy excelled. Its logistics quickly became disorganized. Though united in their early days of sheer victory, when confronted with the first reverses the offi-cers of the Egyptian High Command relapsed into their traditional quarrels and could hardly agree on how to liquidate the Israeli pocket on the west bank. This made the situation worse, especially since, freed from all pressure on the Syrian front since 13 October, the Israeli army could concentrate solely on the Egyptian front, where American military aircraft were unloading tons of equip-ment directly onto the El Aris airstrip in Sinai.

It was in fact on the Syrian front where there was the greater danger in the beginning for the Israelis because of its proximity to the Palestinian territories on which they had established their State in 1948. Their defences there were therefore much better stocked with men and equipment than on the Bar-Lev line on the Canal. Until 9 October, the Syrians were successful in their offensive, progressing 20 kilometres beyond the cease-fire lines of 1967. But their losses in equipment were so great that on 10 October they withdrew to their starting points. From 11 to 13 October, the Israelis mounted a counter-attack and achieved a 20 kilometre breakthrough on the north-west flank of the Syrians, without however totally routing their opponents, who had been reinforced by the arrival of Iraqi forces. The Syrians in fact withdrew in good order and their new defence lines did not succumb to Israeli pressure. With the Syrian front thus stabilized, the Israelis did not persist in this sector but turned their attention to re-establishing the military balance on the Egyptian front where, until then, they had been doing badly, losing considerable amounts of equipment in ineffective counter-offensives (more than 600 tanks, as against the Egyptians who, until 13 October, had kept their losses down to 300 tanks). Having given full military and diplomatic support to the Israelis, the United States government did not wish to leave them to negotiate with the Arabs from too weak a position.

It was out of this situation that the escalation developed between the two big powers. For attached to the fate of the belligerents' arms was the prestige of the arms suppliers, who were at the same time the combatants' political patrons. In the first few days of the war, the Arab armies had mounted a dazzling demonstration of the effectiveness of Soviet equipment in wreaking havoc in the Israeli armour and air-force. The United States could not accept a success of this kind which jeopardized the gains of their policy. This explains the scale of the American airlift and delivery of the most sophisticated equipment, in particular electronic systems for deflecting missile paths. The United States being about 10,000 kilometres from the field of operations the airlift was a logistic feat in itself, with continuous delivery in the heart of Sinai from 12 October of thousands of tons of equipment, including heavy tanks. Though the Russians are only 3000 kilometres from the Near East, their no less spectacular airlift was not such a logistic feat, though in their case they had to supply two different armies. But they also transported less tonnage than the Americans, 15,000 for Egypt and Syria, against 27,895 tons to Israel of which 5500 was transported by aircraft of the Israeli commercial line, El Al.[13]

This makes it easier to understand why the Israelis ignored the cease-fire declared on 22 October by the Security Council after it had been negotiated by Kissinger and Brezhnev in Moscow on 20 and 21 October, dates on which the Egyptian and Israeli protagonists arrived at a draw on the field of military operations. This the Israelis had wanted to avoid at any price, for when negotiations came they would have nothing new with which to drive a hard bargain. This was especially necessary this time, as opposed to in 1967, for they would be held doubly accountable. They had to answer to international opinion which, in spite of everything, believed that, although the Arabs had been the first to attack, responsibility for the war lay on Israel for its continued occupation of territories conquered more than six years before, and in its stubbornness in not recognizing the existence of a Palestinian cause. But they would also have to answer to Israeli opinion at home on the eve of the Knesset elections due in December. The Labour government would be asked if it had tried hard enough to come to a settlement with the Arabs, and if so, why the first days of the war had been such a disaster, when anyone could foresee that the Arabs would try to regain their lost territories by force. Hence the need to ignore the cease-fire and keep going until the suburbs of the town of Suez were reached, encircling the Egyptian Third Army in the process. Only then did Israel consider it had gained enough to negotiate an effective end to hostilities and disengagement of troops, whose positions had become inextricably mixed up. But meanwhile, the peace of the world was put in danger and there was the famous incident when the anger of the Russians provoked the American nuclear alert of 25 October.

Launched without consultation with their NATO allies, the American alert was in all likelihood an over-reaction, but it was clearly understood by the Soviets who, on the 26th, abandoned their plan of an American-Soviet force to separate the combatants. This enabled the United Nations Security Council to vote on the same day for a resolution setting up a United Nations Emergency Force (excluding its permanent members) to ensure the effective implementation of the cease-fire. On 29 October Israeli and Egyptian military personnel began discussions at the now famous milestone 101 on the road from Cairo to Suez. The fourth Arab–Israeli war had ended.[14]

The ambiguities of a war: the blood of the poor and the gold of the rich

Having begun in an extremely ambiguous context for the Arabs, with strictly limited military objectives, especially on the Egyptian side, the war ended in total confusion. The oil embargo, which was so important as an Arab counter *vis-à-vis* the West, had hardly fulfilled its role as a weapon and was being diverted from its objective. The international oil market had abruptly seized the opportunity to correct a fundamental imbalance that had lasted too long. From then on, the problem of oil prices and the avalanche of petro-dollars descending on the international financial system, riveted world attention. Firstly in the industrialized countries, where aroused anti-Arab prejudice was all the more pernicious for having to be hidden so as not to endanger economic interests that had become far too important. But also in the OPEC countries, particularly Saudi Arabia (with the most swollen petro-dollar coffers of all its oil colleagues) as well as in other Third World countries for which oil costs had become a serious problem. Oil had thus become a double-edged weapon, one which, incidentally, the Arabs had never much liked considering that they had hardly ever used it before, because of the risk of alienating the West, whom they had courted with so much passion since the time of Muhammad Ali.

The Arab armies lost their military advantage during the first week of the war. Admittedly they had shown that from now on they would be different from what they had been in 1967 and had achieved an important qualitative leap in handling sophisticated military equipment. But subsequent reverses also showed that they were far from having mastered the complex problems of mobility and co-ordination between military units which a war of movement demands. It must once more be borne in mind, regarding these reverses, that Israel enjoyed the aggressive support of its American protector, thereby pushing its superiority in the war of movement to the limit, and practising its traditional policy of ignoring cease-fires. On the Arab side, the Russian protector was highly cautious in its support, especially during the years when Brezhnev was seeking detente with the capitalist West, in the hope of extending the economic co-operation which Russia so urgently needed.

The question now was whether these unfavourable political and military factors would undermine the basic Arab attitude and lead to the Near East falling, perhaps permanently this time into the Russian orbit, with a renewed radicalization of the elite. And further, whether the ambiguities and confusions of the October war would enable the Palestinian resistance (whose Left wing had conducted all those spectacular operations since 1968, overseas, in Israel, and even in the Arab countries) to tip Arab society into a bitter, uncompromising revolutionary upsurge avenging all sorts of economic, social and political oppression. These issues came to characterize the Near East and dominate the development of events.

These would be fierce and bloody. For although the war ended on 29 October 1973, when Egyptian and Israeli military personnel started talking at milestone 101, Arab blood had only just begun to flow. The October war had certainly seen the biggest tank battles in contemporary history; but although the cost in hardware had been very heavy, bearing in mind the extent of the fighting, it had been light in human lives. It was only later that the Arabs experienced the real cost in human life resulting from the ambiguities of this war in the shape of the terrible Lebanese civil war and the horror of continuous Israeli reprisals (which incidentally had not stopped since 1968) against innocent Palestinian and Lebanese civilians, from the extreme south to the extreme north of this tiny territory, whose only faults were to be wedged in geographically between Syria and Israel and to have the most decadent political elite in the Arab world.

But for the time being, at the end of 1973, there was a certain euphoria in the air, for talks were at last in sight, in which, the Arabs being now on a more equal military and economic footing, a way might open through an intolerably deadlocked situation. Despite its acute anxieties about oil, the West too was thinking in terms of the serious dialogue with the Near East which was so vital to its survival. Westerners were well aware, however, and had been since 1950, that they had entered into an equation with the Arabs which Israeli intransigence had so far made it impossible to solve. Their position was clearly untenable what with the unqualified 'yes' to Israel and 'no' to all Arab demands, including those legitimized by United Nations resolutions they themselves had approved and voted for; as well as the 'no' to a Soviet presence in the Near East in support of the Arab and Palestinian cause, making it necessary for the West to seek preferential cultural, economic and military ties with the principal countries of the region.

Arab socio-political developments between 1967 and 1973, the events of the 1973 war, and the initial crushing blow at the Israeli army together created circumstances favourable to normalizing the situation in the Near East. Because of its oil, this highly important region, geopolitically, had acquired a strategic economic dimension even more important than the opening of the Suez Canal in the last century. The old American dream of uniting Israel with its neighbours in a military alliance to contain the Russian giant rose from the ashes and found itself in the company of the anti-Soviet phobia of two of the principal Arab Heads of State, King Faisal and President Sadat. This phobia was stimulated by the deep attraction of the Arabs for the Christian capitalist West, an attraction which had been long frustrated by the existence of Israel and by its massive support in the West.

From this encounter, and from the excesses that it led to, a new and unhappy phase was born in the history of relations between East and West. The separate peace signed between Egypt and Israel in 1978 created a deep fissure in the Arab world, which in 1973–4 believed that it had at last refound unity in action, if not a unity of States and territories: a peace all the more serious, in that through the first Camp David Agreements it laid the foundations of a Palestinian 'Bantustan', so desired by Israel in order to be freed from pretending to ignore the existence of an Arab population on the Palestinian soil it had conquered in 1948 and 1967.

To this scenario was now added the outbreak of oil tyranny, in both East and West. After the October war, billions of dollars came down in a frenzied torrent onto the deserts, semi-arid mountains and olive trees of the Near East, shaking Arab society to its deepest foundations, creating all sorts of double-dealing officials and speculation and bringing social disorder and economic anarchy in its wake. A golden calf ruled in the lands of mysticism. In this state of misfortune, thrones tottered and all the God-crazed political figures whose presence have always studded the history of the region, cradle of religions, reappeared. Although religious fanatacism was to explode under Ayatollah Khomeini in Iran, in reality it had long been rumbling in the whole of the Near and Middle East, finding its strength in the popular religious brotherhoods everywhere left intact behind a facade of modernization.

Not even secular Turkey, Baathist Syria or Mediterranean Egypt would be exempt.

The West, for its part, also adored this twentieth century golden calf and did nothing to help the East. A frantic rush began to lay hands on the billions of dollars passing East-wards by 'recycling', as economists call it, a technical term concealing highly dubious transactions and lunatic projects sold to the Arabs and to other monarchs of oil. These merely accelerated the destruction of the social fabric of these societies which decades of abortive moderniz-ation had made more and more fragile. There was also Western blackmail and brutal pressure of all kinds on these countries whose apparent excess of economic power merely reflected the depth of their underdevelopment. This went as far as threats of military intervention, which Kissinger so jauntily did in an interview to an internationally renowned American economic journal,[15] considered to be the mouthpiece of the United States business community. *Newsweek*,[16] another American weekly with a world-wide circulation, had previously discussed in graphic detail stra-tegies for taking the oil 'sheikhs' by the throat, including military intervention. The West also pressurized the more docile of its oil allies into increasing their production in the vain hope of lowering prices. Such increases only complicated and worsened the financial difficulties posed by the increasing and destabilizing flow of petro-dollars.

Finally, a last unfortunate consequence of the ambiguity of the October war was that those who had fought were the poorest of poor Arabs, the destitute peasants who formed the main strength of the Egyptian and Syrian armies, and the refugees in the Palesti-nian camps, proletarianized to the last degree, whose suicide oper-ations maintained tensions in the region and prodded immobile Arab regimes into action. But it was the feudal lords of the Arab world on whom the dollars and the honours rained. This goes towards explaining why the Egyptian leader, exasperated by the new wealth of some of his peers who had not entered into battle and from whom he constantly had to ask for charity, decided to go it alone, and by the shortest route, to the source of all power and prosperity, the United States.

It was Boumedienne, the Arab of the West *par excellence*,[17] and perhaps because of this well versed in the industrial language of the West who sought to get the most out of the complexity of events and situations. Disappointed, as in 1967, by the Arab armies' acceptance of a cease-fire, as well as by Soviet caution, he threw himself wholeheartedly in with the Shah of Iran to bring about a programme of international economic reform. His aim was that the Arabs' new-found oil power should be put to constructive use to accelerate Third World industrialization and introduce at least minimal international economic justice, so that the oppressed of this world could at last lift up their heads a little. From such action he felt that the Palestinians could not help but profit. He was not mistaken. The big Third World movement his strong personality crystallized, and the very high standard of his dialogue with the West, led to the appearance at the United Nations in 1974 of the PLO leader, Yasser Arafat, amid scenes of indescribable enthusiasm. In his speech, olive branch held out to the world in one hand, gun in the other, Arafat, Palestinian come from afar, pathetically shared his dream of democracy, secularism and equality between the Jews and Arabs of this land in which the dual tyranny of oil and religion, Judaism and Islam now ruled supreme.

The man the Israelis were gunning for with such blind violence and so fiercely accused of being the leader of Middle East terrorist gangs was now, only one year after the October war, sitting next to the world's most important figures – a notable result in a dramatically short time. Nevertheless, seven years later, Arafat, in 1974 on the way to turning into a Head of State overnight, remained only a skilful co-ordinator of resistance movements, without controlling a single square metre of Palestinian territory. His territory was that of another State, the Lebanese Republic, and his armies were foreign troops on the soil of another people, the Lebanese. We have to ask what forces these were that distorted the Arab Near East's destiny in this way and to such an extent? Many have already been identified. We shall now have to see them at work.

5 OPEC or the PLO?: 1974–5

An Arab paradise or the space of a morning

In retrospect, it is now evident that at the beginning of 1974 the Arab Near East entered into a phase of acute turbulence caused by the ambiguities of the October war, which in turn stemmed from the factors mentioned in the previous chapters. These included the cultural dissonances that affected major political decisions, the telescoping of epochs in which points of difference confronted one another and insoluble foreign policy equations. The economic, financial and social shocks caused by violent readjustments of the oil market in the oil-exporting countries now added to the causes of tension that had been weakening Near Eastern society for at least a quarter of a century.

At the time, however, the year 1974 seemed to open under eminently favourable auspices. On Kissinger's first visit to Cairo in November 1973, Egypt re-established diplomatic relations with the United States. Egyptian and Israeli military personnel were involved in lengthy discussions at the famous milestone 101, the first ever face-to-face in the history of Arab–Israeli relations and which succeeded in establishing a six-point cease-fire.

To implement the United Nations Security Council Resolution 338 of 22 October enjoining the warring factions to cease fire a peace conference was finally held in Geneva on 21 December 'with a view to establishing a just and lasting peace in the Middle East', as stipulated in the Resolution. The conference also officially brought Arabs (Egyptians and Jordanians) and Israelis together for the first time. Syria remained absent, but had, on the other hand, attended the sixth summit of Arab Heads of State held in Algiers at the end of November. Iraq and Libya boycotted the November conference on the grounds 'capitulationist' tendencies were arising in other Arab countries. The summit was in fact destined to co-ordinate Arab action with a view to peace talks.

As a follow-up to Kissinger's shuttles, a disengagement agreement amounting to a formal armistice was signed by Israel and Egypt on 18 January 1974. The text referred to the agreement as constituting 'a first step forward towards a lasting, just and permanent peace, in conformity with the provisions of the Security Council's Resolution 338 and within the framework of the Geneva Conference'. Syria's turn to sign an equivalent agreement came on 31 May 1974, after violent confrontations between the Syrian and Israeli armies on Mount Hermon during the month of April. As a result of these two agreements, for the first time since the birth of the State of Israel (with the exception of the occupation of Sinai in 1956), the Israeli army evacuated territories conquered by force. Even if, for the moment, these only represented partial and minor withdrawals in comparison with the occupied territories as a whole, the gesture was nonetheless highly symbolic of the beginnings of a change in the balance of strength, until then so unfavourably weighted against the Arabs.

Israeli troops accordingly left the right bank and withdrew to about 30 kilometres east of the Canal, to the rear of the Egyptian force on the left bank. In Syria, they evacuated the town of Quneitra, the capital of Golan, but only after dynamiting it practically out of existence before leaving it to the Syrians. Syria, which had refused to follow Egypt's example of negotiating directly with the Israelis, then signed a disengagement agreement in Geneva, as set out by the peace conference it had boycotted in December 1973.

In June, some days after re-establishing diplomatic relations with the United States, Syria received President Nixon in Damascus. Nixon was on a triumphant tour of the Middle East which had taken him to Cairo, Jerusalem, Amman and Saudi Arabia. After being psychologically cut off from the Arab world since the death of John Kennedy in 1963, the United States had now vigorously re-surfaced in the region. One of the major objectives of the 1973 war appeared to have been achieved.

For the rest, at the beginning of 1974 the Arabs seemed transformed, as if the nightmare of shame and isolation due to the crushing defeat of 1967 had at last ended. Thanks to the quadrupling of oil prices, material prosperity was henceforth added to their partial military successes. The Arabs, for so long targets of racist denigration and colonialist resentment suddenly advanced into the international spotlight and established by oil and petro-dollars as indispensable partners in the new international order, now became entitled to proper respect. Though every now and then the West resorted to threats – as we've seen it did not deny itself the privilege – it no longer seriously envisaged punitive military expeditions. The United States, still experiencing the intense trauma of Vietnam, was in the throes of the Watergate scandal, which was paralyzing the presidential authority. Through Syria, Iraq and South Yemen, the Soviet Union had once again ensconsed itself in the Near East. Soviet arms had made the victory of 1973 possible, and the Soviet presence could not fail to dissuade the United States from undertaking a new colonial military adventure. As for Europe, taken by the throat as it was by its dependence on oil for its energy requirements, there was no question of it turning its back on the Arab world.

These circumstances enabled the Arab countries to make a dramatic international breakthrough which, with the help of Iran, involved the whole of the Third World. It was this development that led to the historically unique meetings known as the North-South Dialogue, in which rich and poor countries held interminable discussions at global level on the need to reform distribution of wealth in the world. As we have shown, the instigator of this action was of the East, Boumedienne's Algeria. What the Marxist ideal in all its incarnations had failed to achieve, whether Bolshevism, Guevara-type guerrilla warfare in Latin America or Chinese Cultural Revolutions and what the liberal creed of free enterprise democracy, with the enormous technical progress created in the capitalist West, had been unable to concretize the oil of the poor was at last due to achieve. That is to say, in the service of ideals of modernization and freedom, to ensure a minimum of international economic justice that would enable the oppressed of this world, two-thirds of humanity, to exist in dignity, integrated into the great current of scientific and technical progress, in which the West had led for the past four centuries.

Such was the Algerian President's vision as expressed in a speech of a high order to a United Nations Extraordinary General Assembly on 10 April 1974, in which he made an emotive plea for an economic emancipation of the peoples of the Third World which would 'not be the revenge of the poor countries on the rich, but victory for the whole of mankind'.

The oil of the poor at the service of international justice

That Assembly had been held at the initiative of Boumedienne, then in his term as President of the Non-Aligned Movement. Its debates on oil, raw materials and Third World developmental problems were to lead to the gradual creation of a new international economic order deriving its basic ideas from the big guns of classical political economy, David Ricardo and Adam Smith. This was because Boumedienne was above all a man of the West, who was acutely conscious of the historical backwardness of the underdeveloped countries in comparison with the developed counties, a condition aggravated by colonialism. For him, this backwardness could be remedied only through intensive exposure to the industrialized world and by international co-operation, 'in the fullest sense of the word, founded on the equal rights of all parties, mutual respect of national sovereignties and reciprocity of advantages'.[1]

He was hostile to all autarchy and to any form of fundamentalist return to roots which would nullify the evolution of society and its modernist acquisitions. A few days before the United Nations debates, at the second summit of Islamic Heads of State held in Lahore, he minced no words in affirming that Koranic verses could not feed hungry people. For this pious Muslim was above all fanatical about freedom and emancipation which, for him, could be achieved only through the gains of modern science. A cursory glance at the Lahore speech reveals that an intensely modernist Islam existed among the Arabs, today somewhat smothered by the dramatic revival of religious fundamentalism. For Boumedienne, Islam was first and foremost a 'spiritual bond'. Islamic co-operation made sense only in terms of economic liberation, for 'men don't wish to go to heaven on an empty stomach', and experience had shown that religious spirituality was not immune to the 'batterings of poverty and ignorance'. It was pointless, he considered, to philosophize about Islam, to affirm its totality for the social order and its universal validity, for, 'whether one liked it or not, power in the world today is based on the economy and energy sources.' To refuse to recognize this situation was to condemn oneself to remaining 'subjugated and submissive' forever.

This was at the opposite extreme from the discourse of fundamentalist Islam, earlier expressed through Saudi Wahhabism,

Sudanese Mahdism, or Libyan Senussism, and now by Iranian Khomeinism. It is true that Boumedienne was carried along by the strong wind of brotherhood and universal liberation blowing in the Third World since the nationalization of the Suez Canal, and by the great rationalizers and theoreticians of the progress of mankind, Adam Smith, David Ricardo and Hegel as well as by Marx, Lenin and Frantz Fanon. The great adventure of oil which had only just begun, was the bearer of all hopes, and nobody realized what tragedies its tyranny would bring about in so few years.

The fundamentalism which arose some years later to confront it with total difference, irreducible specificity and anti-modernism was the product of this adventure that turned out so badly. The adventure involved Egypt in the dubious and isolated reunions with the West that cost Sadat his life. It also provoked rioting in Mecca and toppled the throne of Iran, the Middle East's oldest monarchy. It dogged the steps of the Syrian President, Assad, heir to the secularism of the Baath party, with an unceasing terrorism through the various groups of the Muslim Brotherhood. It dragged his Iraqi colleague, President Saddam Hussein, the last survivor of unitarian, modernist and secular Arab nationalim, into an unfortunate war. And height of irony, in Algeria itself, so turned towards the West and where death had removed Boumedienne from the scene in 1979 after long illness, fundamentalist groups, which had already shown their strength during the 1975 talks over the draft of a national charter, began to multiply.

Alongside this monstrous picture, but no less grotesque, was the perpetuation of Palestinian wandering in Lebanon, land of traditional co-existence of Islam and Christianity, but now ploughed up by the bombs of a State officially based on the Mosaic law honoured by destruction and occupied or evacuated within the general indifference.

To understand this brutal descent from Heaven into Hell, it is first necessary to explain the failure of those international dynamics on which the Arabs had placed all their bets, and for which the West was largely responsible. It also involves further reference to the cultural discordance due to immense wealth suddenly sprouting amidst great poverty and to the economic uprooting that followed.

The irresistible rise of Arab diplomacy

During the whole of 1974, and at the beginning of 1975, international dynamics seemed fully successful for the Arabs. Boumedienne's strategy appeared to be bearing fruit, namely, via the OPEC to maximize the leverage effect in international relations acquired by the four-fold increase in oil prices accompanied by a quickening of Third World solidarity in which international recognition of the Palestine resistance could be achieved – all with the aim of establishing a constructive and integrating dialogue with the industrialized capitalist world. At that time it looked as if the OPEC-equals-PLO equation might well solve itself out.

It was the Arabs who first recognized the PLO as the Palestinian people's sole legitimate representative. This took place at a summit of Arab Heads of State in Rabat in September 1974, when the PLO was officially recognized thereby nullifying any Hashemite claim to legal sovereignty over the Palestinian territories occupied by Israel. The 1948 mistake of King Hussein's grandfather, King Abdullah, in occupying Palestinian territories not included in the State of Israel (for which he was assassinated in 1951), was thus remedied. Egypt, which had administered the Palestinian territory of Gaza from 1948 to 1967, was likewise affected by this decision.

The following month, the United Nations General Assembly invited the PLO to take part in the debate on the Palestinian question, and this as the representative of the Palestinian people. The decision was accepted by an overwhelming majority, 105 votes to 4 (the United States, Bolivia, Israel and the Dominican Republic), with 20 abstentions, including six EEC countries, France, Italy and Ireland voting in favour. The solidarity of the Third World and the sympathy of some Western countries had made this historic decision possible. Arab diplomacy had achieved a remarkable feat, especially among the African countries, which had for the most part broken off diplomatic relations with Israel, thanks to the active interventions of Algeria and Libya. In future a united Third World would automatically be able to command a majority in the principal United Nations bodies. Western countries headed by the United States would complain continually about this majority, especially when resolutions hostile to Israel were systematically adopted or when too uncompromising positions were taken over international economic reforms.

This was the case, for example, with the famous United Nations General Assembly Resolution of 10 November 1975 which compared Zionism to 'a form of racism',[2] or with the Charter of States' Rights and Economic Duties establishing the right to nationalize natural resources. The General Assembly voted for the latter on 14 December 1974, with a majority of 120 votes in favour of adopting the Charter, with 6 votes against (the United States, West Germany, Great Britain, Belgium, Luxembourg and Denmark) and 10 abstentions (France, Japan, the Netherlands, Austria, Canada, Ireland, Italy, Norway, Spain and also Israel). This effective solidarity also led to the United States withdrawing its support in 1977 from the International Labour Organization (ILO), which it considered too politicized by the Third World resolutions it had adopted, especially against Israel.

Arab diplomacy in fact succeeded in setting off a remarkable amount of hostility towards the State of Israel on most international platforms, especially at the United Nations General Assembly and at UNESCO, where Zionism, the Israeli State's basic political doctrine, was compared with colonialism and racism. However, a hardening of Western opinion took place: although the Palestinian tragedy was now better understood, yet the creation of the Jewish State having been supported and its legitimacy unhesitatingly accepted, it was hardly prepared now to have it tainted with colonial sin and still less to envisage that the traditional victims of racism should themselves be accused of that shameful practice. This is not the place at which to discuss the Western Christian world's ambiguous relationship with the commitment of political Zionism to creating a State. At this stage[3] it is sufficient merely to point to this atmosphere of confrontation, hardly conducive to a dispassionate solution of the Palestinian tragedy which Yasser Arafat, President of the PLO's Executive Committee, described to the whole world on 13 November from the platform of the United Nations General Assembly.

Drawbacks of idealism in matters of diplomacy

The importance of this event has already been emphasized. It is nevertheless useful to recall the contents of the Palestinian speech at the United nations and to compare its utopian idealism with that of the speech on international economic justice delivered by Boumedienne in the same place some months earlier. Sadat's

speech to the Israeli Knesset three years later, which was as
outstanding as Boumedienne's and Arafat's to the United Nations
in 1974, once again brought out the naive political idealism of
these three major personalities of the Arab world. These three
great speeches, each a masterpiece of well-articulated political
eloquence on the most noble and humanitarian ideals, sublimely
ignored the reality of the regional, international, political and
economic balance of power.

Boumedienne wanted to see a better distribution of wealth in
the world, which he would regard not as the revenge of the poor
on the rich, but as a 'victory for the whole of mankind'. He failed
to realize that the economic development of a nation had to be
achieved by its own strong arm and was not to be acquired at an
international negotiating table where the rich voluntarily handed
over a little of their comfort to the oppressed.

Arafat dreamed of a secular and democratic Palestine, free of
all sectarianism, where Jews, Muslims and Christians, whether
ethnically Arab or not, could live together in friendship. He failed
to understand the essential character of the Zionist movement
and its manner of penetrating the Western consciousness. More
seriously, he took no account of the effective balance of power in
the area between the resistance movements and the various Arab
States between the Arabs and the Israelis and especially between
isolated Palestinians and Israelis.

Finally, Sadat, putting aside all the taboos, resentments and
hatreds, courageously set out to embrace yesterday's enemies in
occupied Jerusalem, over which all Arabs had been lamenting
ever since 1948, and especially since 1967. Before the Israeli
Parliament he made a marvellous plea for reason, peace, friendship and justice but without thinking how he was going to obtain
satisfaction from a conquering warrior State based on religious
mysticism. He did not even leave himself a way out in case of
failure or point out to the Israelis the cost of intransigence. For
while the 'revolutionary gun' Arafat mentioned in his speech as
an alternative to the 'olive branch' (which would be refused)
hardly bothered the Israelis militarily, Egypt's armed strength
could well have done so. But Sadat had already announced that
he no longer wanted war with Israel and several of his measures
tended to prove this quite clearly, especially the opening of the
Suez Canal in June 1975 and the rebuilding of the destroyed
towns even before any agreement had been reached on an Israeli

evacuation of Sinai. His speech in 1977, therefore, was also that of an idealist, far removed from the bitter realities of the struggle for survival people have to face.

The similarity in the absurd political utopianism of these three speeches was striking. Their naivety was nevertheless a poignant indication of the thirst for dignity felt by humiliated people who remain beyond the pale of progress and at a modernity well impregnating the social fabric. Sadat said as much when, back in Cairo from his historic trip to Jerusalem, he addressed the Egyptian Parliament and several times emphasized the need to solve problems 'as civilized people'.[4] But in the case of the Arabs, there was more to it than that, namely, the ambivalent relationship with the West, which was not shared by the people of the Far East, seemingly better protected by distance and by a more specific cultural identity from complexes about Western technical and cultural power.

These are complexes particularly of the Near East, as well as of the Maghrib – the North Africa so close to Europe. It was therefore no accident that these three speeches, their authors each equally dreaming of an integration into the rationalist and humanist values of Western culture, came from the Heads of Arab States bordering the Mediterranean. A Wahhabi king would never have spoken thus, much less an Iranian sovereign. Though the Shah of Iran admired the West, he saw himself as its equal and projected his image as the leader of a big military power, an arrogance never attempted by the Arabs. Khomeini, his successor, turned his back on the West to dig himself into a continental Islam believing itself able in the twentieth century to live completely turned in on itself.

The Arabs of the Near East and North Africa, on the other hand, seemed condemned to an ambivalent relationship with the adjacent West. Nasserist Jacobin nationalism, ultra-Left revolutionary romanticism, the gentlemanly civility of a certain style of Sadatism, Boumedienne's economic Thornism were all, whether in frustration or in friendship, devised for or in terms of the West. It should never be forgotten that although the Near East shares its culture with Asia, it does so even more with the West, especially through its Greek, Roman and Byzantine inheritance. The main threads of this relationship, from Muhammad Ali to Nasser and Sadat, have been described. In the mid–1970s, the threads became unusually tangled and of this the West evidently had no idea.

How the really rich protect themselves

Meanwhile, the industrialized countries busied themselves with plugging the breaches that had been forming in the structure of domination and power. The rich dislike even the smallest diminution of their privileges. In the debates of one interminable conference after the other the West proved more expert than Third World countries. Subdivision of debates, creation of committees and sub-committees, reference back to specialist bodies, dubious compromises that merely opened the door to new controversies – all these tactics were employed to avoid any serious global discussion of the economic inequality between nations and the means of remedying it.

The complex bureaucracy of the United Nations lent itself well to this game. France achieved the first big diversionary manoeuvre by holding a conference on international co-operation in Paris, the delegates to which were apportioned by groups of countries, this itself creating discord within the Third World. Invitations were sent to three categories of countries: the industrialized, the Third World oil-exporting and the Third World oil-importing. To make matters worse, discussions about the global nature of the problem of underdevelopment, which Boumedienne and the Non-Aligned Movement were keen to present, were prevented by splitting up the conference into five specialized commissions. The North-South dialogue went on for two years (1975–7), naturally without reaching the least concrete conclusions.

No more tangible results came out of the Euro-Arab Dialogue set up between the EEC and the Arab League in 1974, as part of the same big step forward in international economic diplomacy started by the Arabs. It was the same with other big international meetings it would be tedious to list, in which great hopes invested by the Third World were effectively resisted by the industrialized countries, both by a 'war of position' and continual 'guerrilla' action.

The hard core of this resistance was formed by the Big Three industrialized countries, the United States, Japan and Germany, with France and Italy taking a less rigid stance and Norway, the Netherlands and Sweden, which unfortunately carry little economic weight, sympathetic to demands for international economic justice. But all that the thousands of hours of energy expended by the best brains of the Third World managed to achieve was the creation of an Agricultural Development Fund, for which the OPEC countries had to advance nearly half the capital, whereas the total of their gross national products (GNP) did not come up to that of a country like Japan.

The West in effect managed to put the OPEC on the defensive *vis-à-vis* international opinion and to relay to the latter's member countries the industrialized countries' aid commitments to developing countries. The OPEC was accused of all the crimes of mankind: of creating unemployment, inflation, balance of payment deficits, and of worsening the evils of underdevelopment. Its member countries were, however, themselves underdeveloped, poor and thrown off balance by the violence of the oil flows. But clearly this reality was forgotten amidst the hullabaloo of the Western medias over petro-dollars and the fantasies of some of the poor who saw themselves becoming rich quickly.

By various mechanisms the OPEC countries were thus led into giving other Third World countries an average of from 6 to 7 per cent of their annual GNPs, while the rich and powerful West donated hardly 0.3 per cent. This new aid flow was of course translated into orders for the finished goods and capital equipment of the industrialized countries. So far from the OPEC donor countries deriving any profit from it, no matter what their generosity, they remained in the dock under the accusations of the Western media. In this atmosphere, OPEC solidarity, basic element of Boumedienne's strategy for Arab international policy, rapidly crumbled.

From the middle of 1976 a widening split occurred between the 'hawks' and 'doves' and came to a head at the end of 1976, when Saudi Arabia only partially complied with a 10 per cent price rise. From then on, with its productive capacities considerably increased, the Wahhabi kingdom went it alone, more often than not trailing two Gulf Emirates, Qatar and Abu Dhabi, in its wake. For reasons already explained,[5] it aligned itself faithfully with Western interests. By 1979, the OPEC was completely paralysed by the differences between its principal members. In 1980, a summit of OPEC Heads of State that was to be held in Baghdad had to be cancelled because of the Iraq-Iran conflict.

What a contrast this was with the success of the first summit of

OPEC Heads of State held in Algiers in March 1975, when all ranks were completely united and the OPEC announced its wish to make a 'positive contribution to resolve the major problems affecting the world economy and to promote a process of real co-operation, key to the establishment of a new international economic order'.[6] Despite their serious historical and geographical disputes, it was during this summit that the Algerian President achieved the new feat of reconciling Iran and Iraq. The Shah of Iran gave up his support to the Kurdish resistance, which was hampering Iraq's economic and political expansion; with the Iranian border closed, the revolt of the Iraqi Kurds collapsed. In return, Iraq recognized Iran's sovereignty over the waters of the Shatt el-Arab, though, as the Iraq-Iran war launched in 1980 was to prove, this agreement was hardly a model of political morality. Nevertheless, the point of it was to ensure a completely united stand by the OPEC countries, both among themselves and towards the outside world.

OPEC as hostage: a strategy detailed

After its 1974–5 period in Paradise, the OPEC rapidly slid down towards Hell. This Dantean descent happened at the same time as Arab solidarity collapsed and the Palestinian situation grew worse. The most dramatic and symbolic moment came in December 1975, when all the oil ministers of the oil-exporting countries meeting in Vienna were taken hostage by a group of guerrillas, led by the celebrated Carlos. The group, claiming to be the 'Right Arm of the Arab Revolution', were trying to sabotage international deals that confirmed the Zionist annexations. These poor oilmen were certainly among the unloved. Not only were they hammered at by the capitalist West and its propaganda, but were also taken as hostages by international desperadoes claiming their actions to be expressing the oppression of the have-nots of this world. Everything was combining to ensure the failure of the Arab strategy of the 1970s.

There were, in fact, numerous signs of the derailment of this strategy. Firstly, the resignation of President Nixon as a result of the Watergate scandal and the relative paralysis of American foreign policy. But above all, and even before the October war, there was the recrudescence of Arab ultra-Leftism in the Palestinian and Lebanese movements. Terrorist operations were now no longer directed only at Israeli targets in Palestine or abroad, but also at Arab ones. For example, in March and September 1973, Palestinian commandos attacked and took hostages at the Saudi Arabian Embassies in Khartoum and Paris respectively. With the active support of Iraq, refusing to agree to any peaceful solution to the Arab–Israeli conflict, Left-wing Palestinian organizations broke away from the PLO. It should however be remembered that two 'brother-enemies', both claiming the same Baath legitimacy, ruled in Iraq and Syria, and so if Syria moved to the Right, Iraq would move to the Left, and vice versa.

It was at Beirut that bombing attacks and urban guerrilla operations multiplied. On 18 October 1973, the head office of the Bank of America was attacked and some months later it was the turn of another American bank, the First National City Bank of Chicago, then of the Kennedy Centre, and of Iran Air, etc. Two movements claimed responsibility for most of these attacks – a Revolutionary Socialist Organization in Lebanon and an Arab Communist Organization. In September 1974, the latter manifested itself in Damascus by attacking the American information centre and the pavilion at the Damascus Fair. This ultra-Leftism, which seemed linked to Trotskyism and to the Latin American Tupamaros, was also hostile to the Soviet Union, which the PFLP leader, George Habas, openly criticized in August 1974, thereby earning himself the Muscovite accusation of 'pseudo-revolutionary'.

Libya on its part, avoided by the other Arabs, decided to approach Moscow, and this after having been the most violent opponent of Soviet influence in the Near East.[7] For Gadaffi was in the beginning trying to remain faithful to himself and preserve the unionist legacy of Nasser. When first the Federation of Arab Republics and then the Egypto-Libyan Union failed in 1971 and 1972 respectively,[8] he turned to Tunisia, with which Libya was united for exactly forty-eight hours in January 1974. This new farce was especially shocking since Bourguiba did indeed sign the unity agreements but repudiated them immediately afterwards, dismissing his Minister of Foreign Affairs who had been instrumental in setting them up. Decidedly, the Libyan President, burning with desire to glorify his name on behalf of the Arab homeland, was not much liked by his Arab peers. The subsequent development of this ambitious and idealist young man can only be understood in relation to all the snubs he was to receive from them. A month after the unhappy attempt at union, he retired in disappointment, leaving the management of the State to his second-in-command, Major Jalloud. His real ideological and political adventure, to which we shall return, then began at both domestic and foreign levels. But for the time being, there was no doubt that he definitely swung over into a rejection of the whole established order.

In addition, anyone observing Lebanon during this same year, 1974, would have soon realized that clouds were gathering over the Near East. Though saturated with oil wealth, the gateway to the East was beginning to creak a little here and there. If banks sprang up in increasing numbers and luxury and wealth flaunted themselves, chaos had already begun to appear in political and economic life: strikes, student movements, Cabinet instability, inflation, kidnappings, restlessness in the Shia community, the most under-privileged in the country, which was becoming organized behind the religious charisma of the Imam Musa al-Sadr,[9] of strange destiny. But this chaos was screened by the outbreak of reprisals carried out on Lebanese territory by the Israeli airforce whenever there was a Palestinian operation against an Israeli target. In the course of 1974 alone there were several hundred Lebanese and Palestinian victims. None of the big Arab countries directly involved in the conflict with Israel came to the help of the Palestinian-Lebanese martyr. The guns had finally been silenced on the Syrian and Egyptian fronts since the spring of 1974. The Lebanese and the Palestinians floundered tragically alone in blood, mud, luxury and poverty, in their quarrels and chimeras, their diversities and their respective factions.

Lebanon's traditional protectors, the big Western powers, were for their part much too occupied with the new oil situation to cast more than a cursory glance at this country, clear example of the way things were drifting. At best, Lebanon retained its importance as a place for making symbolic rather than effective gestures at the Arab-Palestinian level. The French Minister of Foreign Affairs, Sauvagnargues, for example, came to Beirut in October 1974 so that the international press could photograph him shaking hands with Arafat. It didn't really require much perspicacity to look through the Lebanese prism and see all the contradictions of Arab society and the dead-ends of its political actions.

Hell: an avalanche of petro-dollars

In reality, the tyranny of oil had muddled all minds in 1974–5. The diplomatic activism it unleashed covered up still further the real problems of Arab society. For it either provided a flight from reality into an all-encompassing idealism, this being most often the case, or provided an opportunity to return restless minorities and unrepentant schismatics to the adventurist ultra-Leftism of 'rejection'. For the West, this activism was a marvellous method of playing for time against the rise of the new trade union of the Non-Aligned Movement countries under the leadership of OPEC bigwigs, including the former fellah, Boumedienne, and the Persian monarch, the Shah of Iran. But since social, historical, regional and international reality developed outside the diplomatic stage, all this activism had a rather unreal quality to it.

The real tragedy was that this activism, so strongly associated with oil and petro-dollars, polarized the attention of the political elites and accelerated the breakdown of social structures, both in the East and West. Khomeini, at first seeming no more than a religious fanatic, was thus able to strike a chord in the castaways of both. His unbridled imprecations from under his Neauphle-le-Chateau tent against all the materialistic arrogance symbolized by Iranian royalty found a disproportionate echo in the Western media as among all the rejects of the tyranny of oil in the East.

Since 1974 official life in East and West had marched in step with the rhythm of oil. On those deserts, which the flow of oil now bound solidly to the West, a constant stream of Heads of State, Ministers, directors of banks, contractors and executives of multinationals descended at a crazy pace, with speculators, middlemen and adventurers of all types close on their heels. Those oil States, with small populations, hardly knew what to do with the 'hundred million dollars a day'[10] pouring into the coffers of their primitive or non-existent bureaucracies.

This is especially the case in the countries of the Arabian Peninsula, which sometimes lacked even a central bank (Qatar, the United Arab Emirates, Oman), and if they did have one, as in Saudi Arabia and Kuwait, it was no more than embryonic, with hardly more than a few dozen employees. Oil receipts were consequently sometimes entrusted to Finance Ministries (Kuwait, United Arab Emirates), but as these, like the Saudi Central Bank (the Saudi Arabian Monetary Agency), had to rely on foreign institutions and experts, their petro-dollars were automatically and directly recycled towards the West.

Countries with more substantial populations (Algeria and Iraq in the Arab world, Iran in the Middle East) were better placed to derive immediate benefits from this money flow. Their capacity to import was almost limitless: consumer goods for impoverished populations and capital goods for those Heads of State devoted to accelerated modernization. From 1975, only one year after the four-fold increase in oil prices, Algeria and Iran had run up large balance of payments deficits, to meet which they had to borrow substantial amounts on the international market. This sufficiently indicates the extent of unsatisfied needs. It is true that massive arms orders partly account for this state of affairs in Iran, but not in Algeria, Nigeria, Indonesia and Venezuela, all big oil producers but despite their new wealth heavily in debt.

Wealth descending on the poor actually releases a frenzy of consumption, often of an ostentatious kind. This greed is inevitably translated into unrealistic development plans into which are fitted large projects that cannot possibly be carried out by the primitive and 'lethargic economies'[11] concerned. Violent inflation inevitably results and all kinds of bottlenecks are created, especially in the form of shortages of building materials. Obviously the under-privileged classes are hit the hardest, but so are the middle classes on fixed incomes, civil servants, teachers, and employees. In the Arab world, it was not only the oil-exporting countries that suffered, but the others as well. The social security system set up at Khartoum had expanded considerably after the 1973 war and this increased the flow of capital to other Arab countries. In addition, Syria, Sudan and Egypt relaxed their exchange regulations and relaxed State control of their economies.

Especially in Egypt and Sudan, the way was opened up for the direct introduction of foreign firms – the economic liberalization so dear to Sadat's heart. At one stroke all kinds of speculations became possible. There began a veritable stampede of rich people from the Gulf and of foreign banks to buy up the finest blocks of flats and the best plots of land. It was not uncommon for the rent to be multiplied a hundred-fold when a flat was let to a foreigner. Salaries also came under terrible pressure, for the best technicians and employees were snapped up by foreign companies if they had not already emigrated towards the Gulf in search of fortune or lucrative employment. In these countries, characterized by extremely stable prices and salaries that had till then stabilized the social order, the door actually opened to all manner of adventurism. This development was all the more serious because the situation in the countryside, already none too satisfactory, was worsened and the rural exodus speeded up. Everything thus combined to de-stabilize the social order.

Lebanon was the first to be affected. It was in the poverty belts of Beirut that the bloody events of 1975–6 began. But there was also the terrible riots in Cairo in January 1977 against the rise in the price of bread and other basic foodstuffs imposed by the International Monetary Fund (IMF). Sadat had to backtrack and annul the increases.

In the deserts of the Arabian Peninsula, a gold rush set in. Not since the fall of the Abassid Empire had the Arab world seen population movements on such a scale. Like Libya, the oil-exporting countries of the Gulf barely had sufficient manpower, managerial staff, technicians, employees and teachers to meet the needs and projects this new oil wealth gave rise to. Other Arab countries were suddenly drained of the most dynamic among their active populations, which further undermined their already eroding social structures. Expatriates earning high salaries remitted savings to their home countries, thus increasing the flow of capital and the craving for consumption and, consequently stimulating inflation.

The flux of wealth and of human beings accelerated changes everywhere in the Arab world, not only in basic economic and social structures but also in the urban and rural landscape. In demographically compact countries (Syria, Egypt, Iraq, etc.) these changes often introduced contradictions into the preceding period's legacy of state socialism, thus adding to the complexity of the problems. The traditional landscapes of the demographically poor desert countries were ruined with unimaginable rapidity. For example, beautiful *pisé* buildings in Jiddah and Riyadh, in Saudi Arabia, disappeared without trace to make way for blocks of concrete and glass panelling which turned these already hot towns into infernos of heat and architectural horror. Furthermore, Arab immigration being insufficient to meet the needs, a wave of Koreans, Pakistanis and Filipinos entered the region, with Europeans and Americans in all the key posts. In its turn, the human landscape became intolerable.

This state of affairs is not confined to the Arabs. It is certainly found in Iran as well, but also, although with obvious differences, in Venezuela and Nigeria. In looking back at the situation, one might well wonder why the social disorder provoked by the eruption of religious fundamentalism did not manifest itself earlier, more intensely and in a more generalized way. When social and economic structures suffer such mutilations, is there any alternative to ultra-reactionary religious fundamentalism or to systematic ultra-Leftism? The Iranian revolution was to combine in spectacular fashion the dual ambiguity of these two ideological modes, which are the usual responses to the deep distress of societies undergoing chaotic, sudden and continuous change.

The power and selfishness of the West

The West was certainly able to defend itself better. A developed society is in effect one which, through its accumulation of knowledge and power entirely interiorized in the social order, is capable of transforming the ordeals it has to face into new sources of knowledge and power. An underdeveloped society, on the other hand, is one whose very advantages and potential sources of power become causes of additional weakness, increased dependence and new imbalances. Thus, in the West, the oil 'crisis' became the source of new technical progress in every form of energy production and of industrial readjustments, in any case necessitated by profound changes in the technical and economic competition of the big capitalist countries among themselves. In the East, oil 'wealth' destroyed the social fabric to the utmost disorder, created serious food shortages[12] and almost total dependence on oil production, thus placing rickety economies at the mercy of developed countries, particularly the Western ones, and therefore in a position of absolute vulnerability.

For the West in any case, in the absence of new technological break-throughs in the field of energy, oil prices could not remain at existing low levels. The price rise was therefore essential to the survival of the industrialized West, both in saving energy and in creating new sources of it. OPEC had done it an enormous favour. That the consequential adjustments would be painful also for the West was never in any doubt – the number of unemployed bears this out – even though a country like Japan, precisely because it is a pioneer in several big developments in technology, suffers from neither the unemployment nor the inflation experienced by other industrialized countries. Other examples in the industrialized world also exist. In any case, there was neither chaos nor breakdown. There is no comparison between the lot of an unemployed person in the West and the social and economic marginality without any cushioning reserves into which oil rapidly pushed people in the underdeveloped countries. It proved impossible for all these rural populations, small craftsmen and minor officials to keep up either with the rate of inflation or with the sudden and chaotic changes of their cultural, economic and social landscapes.

The tragedy of the oil crisis actually lies in the absence of any serious dialogue in the matter of development and for this the West must bear a large part of the responsibility. Boumedienne was correct in his approach, but in his idealism under-estimated the selfishness of the rich. The oil countries were well and truly trapped in a vicious circle. If they reduced their production to conserve the energy sources necessary to any real future industrialization, the West would protest violently about being strangled and would turn it into a veritable *casus belli*. The alternative practised by all the underdeveloped oil exporting countries was to maximize financial resources and thus expand wealth in the midst of poverty and underdevelopment, the very thing at the source of all the unrest. The results of this can clearly be seen when some Arabs are able to buy up New York skyscrapers or Parisian tower blocks, while for the average Arab finding somewhere to live is a real headache, and can cost him more than half a month's income. Or again, while the price of a car remains prohibitive for tens of millions of Arabs, some of their governments own substantial holdings in Mercedes or Fiat. It means that a country can possess the most highly-equipped steel or petrochemical works, as in Iraq or Algeria, but lacks pins or plastic toys for children, not to mention the thousand other absurdities of a 'development' recycled for the sole profit of the multinationals, another symbol of Western power.

For the poor, therefore, oil is a dead end. The theoreticians of the Iranian revolution understood this, but the rest of the Third World is even today barely aware of it. It is the West that profits, for the Near or Middle East can now easily boast the highest number of millionaires in the world, who run prosperous businesses in Paris, London, New York or Geneva, and content themselves with only short holidays at home. These rich people are strangely like their Western brothers and certainly know how to tuck away the wherewithal of their power in safe places.

The never-to-exist Palestinian government: a return to Arab ultra-Leftism

With the OPEC thus blocked, what were the PLO's chances of getting somewhere? Frankly, none. Arafat had, of course, been triumphantly received at the United Nations General Assembly, but we have seen how much efficacity there is in international forums. The General Assembly is, besides, without effective power; this resides in the Security Council, where the Americans vigilantly guarded their Israeli protégé's interests. In any case, Israel totally disregarded United Nations resolutions and did not mind saying so openly. For Israel, reality was to be found on the ground and only in concert with the American big brother.

Having been received at the United Nations, the PLO was also and at last set up by the Arab Heads of State meeting in Rabat as the only legitimate representative of the Palestinian people. But it still possessed not one square kilometre of Palestinian territory, whereas the King of Jordon remained a silent and formidable competitor in possession of a State and a considerable fund of sympathy in the West and even in Israel. Further, the PLO became a full member of the Arab League in September 1976, two years after the Rabat summit; until then it was only an observer in the Arab organization.

The situation could have been changed if a government in exile, similar to the Algerian GPRA, had been formed at the beginning of the prevailing exceptional state of affairs. Egypt, the Soviet Union, Algeria and several others pressed Yasser Arafat to do so. Such a government would have then been recognized by the whole of the Third World, by the socialist bloc and by at least some, if not all, of the Western countries. Had it existed in 1975 and 1976, when the West Bank's population was in open rebellion against the Israeli military administration, it would certainly have helped reduce the intransigence of Israel's claim to this last remaining province (with Gaza) of Palestine. But to imagine a rational and reassuring solution such as this, which would very likely have avoided the bloody tearing apart of Lebanon, is to fail to realize that the PLO itself is rent by all the same fissures of Arab society.

As a federation of resistance movements sustained by the centrifugal forces paralysing Arab political life, the PLO was kept together partly by the skill of its leader and the support Arafat's movement, al-Fatah, enjoyed among Palestinian opinion. But although al-Fatah was the pivot around which the PLO revolved, it was itself shaken by the most diverse currents, the same Arab kaleidescope that veered between Islamic fundamentalism and staunch ultra-Leftism. Around al-Fatah, with the PLO, there was a continuous movement of groups of very variable importance, evolving in disorganized fashion, depending on the circumstances, the interests of the Arab States that supported them and the ideological moods of their leaders. Alliances were made and unmade and splits and schisms reduced or increased at will the number of the PLO's Executive Committee.

The Palestinian resistance did, of course, manifest itself in the field as shown by its continual operations against Israeli targets, especially since 1968. Nonetheless, its unity and political cohesion remained precarious. Consequently, Yasser Arafat's skill has so far been a major asset for the PLO whose representativeness remains endangered in international law, repudiated as it is by the Israeli enemy on the one hand and threatened with disintegration on account of the differences among the Arab brothers on the other.

In 1974–5, within the PLO the partisans of 'no-compromise' had the wind in their sails. It was they who carried out most of the big overseas operations, particularly the hijacking of aircraft, which al-Fatah manifestly and openly disapproved of. These operations did not stop until after the Entebbe incident in June 1976 during which the Israelis undertook a military raid into Uganda to rescue Israeli hostages who had been captured during a plane hijack. Theirs also were the daring operations in Israel from Lebanese territory. The leading figure of this intransigence and revolutionary orthodoxy was Dr George Habash, whose charisma derived from a simple life in the service of the poor. He was then supported by Iraq, which had become the bastion of 'no-compromise', and of course by Libya.

The PLO was, moreover, from its creation in 1964, an emanation of Arab governments, particularly Egypt, and not a true resistance movement. The Palestine Liberation Army (PLA), which was also created at the same time under the aegis of the Arab League, was made up of scattered battalions under the control of the Arab armies. Its first leader, Ahmad Shuqairi, was typical of the bureaucrats of the Arab League, real men of the Cabal.

The resistance movements came into being in this same period, but underground and outside Arab official structures. These movements were hounded by nearly all the Arab countries, which saw in them a risk of internal subversion, as well as a potential for useless provocations against Israel. This explains why most of their leaders at some time or another spend time inside Arab gaols.[13]

It was only in 1968 that the resistance movements took over the PLO. By discrediting the Arab regimes, the 1967 defeat raised a fair wind for the former by proving that their revolutionary theories had been correct. Shuqairi was not re-elected to the presidency of the PLO and in 1969 Arafat became its leader and was borne along on the crest of a wave of extraordinary popularity, among both Palestinians and Arabs, who began to adulate al-Fatah as the revolutionary ideal and to detest the weakness and compromises of the Arab regimes. This was the great adventure of Arab ultra-Leftism, already discussed in Chapter 2.

These facts must be kept in mind in order to understand the PLO's behaviour: the absence of a programme with any hold on reality. For to maintain its character as a representative organization internationally, the PLO had to reach virtual unanimity in the positions it took up. Although al-Fatah, under the domination of Arafat's personality, had been searching for a rapid and peaceful settlement since 1974, this was not at that time the case with the other movements. They remained maximalist and refrained from taking part in the PLO Executive Committee's meetings whenever there was any question of negotiations and concessions, any such implying amendment of the famous Palestinian Charter of 1948 which denied the State of Israel the right to exist, but recognized the legality of the existence of those Jews in Palestine before the creation of the State.

It was only in March 1977, at the 13th Palestinian National Council – the Palestinian Parliament in existence since 1964 which elected members to the PLO Central Committee – that Arafat managed to get the principle adopted of creating a Palestinian State on any liberated part of Palestinian territory. This was the maximalists' first defeat and largely a result of the Palestinian-Lebanese troubles of 1975–6. Already in December 1976, however, the PLO Central Committee, meeting in Damascus, had accepted the creation of a Palestinian State but without clearly defining its frontiers. In other words, it had relinquished the integrity of Palestinian territory and the ideal of a secular and demo-cratic Palestine to replace the State of Israel. This session was boycotted by the 'Rejection Front' organizations. But in 1977, it was already too late. It was the eve of Sadat's visit to Jerusalem, which would throw all into confusion and give new energy to all versions of 'rejection'. It was also too late because the tearing apart of Lebanon in 1975–6 had once more allowed Israel to make new territorial and political gains in this adjacent Arab country whose territory had until then remained intact.

Supporters of the Rejection became increasingly bitter and consequently authentic representatives of Arab ultra-Leftism. For them, the loss of Palestine, the absence of Arab unity, the social injustice and the military and political weakness so characteristic of twentieth-century Arab society, were merely results of the Arab political elite's deals with imperialism. The struggle for Arab unity could not be separated from the struggle for Palestine. Liberation could be achieved only through a single-minded internal and external battle against the defeatist governments, reactionary monarchies or autocratic petit-bourgeois regimes which were the objective allies of that imperialism of which Zionism was only an emanation. This context illustrates the logic of the geographically bizarre strategy whereby the road to Tel Aviv had to pass via Damascus, Amman, Beirut and Cairo. It was hardly surprising that Iraq and Libya became, as States, the two pillars of the Rejection.

Iraq was actually the only Arab country to allow the Palestinians to continue to exist when they were silently suffocating. In 1959, General Kassem was, in fact, the first to speak of a Palestinian government in Gaza and the West Bank and to train Palestinian volunteers and create a Palestinian tax. It was thus from Iraq that the second wave of Palestinian nationalism was launched, following that of 1919–39, which had fought against Jewish settle-ment in Palestine but had been betrayed by the shady deals of its leaders. In 1964 Egypt and Jordan tried to bring this nationalism under control by setting up the PLO and the PLA, resultants of the Arab political and military bureaucracies of the period. In the 1970s, Iraq was Baathist and strengthened by the legitimacy conferred by those founder members who had been driven from Syria to take up refuge in Baghdad, at any rate so far as Michel Aflak was concerned. Iraq had oil and an uncompromising Arab nationalist, anti-imperialist ideology, whereas its rival in

Damascus had veered to the Right and become much closer to 'imperialism'.

As for Libya, we have seen what affronts Gadaffi's unitary and revolutionary orthodoxy suffered at the hands of his Arab peers, particularly his two African neighbours, Sadat and Bourguiba. But having oil, i.e. resources, Libya was under no pressure to compromise with imperialism. Even if the Arab world turned its back on the orthodox revolutionary ideology of the *Green Book*, there was still room for an Islamic and 'progressive' sphere of influence in Africa, not to mention all the doors open from material interest (Malta, for example) or from political and ideological necessity. Further, after having vehemently criticized Soviet influence in the Third World, from now on Libya drew closer and closer to Moscow.

All this goes to show that an Algerian path would not have been feasible for the PLO in the Near Eastern context. The creation of a government along the lines of the GPRA presupposed a unity the Palestinian resistance movement never possessed. The Algerian NLF had achieved its unity before the provisional government was set up in Tunisia, and not without much bloodshed among its militants. The Palestinians on the other hand were very attached to their diversities and reluctant to shed blood in order to stamp out factionalism. Besides, such a course would have opened the way to even more interference by the Arab States in the affairs of the PLO. The emergence of a Palestinian government in 1974 or 1975 would have indicated willingness to negotiate and thus to compromise, and this would have meant renouncing the ideals of a complete recovery of the homeland in a surge of newly found revolutionary Arab unity. Supporters of the Rejection, though indeed in the minority, yet with powerful protectors, would never have accepted this. Their failure to participate in a government-in-exile would have reduced its representativeness and deepened its schisms. Yasser Arafat had never wanted to take this risk, for the least suspicion of non-representativeness would have tainted his own political and diplomatic legitimacy at the international level as leader of the PLO.

A new and impossible equation thus appeared of the tensions and contractions as well as the cultural and economic discordances of Arab society in the Near East. The PLO was to pay the price when, twelve years after its Jordanian setback, it was thrown out of Beirut by the Israeli army in the summer of 1982.

It was in fact in an attempt to resolve this impossible equation of the Arab–Palestinian front that Lebanon was torn apart. The 1973 war had tried to change the terms of the situation left by the Khartoum summit, which contained so many ambiguities and limitations. From then on, open to the harsh winds from every quarter, Lebanon was where efforts were made to clarify those ambiguities, by trying to unblock the paralysis, at the Palestinian level, created by the permanent schisms embedded in the historical heritage of the Near East, and by undoing the limitations the October war and the failure of Arab diplomacy in 1974–5 had imposed on any solution to the Arab–Israeli conflict.

This is the key to the civil war to which the Arabs abandoned themselves in Lebanon, parallel to an explosion of tensions between Lebanese communities and an extraordinary drive on the Arab and international stage by an ever-mysterious Syria. As in the 1973 war, of which it was merely an extension, the war in Lebanon cost the Arabs many opportunities. When, over a period of several months in 1975–6, the inhabitants of the West Bank were in a state of massive ferment, not only was there no internationally recognized Palestinian government to speak on their behalf, but the PLO was bogged down in Lebanon in the most ambiguous of all situations. World attention was focused on a chaos in Lebanon which was all the more spectacular since nobody could really say who was fighting whom and why. Christians against Muslims, Right against Left, Palestinians against Lebanese, Lebanese amongst themselves, Palestinians amongst themselves: the frightful mêlée reflected the profound disorder afflicting all the socio-cultural structures of the Near East.

The Israelis watched in derision as all the PLO's United Nations-style dreams of democracy, secularism and dialogue collapsed. In the prevailing confusion they acquired gains which reinforced their intransigence still further and to which Egypt, pivot of the Near East, succumbed in 1977.

Two wars, for nothing, one external in 1973 and one internal in Lebanon in 1975–6. Was Arab society then really in deadlock? To answer this question, we must decipher the messages of violence that began the destruction of Lebanon.

6   The disintegration of Lebanon: 1975–6

Lebanon, a microcosm of Ottoman society

The disintegration of the State and of Lebanese society in general since 1975–6 presents the observer with a complex set of messages about the situation in the Near East. Attention is primarily focused on the extent of the violence and the nature of atrocities committed, all the more shocking in that Lebanon had always seemed so peaceful and easy-going a place, in comparison with the rough and often dramatic history of its neighbours. But this appearance was deceptive, as amply proved by the horrors that took place in a country often mistakenly thought of as the 'Switzerland of the Middle East'. Rarely has the image of itself presented by a society to the outside world been so far from the real truth. Although a veneer of Westernization contributed to concealing the real nature of Lebanese society, the Lebanese political and cultural elite for its part showed a quite extraordinary degree of political shortsightedness. Once again, in the case of Lebanon, East and West made a contact with each other all the more unhappy because so often eulogized as a perfect example of the meeting of cultures.

It is no historical accident that, once again deadlocked in the Arab–Israeli conflict, in 1975 the Near East was disrupted at its weakest point, Lebanon. Of all Near Eastern societies, Lebanon was in fact the only one that continued unchanged, ruled by the same political and cultural plutocracy ever since the mandatory power, France, proclaimed a Greater Lebanon in 1920. The disintegration of Lebanon was illustrative precisely because it showed the true face of an Arab society that in its basic structures had remained untouched by the evolution of the contemporary world. This helps explain the difficulties of analysis and the paradoxes that appear. On the one hand, Lebanon, apparently 'modern', democratic, pluralist and economically advanced; on the other,

the neighbours, especially Egypt, Syria and Jordan, still economically backward and consequently preserving entire sectors of
society in traditionalism, not to speak of regimes politicially authoritarian and rejecting all pluralism. And yet it was Lebanese
society that dissolved into anarchy and generalized violence, while
the others in the Near East seemed to survive all ordeals, military
defeats, *coups d'états*, economic imbalances and the challenges of
the Palestinian resistance movements. Lebanese 'modernity' was
thus only an illusion, and an illusion to which the country's stability and the apparent democracy of its institutions were rather
too facilely attributed. This while in the neighbour countries social
stability survived despite the *coups d'état*, the changes in the elites
in power and the successive upheavels in socio-political institutions
which gave an impression of incoherence and instability and a
seeming rejection of rationalistic modernity.

Of course, today, the ravages of oil in Arab society as well as
the perpetuation of the Arab–Israeli conflict have undermined the
societies of the other Near Eastern countries as well. The rise of
religious fundamentalism and the terrorism practised by certain
of its adherents, notably in Egypt and Syria, constitute the most
evident manifestations. The disintegration of Lebanon must be
interpreted in a wider context for this reinforces its exemplary
character at the regional level and justifies close and detailed
analysis. For the violence let loose in Lebanon in 1975 was in
reality only a forewarning signal of a general destabilization of
the socio-cultural and political structures of the Near East, caught
between an active traditionalism and a veneer of modernity and
battered by the eruption of an oil wealth uncontrollable in volume
and distribution. In these conditions, it is not surprising that
Lebanese violence had the use of a considerable military arsenal,
a heterogeneous ideological vocabulary and a context of return to
profound traditions within society.

Lebanon had in fact remained a pure microcosm of Ottoman
society whose institutions had overpaid Arab society for four
centuries. It had known neither *coups d'état* nor the changes of
elites or socio-economic systems that had affected the principal
countries of the Near East.[1] It has also preserved Ottoman
traditions of tolerance and pluralism intact in circumstances
whether stable, violent, fanatical, dangerous or difficult. Western
images had often presented the Ottoman Empire in the darkest
colours of religious fanaticism and rule by army rabble. Yet this

Empire can be counted among the great achievements of history and for most of time as a model of tolerance and pluralism. Under its rule, all the ethnic groups and minorities its sovereignty encompassed, such as Armenians, Kurds, Berbers, Serbs, Montenegrians, Croats, Rumanians, Hungarians, Greeks, Arabs, Near Eastern Christians, Jews, etc., lived in harmony and without any hint of religious or cultural restrictions. Its traditions of tolerance towards Jews and Christians was deeply rooted in the politics of the great Turkish conquerors since the time of the Seljuks (eleventh century), with antecedents among the Arabs of the Islamic Conquest, especially during the reigns of the first four Caliphs, called 'the Just'.

It was Western advance in the East from the eighteenth, but above all in the nineteenth century, that put the Ottoman Empire on the defensive, forcing it into abandoning its traditional policy of racial and religious tolerance, by creating clienteles among the different nationalities and religious minorities under Ottoman sovereignty and encouraging them into dissidence. The European powers were in effect trying to undermine the Empire from within. Thus arose the 'Eastern question' of the eighteenth and nineteenth centuries, which the great English historian, Arnold Toynbee, declared was really a Western question, meaning that an Eastern question existed only because of European great power rivalry in the East. Between 1840 and 1860 the Lebanon was in fact a victim of this. The damage done to the Lebanon in the last century bears an uncanny resemblance to that being done today, thus indicating the permanence of certain elements, particularly the unhappy relations of East and West crystallizing in this frontier region between two worlds.

Already in the last century, Great Britain, worried by the progress of French influence in the Near East, had stirred up elements of discord in Lebanese society. France had made a strong cultural, commercial and political impact in the Near East from the time of Bonaparte: in the Lebanon, thanks to its protection of the Maronite community in the name of safeguarding the Christian minorities of the East, and in Egypt from the important cultural work undertaken as part of Napoleon's expedition and which earned him the open sympathies of Muhammad Ali, Viceroy of Egypt. This aroused British fears for the control of the route to India vital for her Empire. A heightening of rivalries, tensions and intrigues resulted, of which the Lebanon was the victim. It was now that Whitehall hatched the first Zionist plan to take British and European Jews back to Palestine in an attempt to build up a local client as a counterweight to the influence of France among the Maronites. At the time the plan aroused little enthusiasm among the European Jewish communities, which, emancipated by the permanent results of the French Revolution, dreamed only of integration and assimilation. The British had consequently to be content with supporting the Ottomans in their efforts to maintain control of Egypt and the Lebanon, both of which, in close alliance, were trying to escape the Empire's sphere of influence.

Mountains and minorities in the Near East

The Lebanese escarpment had actually always been difficult to govern and to unify. A steep ridge dropping directly onto the Mediterranean, it had for centuries provided refuge for religious schismatic groups persecuted by the orthodoxy of the central power, Byzantine or Muslim. Thus, in the twelfth century, the Maronites found refuge there from Byzantine persecution; later under Islam it sheltered the Shias and Druze, while to the north of Mount Lebanon, in Syria, another chain of mountains became a stronghold for the Alawis. During the centuries these strong natural fortresses have been permanently installed in the main urban centres of the region, i.e. Damascus, Tripoli, Aleppo, Beirut, Saida and Acre in Palestine. Although the central Islamic power was obliged to respect the cultural and religious autonomy of the Christian (and Jewish) communities, as prescribed in the Koran itself, this did not apply to heterodox Islamic sects like the Shias, Druze, Ismailis and Alawis. Hence the constant punitive raids, which affected the Christian communites living in socio-cultural symbiosis with the heterodox Islamic sects and who were quite as unruly as the latter. These Lebanese mountain dwellers (Maronites, Druze and Shias) were a lot of braggarts controlled by a turbulent aristocracy that had become powerful as farmers of the revenue for the central authority and had kept profoundly alive the tribal values of pre-Islamic Arabia. Till the beginning of the eighteenth century these Lebanese feudal lords fought one another savagely in the mountains, not over any theological or religious questions but to affirm the primacy of one ancient tribal origin over another. In this sense, through its diversity and contradictions, Lebanese society has retained right up to the contemporary period 'the actual image of the Arab family and its original structure',[2] as one of the best informed French observers of Lebanon has put it.

Internal struggles for power in the Lebanon have always had a markedly tribal character, which the central Ottoman power exploited to prevent any suggestion of emancipation. But in their incessant internal quarrels, the local aristocracy, in turn, never hesitate to call in governors of neighbouring provinces and, since the Renaissance, the Europeans as well. In the sixteenth century, two leading aristocratic families succeeded in rising above the mêlée and imposing their rule in the Lebanese mountain. Firstly the Druze emirs of the Maan family (1516–1697) and the Chehab-emirs (1697–1841), related by blood to the Maan, who were originally Sunni Muslims but converted to Christianity in the eighteenth century. Their conversion contributed quite considerably to the transfer of political supremacy in the Lebanon from the Druze aristocracy to the Maronites. But to this it must be added that the power of these emirs was permanently threatened first from within, usually from close family rivals, then from outside, from the Ottoman governors of neighbouring provinces, and finally in an indirect manner from European designs on the Near East.

In the last resort it was nineteenth century Europe that contributed probably the most to the disappearance of the Lebanese Emirate. Growing French influence seriously disrupted the balance between the communities. In the economic sphere competition from the silk mills of Lyon led to the decline of the mountain region's principal acitivity, breeding silkworms, while aggressive French commercial competition in general contributed to the general decay of local cottage industries. These developments enfeebled the aristocracy and impoverished the peasantry. Among the Maronites, where French cultural and economic influence was strongest, the clergy, until then kept in check by the aristocracy was strengthened and an embryonic bourgeoisie began to form within the framework of that influence. A logical result was growth among the Maronites of a feeling of aloofness from the Druze and Shiites, who had been left behind by the wave of 'modernization'. French policy encouraged this feeling by painting a glowing picture, especially to the Maronite clergy, recruited largely from the peasant masses, of the possibility of a Christian State in the Near East ruled by the Maronites under French protection. Furthermore, since the eighteenth century, the Maronites had been undergoing a considerable demographic and territorial expansion in comparison with the other communities, which reached a peak in the middle of the nineteenth century.

These factors explain the period of bloodstained troubles the Lebanon experienced between 1841 and 1861 when class revolts, inter-community troubles and violence, rivalries between the European great powers and Ottoman attempts to resist these pressures were all intimately interwoven. The period began when Muhammad Ali withdrew Egyptian troops from Syria and the Lebanon in 1840 in accordance with the agreement with the European powers guaranteeing the Pasha the government of Egypt in return for abandoning his claims to the Ottoman Near East.[3] Emir Bashir Chehab II, who had linked his fate to the Egyptian presence in the Lebanon, was forced to relinquish power and with him went the last great figure of the traditional Lebanese aristocracy. He left the Lebanon on the verge of disintegration, caused as much by his policy of profiting from the Egyptian occupation to decimate the powerful Druze aristocracy, as by the cultural and economic shock caused by destabilizing Western influence on the symbiosis of the three main Lebanese communities.

Three big outbreaks of violence between Druze and Maronites occurred in 1841, 1845 and 1860 and also an important revolt in Kisrwan of the Maronite peasantry against its own aristocracy (1858), which had been preceded a year earlier by a rebellion of the population of Zahle, a large Christian town in the Beqa'a Valley, against the authorities. During this period, scenes of fraternization between Druze and Maronites alternated with the massacres, often started from the most trivial reasons (that of 1841, for example, arose out of a disagreement between individuals over hunting rights.)

Western influence on Near Eastern minorities

It is clear, however, that behind all the chaos, Western pressure on the Ottoman-dominated Arab Near East crystallized around the fate of the Lebanon. The complexity of its socio-religious structures offered an open arch to intra-European rivalries which allowed the Ottoman Empire to resume the direct administration of the Lebanese territory it had until then been conceding with more or less good grace to the local aristocracy. This direct administration was, however, closely scrutinized by the European consuls posted in Beirut, who were on constant alert to ensure that none of them acquired overwhelming influence in the affairs of this unfortunate mountain territory.

The Lebanese question was settled in 1861 when French troops landed in Beirut in the name of the powers to protect Lebanese Christians. The settlement was actually drawn up by an international commission on which the Ottoman Empire and the five European great powers (France, England, Austria, Russia and Prussia) were represented. The agreement of 9 June 1861, which included an appendix on the legal status of Mount Lebanon, left the Lebanese mountains under Ottoman sovereignty but with the Beqa'a Valley and the South Lebanon territorially amputated. It also gave the European signatories control over the administration of the Ottoman governor through the agency of their consuls in Beirut. This was a noteworthy event which established Christian domination in the Lebanon, for under the agreement the Ottoman governor had to be of the Christian faith.

It should also be pointed out that between 1843 and 1861 the Lebanon was subjected to an untenable legal statute which divided the country into two prefectures (*kaimakamates*), the one Druze and the other Maronite. This statute clearly enabled the Ottoman Empire to confirm the break-up of the Maronite-Druze symbiosis which had characterized the best days of the Lebanese Emirate, and thus the better to consolidate its direct hold over this mountain area so coveted by the West. But it also enabled the European powers to find greener pastures for their manoeuvres and intrigues.

The picture of the nineteenth century troubles of the Lebanon must include the 1860 massacres of Christians in Damascus, once capital of the Umayyad Empire, which had seen the best days of peaceful co-existence between Christianity and Arab Islam at the beginning of the Islamic Conquest.[4] The Umayyad mosque in Damascus, a high place of Arab civilization, was for long a place of dual worship, where Christians and Muslims, each following their own faith, prayed side by side. Though there were many and complex reasons for this community violence, it was in essence caused by the economic and cultural aggression of the industrial West, triumphant over a prostrate East and using the Christian minorities to strengthen its position.

As in the Lebanon, the bourgeoisies that emerged from the

Christian communities of Syria owed their prosperity to their role as commercial intermediaries for the European powers. Christian prosperity was thus built on the weakening of traditional socio-economic structures. A wave of Islamic fundamentalism then followed, directed against the Arab Christians, obvious symbols of Western power and Eastern dispossession. This fundamentalist movement rejected all the new ideas of equality, freedom and fraternity coming in to the East ever since Bonaparte, which Muhammad Ali had put into practice in the Near East and the Ottoman sultans had eventually adopted in reforms of 1839 and 1856.[5]

The scapegoat Christians, who had provided the West with the pretext for colonial-type penetration of the East, played this role once again in Iraq in the 1920s when they were unscrupulously used by the English to repress local uprisings. It will also be remembered that at the beginning of this century the Ottoman Empire crumbled away in the infamous massacres of Armenians and Greeks, for which the European powers as well bear considerable responsibility. All this, of course, passed into the collective unconscious of the minorities and it was certainly not by chance that the rise of a powerful Arab Christianity in the Lebanon, personified by the Phalangist party, coincided with the emergence in the twentieth century of a new wave of Islamic fundamentalism.

Apart from the traumatic aspect of community violence, what is striking in retrospect about these nineteenth-century events is that recurrence of social convulsions caused by abortive attempts at modernization and expressed through a rebirth of religious fundamentalism. The remark of our well-informed observer of Mount Lebanon about the Near East during the European Industrial Revolution in the nineteenth century applies as well to the Arab world of the twentieth century faced with the sudden wealth of the energy revolution. 'The industrial revolution coming from the outside remained exterior to it.'[6] Evidently the East-West encounter has resulted in anguish and misfortune for the East. Already an important cause of the major troubles in the Lebanon in the nineteenth century, the overpowerful West was to be so again in the twentieth. For the Palestine that rose out of the ashes in the 1960s and 1970s and came to asphyxiate Lebanon had in fact been seized by the West during its colonial activity, in order to be handed over to another set of Western victims, the Jews.

The historical account already given shows up the Lebanese

political elite as usually unworthy of the power it held. Its deeply anchored tribal and provincial traditions are in inverse proportion to the small size of the mountain area. And of even graver consequence, to conserve its power, it has never hesitated to call on the help of foreigners in its internal quarrels. The twentieth century elite had hardly changed. The influence of the traditional aristocracy may have declined considerably relative to the now all-powerful bourgeoisie business, especially since independence in 1943, but its behaviour is still the same: corruption, sectarian quarrels and clientele-ism/clientelage in relation to the outside world. To this is added a brilliant but superficial varnish of modernism which hides even from the better informed the permanent weight of its historical traditions. These traditions have sprung from insecurity, violent change, interference from local or foreign powers, and arbitrary government. They are not the monopoly of the Lebanese elite; far from it, for one should not forget the exemplary character of the Lebanese situation in the Near East, which serves as the magnifying glass for observing Arab reality more clearly. But in Lebanon the burden of these historical situations is harder both for the individual and collective psychology to bear because of the minority condition which affects all the Lebanese communities.

The psychodramas of Lebanese communities

This crazy Lebanon, set alight in 1975, was a country dying from its minority complex. The Maronites feared the rise of Islam which would question their power. The Druze, who governed the Mountain brilliantly in the sixteenth and seventeenth centuries, had lost all their political and demographic weight, save for the great aristocratic figure of Kamal Jumblatt, central character and principal victim in the drama of these years of violence. The Shias, rejects of Lebanese history and the most crushingly poor of the social groups, were in revolt against their condition. An Iman Musecul Sadt, piercing-eyed and powerful in presence, originally from South Lebanon but who had lived in Qom in Iran, important centre of Shiite theology, galvanized the community by creating a 'Movement for the Underprivileged' which mobilized a large section of poor Shiite youth.[7] This left the Sunnis marginalized by the Maronite ascendancy, the emergence of the Shias and the charisma and dynamism of Jumblatt, authentic representative of the top Druze aristocracy.

In truth, the system set up in the Lebanon by France, Mandatory power from 1920 to 1943, which the Lebanese political elite did not know how to manage after independence, could not help but exacerbate this minority complex.[8] Distributing the highest State and administrative offices between the communities in a strict hierarchy could only make the system more precarious and increase the tendency towards corruption and clientelage.[9] This would have undermined even the soundest social body, and it turned the whole Lebanese democracy into an illusion. Not only did the struggle for power damage inter-community relations but within each community no holds were barred to those seeking to set themselves up as the most 'authentic' representatives. In such cases, there was so much demagoguery that it provided a very effective barrier against alternative elites gaining access to power unless centred on or justified by a community-based system of promotion. Consequently, since 1920 power in the Lebanon remained the monopoly of a closed club in which the logic of circumstance brought together the oligarchies of the principal religious communities. For this reason the local component of the troubles that began in 1975 has been as much a conflict within communities to replace the elites in power as a confrontation between communities. The logic of internal confrontation pushed communities to extremism and as a result accentuated the historical disputes between them.

Thus, among the Maronites, although one family held the monopoly of power within the Phalangist party, struggles were waged, often with violence, to throw out traditional Maronite notables. There was striking proof of this in the two daring and bloody military operations in 1978 and 1980 against Maronite families which had ruled independent Lebanon. Despite being something of a family enterprise, the party successfully reflected the power and aspirations of a Christian middle class recently urbanized in a sub-culture neither Arab nor truly Western.[10] Overtaken by certain local and regional events, the confidence of this middle class was undermined by the spectacular upsurge of political movements advocating revolutionary ideologies, and notably the Palestinian movements so active in Lebanon, and then by the rise of Islamic fundamentalism and the claims of other religious communities as much social as political.

The same phenomenon occurred on the Islamic side. Among the Shiites 'Amal', the political and military arm of the Movement for the Underprivileged created by Imam Sadr, set out to achieve a double objective. On the one hand it sought to discredit and remove all representativeness from the big families of the landed aristocracy, who were monopolizing power within the community and in its share of the management of State affairs to the exclusive benefit of their direct clientele, and on the other hand to increase the community's share of power in Lebanese society and in the running of the State.

Among the Sunnis, various political parties deriving identity from Nasserism took up arms from the beginning of the events, as much to contest the influence of the community's traditional notables as not to be outdone by the Phalangist party's militarization. It was also noticeable that in the Amal Shiite movement, as in the Nasserist parties, young people predominated at the grass roots, while the middle-aged who had never been able to penetrate the exclusive club of the ruling families ran the parties. To a lesser degree, the same applied to the Phalangist Party.

The Kamal Jumblatt phenomenon, however, was quite different. His ascendency over the Druze community was uncontested. On the other hand, the all-powerful position he was acquiring on the Lebanese and Arab political stage rankled both in Lebanon and in the Arab world. In 1972 he became Secretary General of the Palestinian Revolution Support Front which confirmed all the parties in the Arab world claiming to be on the Left. At the same time, he rallied around his strong personality an alliance of all the Lebanese parties of the 'Left' claiming to uphold pan-Arab ideals and Third World progressivism. In 1975 this alliance was formalized by the constitution of the Lebanese National Movement, allied to the PLO. Within a few months Jumblatt became a key figure in the Near East situation at the time when in the spring of 1976 the National Movement force, whose logistics and supply depend for the most part on the PLO, set off to conquer the Maronite fiefs of the Mountain.

Thus the despairing heir of a great aristocracy, deprived of power for two centuries and on the verge of disappearance, was able to rule over Lebanon again for a few months and to play a dominant regional role. This fleeting moment of glory cost him his life. With his assassination in 1977, Lebanon lost an unusually cultured and charismatic figure who might well have been able to build a modern, secular and militarily strong State.

Kamal Jumblatt's passing also symbolized the end of the Jacobin dream of the Arab Left. It was in fact in Lebanon that the Arab revolution, fleetingly embodied in the alliance of Lebanese youth and the Palestinian resistance movements, underwent a second death. For in the spring of 1975, Marx, Lenin, Che Guevara, Mao Tse-tung and Gamal Abdel Nasser met ideologically in Beirut to confront the 'plots' of imperialist Zionism, and Arab 'reaction' against the Palestinian Resistance, which incarnated the 'revolutionary will' of the 'Arab nation'. At a time when the Egyptians and Syrians had already signed military disengagement agreements with the Israelis, when Nixon had been received in Egypt and Syria, the traditional strongholds of anti-imperialism, when oil had bound the monarchies and Emirates of the Gulf hand and foot to the West, when the only basis for an international solution to the Arab–Israeli conflict lay in Security Council Resolution 242, which referred to the Palestinians solely as refugees and not as a sovereign people, how could it be otherwise than that the Arab Left seeking refuge in Lebanon, the only country in which ideology could be freely expressed, should mobilize?

Palestinians in Lebanon or the 'Black September' complex

Like the Lebanese communities, the other minority of the Arab world, the Palestinians, lived in increasing fear, and since the 1970 massacres in Jordan in a 'Black September' complex. Convinced in fact that their liquidation as an armed resistance movement would sooner or later take place in Lebanon, their last refuge, their hard-core Marxism and Pan–Arab socialist movements, felt especially threatened everywhere in the Arab world: they were the least tolerated by the established regimes. All the plane hijackings and other spectacular terrorist operations, sometimes carried out in collaboration with European or Japanese terrorist organizations, were the handiwork of the hard-core elements: the attack on the Saudi Arabian Embassy in Khartoum first in March 1973 during a reception when three Western diplomats were killed, including the United States Ambassador, and then in Paris in September; the incident in December 1973 when the OPEC oil ministers meeting in Vienna were taken hostage; and the taking of hostages at the Egyptian Embassy in Madrid on 15 September 1975.

Al-Fatah, the main resistance movement, which had Centrist tendencies, worried the Arab leaders less. It had never claimed to support this type of operation; on the contrary, it had systematically condemned it. The Phalangist party itself often spoke of 'good' resistance movements and contrasted them with the 'bad', i.e. those tied to 'communism' and international 'subversion'. Until the beginning of the troubles, it had declared its hostility only to the latter, to be rooted out of Lebanon. Thus it was not by mere chance that everything began on 13 April 1975 with the murderous ambush, organized by the Phalangist party, on a bus transporting supporters of the Arab Liberation Front, one of the Rejection movements supported by Iraq.

The Palestinians had another reason for anxiety, namely the implacable determination of the Israelis since 1968 to hunt them down in Lebanon, with intensive bombing of refugee camps often claiming hundreds of innocent victims as well as Israeli army incursions into South Lebanon in order to wipe out the commando bases the Lebanese government had imprudently conceded to the resistance movements in 1969.[11] In April 1973, Israelis came by sea during the night, and in the centre of Beirut's residential area assassinated three Palestinian leaders, including the poet Kamal Nasser, a man in favour of dialogue and appeasement if there ever was.

In all these Israeli raids into Lebanese territory, the national army did not fire a single shot. Even during the Christmas and New Year celebrations in 1968, when an Israeli unit landed by helicopter at Beirut airport in the middle of the night and within half an hour destroyed the whole Lebanese commercial aviation fleet, they were not in the least deterred by the security forces guarding the airport and even less by the Lebanese army units in barracks only a few hundred metres away. The army had probably been ordered not to interfere with Israeli incursions into national territory. The Maronite notables who dominated the State hardly realized that they were signing its death warrant. Their fear of radical Palestinian ideology was stronger than their statesmanship and understanding of the reality of State power. An army that fails to defend the integrity of the national territory in fact loses all legitimacy and can no longer effectively protect the political power.

Lebanese government, an exercise in purblindness

The mode of exercise of power in Lebanon in this period, astonish-ingly shows once again that cultural dissonance already noticed in the Near East in other forms and under other circumstances. Not only did the Lebanese army make no attempt to put up resistance to Israeli incursions, it allowed itself to be used increasingly by the authorities to repress the manifestations of social discontent brewing since the beginning of the 1970s. The traditional sectors of the Lebanese economy were being threatened by the growing importance of regional finance capitalism based on oil. Siphoning off a portion of the oil manna, a dynamic service sector had turned Beirut into an admired banking and commercial centre. Between 1968 and 1975 Lebanese political and military power were both showing signs of rapid wear and tear. Between 1969 and 1973 three half-hearted attempts were made to contain the now omni-present Palestinian resistance movements which, because of the general insecurity and the incursions into Lebanese territory made with impunity by Israel, had become increasingly heavily armed. Equally fearful of being politically overwhelmed and of a check to the great prosperity of the dynamic sectors of the economy, the government did not dare to enter into a decisive confrontation with the resistance movements. This excess of caution was no doubt responsible both for the political crisis and the economic chaos which along with the collapse of the Lebanese army occurred in 1975–6.

The leaders of the Lebanese State had in fact never understood, as the other Arab States had, that to contain the Palestinian Resistance successfully, it was necessary for the national army to have earned legitimacy in the struggle against Israel. Since 1948, the Lebanese army had remained neutral, outside the conflicts of 1956, 1967 and 1973, but when it allowed the Israeli army to operate on Lebanese territory with complete impunity, it condemned itself to impotence. The leadership was derided in 1973 when a corrupt arms deal was exposed which ended with Lebanon asking France to set up an air defence system using 'Crotales' missiles. It must be said however that the Lebanese leaders were afraid of the all-powerful Israeli army's capacity to destroy within a few minutes their small national army (15,000 men), which they mainly regarded as an internal police force. They also knew that the Israelis would not take kindly to any reinforcement of Lebanese defence potential. There was more derision when a military service project was stalled in Parliament for years without being voted on because the political elite were afraid of enrolling young men who harboured dreams of revolution and of slaying the imperialist dragon. The slogan-like phrase repeated for years by the leader of one of the Christian conservative parties well summarizes the piteous aspect of the Lebanese elite: 'The Lebanon's strength is in its weakness.'

This blindness of the club of political notables was due to a certain extent also to their naive confidence in the Western powers and in the protection these were supposed to give Lebanon. Out of date and overtaken by regional events, the 'princes' who governed Lebanon did not grasp in time that, unlike in the 1950s, the Lebanon of the 1970s had ceased to be important to the Near Eastern arrangements of the West. At the beginning of the 1970s, the West was interested mainly in the security of the oil regions and in detaching Egypt and Syria from the Soviet Union and not in preserving communal hierarchies in a small territory without resources or in reinforcing the Christian presence, both of which had involved such high political stakes during the colonial penetration of Near Eastern provinces of the the Ottoman Empire in the nineteenth century.

Through a calculated State Department indiscretion, in 1976 the United States had let it be known that it no longer believed the Lebanese regime was viable in its traditional form. What a respite for Israel in its refusal to recognize a Palestinian existence, this chaos that had descended on Lebanon and enabled the resistance movements to dig themselves in there. A tremendous relief also for the West, which had never much liked being rough with the Israelis.

By trying to liquidate the Palestinian Left in Lebanon, the Lebanese government actually played its last card *vis-à-vis* the West and the pro-Western Arab regimes, a card rapidly lost in the total chaos into which the country had lapsed. Dominated as they were by their respective anxieties, the Lebanese and Palestinians in fact committed a double error. By generalizing fighting and chaos the Palestinians deprived themselves of the only Arab State in which they enjoyed complete military and ideological freedom. For the Lebanese it was yet another attempt to settle by bloodshed the Kistoni conflicts of communities which it would be difficult to integrate into a harmonious social framework afterwards. But how could they think clearly when all the socio-political groups were playing with fire? Instead they flung themselves into a bloody free-for-all, in which all the anguish and frustrations of Arab society were given a free rein.

The rewards of fear

The fear felt by the Palestinians has already been mentioned. Once merged into the populations of predominantly Muslim regions, they distributed arms widely to all parties supporting them and declaring adhesion to Arab Jacobinism. This fear, however, kindled that of the Maronites, who saw in an alliance between the mostly Sunni Palestinians and the other Muslim communities a serious threat to their political existence. And summit of horror, it was a Druze aristocrat, who held by Mirabeau and La Feyette, a formidable political and ideological adversary who gave the lead to such an alliance. But the Maronite Right had forgotten that in the previous century, with help from the Maronite community Emir Bashir Chehab II had opened up the country to Muhammad Ali's armies and had utilized that alliance to crush the top aristocratic Druze families, among them that of Jumblatt. The situation was now reversed; fortified by Palestinian support, it was the turn of the conquered of yesterday to take their revenge.

To denominational fear was added an ideological fear of the Palestinian Left seen as a symbol of subversion and international communism by the new petite bourgeoisie whose gains were quite recent and which was bombarded by extreme Right-wing propaganda, evidently financed by certain Arab regimes. Thus in the regions they dominated the militias of the conservative parties indiscriminately attacked politically unaffiliated Muslims, Left-wing parties with a Christian element (the communists or the Syrian Nationalist party (PPS)), and the Palestinians. None of this made an attractive spectacle and for a long time this Right received a bad press in the West, which could at last have a clear conscience about the Palestinians without having to have a bad one about the Israelis.

A closer look is, however, required, for the horrors perpetrated were just as bad in the opposite camp, where soon it was difficult to tell whether the alliance between Left-wing Lebanese parties and the Palestinian resistance movements was promoting revolutionary Pan-Arab socialism, or whether it had become an Islamic fundamentalist movement (with the tribal traditions from the Lebanese Mountain) to hunt down the Christians. Whole, often unarmed, villages were destroyed, in which sometimes even traditionally Left-wing families perished. The Christian populations, in particular those living in the large urban centres of Beirut, Tripoli and Saida, were never forcibly displaced as the Muslim populations living in Christian urban areas were, but there were numerous and repeated kidnappings of Christians in which the victims usually disappeared without trace.

To these crimes against people were added theft, destruction and looting. On the Right, these activities were institutionalized and well-managed, as shown by the famous looting of the port of Beirut or the destruction of the ancient bazaars. On the Left they were generally less sophisticated, although the armed raids on the strongrooms of certain banks in the centre of Beirut indicated the use of sophisticated equipment. The destruction of State archives carefully preserved by the Right revealed, however, a streak of anarchism in the Left, or perhaps more simply disgust at a State that had become so pusillanimous.

In his conversations with a French journalist some months before his death, Kamal Jumblatt, patron of the so-called 'Palestinian-Progressive' alliance, openly and bitterly expressed his disgust at the mess made by the alliance in practice,[12] which he attributed for the most part to the Palestinian resistance organizations.

The details of this war, which began with the ambush of a Palestinian bus on 13 April 1975 mentioned earlier, are in themselves of little interest. They can be divided, in the romantic revolutionary manner, into three stages. First, a gunpoint revolution (April 1975 to April 1976) when the Palestinian-Progressive alliance had the wind behind it and succeeded in the military conquests aimed at surrounding the Christian zones held by Right-wing Maronite militias. Then a betrayal of the revolution when the intervention of the Syrian army once and for all removed all hope of a seizure of power by the 'revolutionaries' and facilitated the fall of the Palestinian camp of Tel al-Zaatat, stronghold of Left-wing Palestinian organizations right in the middle of the Christian region. This (May–November 1976) was the Arab equivalent of the death of Che Guevara. And finally, the revolution reduced to the commonplace when the Syrian army, with the blessings of Saudia Arabia and Egypt and the symbolic help of 'green helmet' contingents (from Saudia Arabia, Yemen, the United Arab Emirates and Libya), operating under cover of the Arab League, entered Beirut, already battered by months of intensive gunfire between the various districts.

Once again an Arab dream had been blown away by a horrible reality. With the Lebanese Front assembling the conservative Christian parties, the National Movement, the federation of Left-wing parties, and the Palestinian resistance movements, nobody could be proud of the ruin inflicted on the Near East. Fifty to seventy thousand dead, a hundred thousand wounded or disabled, thousands of shells fired between the districts of the Lebanese capital and thousands of millions of pounds' worth of destruction. All this staggering warlike energy was expended not against Israel, but by Arabs against each other for the purpose of reaching agreement over the best way of settling the Arab–Israeli conflict and to 'help' the Lebanese to retain or to change the communal hierarchies and oligarchies that profited from them.

Civil war among the Arabs, new bargaining cards for the Israelis

For the Arab Near East as a whole, the deeper significance of the Lebanese destruction lay in the increased tensions it provoked within the Arab political world between the supporters of a rapid and final solution to the dispute with Israel, in the West's sphere of influence, and those who, for various and sometimes opposing reasons, remained stuck with Third World neutralism, revolutionary romanticism, or unconditional alliance with the Soviet Union. At this level, the Lebanese troubles were first and foremost those of an Arab civil war. Everybody rode his own hobby horse, some several simultaneously or successively depending on circumstances or mood, through the complicated labyrinth of the numerous combatant groups (there were around thirty different movements).

The civil war enabled the Israelis to manage to extract new advantages for themselves: to their right of pursuit and reprisals on Lebanese soil, freely exercised since 1968, they added a good old colonial cause, which they used and abused as they thought fit, namely the protection of the Christians. This happened mainly in the Southern frontier territories, where they gained favour with the Christian villages which had been isolated by the Palestinian

– Progressive troops. Under Israeli protection these villages passed into the control of officers of the now fragmented Lebanese army who belonged to the region.[13] This was the 'good frontier', used in propaganda on all the televisions of the world as an example of Arab–Israeli 'brotherhood'.

This good frontier was subsequently enlarged into a 700 square kilometre strip which these same Lebanese officers, evidently impervious to ridicule proclaimed as 'Free Lebanon' in April 1979. Earlier however, in 1978, they had prevented contingents of the now partly legally reconstituted Lebanese army from resuming control of this good frontier in concert with United Nations. The new encroachment was the result of the Israeli invasion of South Lebanon in the spring of 1978. The troops were subsequently obliged to evacuate the conquered territory to make way for a United Nations peace-keeping force entrusted with the task of intervening between them and the Palestinian resistance movements, whose fighting spirit had in no way been weakened by the war in Lebanon. But no injunction was capable of forcing the Israelis to give up the frontier strip they were holding under the cover of the Lebanese officers acting in breach of due authority.

In addition, Israel had succeeded in keeping the mainly Syrian Arab Deterrent Force (ADF), whose presence in the Lebanon had the support of the Arab League, from the whole area of South Lebanon. This was the famous 'red line' which the Syrians could cross only on pain of having to face the full force of the Israeli army. The Palestinians were thus exposed in South Lebanon where the civilian population more than ever continued to be victims of the Israeli reprisals that followed Palestinian attacks on Galilee on the Lebanese frontier. Lebanon remained a wound from which Arab blood flowed.

After the end of the widespread fighting in the winter of 1976 with the entry of Syrian troops with the backing of the Arab League, it was not only in the South that blood flowed in Lebanon. The agreement between Syria and the main components of the Lebanese Front was broken in the spring of 1978, triggering off large-scale hostilities, particularly in Beirut; Syrian troops then left the Christian quarters of the capital. Clashes between Syrian units and Christian militias began again in the spring of 1981 and were concentrated mainly on the town of Zahle in the Beqa'a Valley and in the surrounding hills. In both cases, the Israelis fanned the flames by setting themselves up in defence of the Christian parties.

In the summer of 1981 occurred the 'missile crisis' in the Beqa'a, when Syria introduced Soviet Sam–7 rockets near the town of Zahle to put an end to Israeli air incursions, which had resulted in the shooting down of Syrian helicopters. There was also an outbreak of wanton violence on the part of the Israelis in South Lebanon, again hitting the civilian populations especially hard. Israel's action was then crowned by a particularly deadly raid (300 victims) on the working-class districts of the capital where certain Palestinian organizations had their administrative offices. All this was, however, only a foretaste of violence and destruction Israel let loose on Lebanon, and particularly on West Beirut, during the summer of 1982.

Nevertheless, during this period the Palestinians, whose armament had become somewhat more sophisticated in quality, again showed their resilience in South Lebanon against Israeli targets on the other side of the border. Since the October 1973 war, the Arab world, bursting with oil, arms and luxury flats in Western capitals, had in fact impassively watched as Lebanese and Palestinians died, just as if South Lebanon had been at the North Pole. During this same bloody summer of 1981, President Sadat met Menachem Begin in Sinai with the embracing gesture that had become familiar since the Camp David Agreements established peace between Egypt and Israel. The situation was hardly any different in the summer of 1982.

A game of poker or a game of chess: Syrian–Egyptian contradictions

As the life-blood of stricken Lebanon drained away the Arabs remained powerless and Israel intransigent. As Israeli politics are the subject of the next chapter, we may at this point look more closely at events on the Arab side. Since 1975 two men had cast their shadow over the Arab stage: the Egyptian President, Anwar Sadat, and the Syrian President, Hafez al-Assad. Of opposite temperaments they had increasing difficulty in finding grounds for agreement as their respective measures became consolidated and events propelled them into the glare of the spotlights in the Near East. Apart from the difference in the two personalities, the conflict between Egypt and Syria had become extremely serious since the dissolution of union between the two countries in 1961. It was Syrian ultra-Leftism between 1963 and 1966 that had pushed Egypt into the disastrous war of 1967 and Syria again which, until 1970, stepped up the level of intransigence.

Hafez al-Assad's accession to power at the end of 1970 ended Syria's isolation. Under its new leader, this other key country of the Near East entered into the discreet move to the Right that would allow reconciliation with the West and thus a rapid solution to the Arab–Israeli conflict, which had been blocked by the Khartoum summit resolutions of 1967. But while the Egyptian President was a man of panache and of dramatic moves, which in a few short years led him to make peace with Israel and to link his destiny to an American presence in the Near East, the Syrian President was just the opposite.

Of seemingly modest and calm appearence, by this quality alone he stood apart from many of his Arab partners, especially self-centred, voluble and febrile Sadat. He preferred to listen rather than to talk. In 1975 and 1976 he spent endless hours receiving Lebanese politicians and listening to the recital of their grievances and their obsessions.

The Syrian President made his moves with a light touch and without roughness. He intervened in Lebanon with half a step forward and three-eighths of a step backwards; and behaved similarly when reorienting his foreign policy. Moreover, unlike Anwar Sadat, he had no anti-Soviet phobia and continued to maintain good relations with both the super-powers. Again unlike Sadat he didn't seem to be a man in a hurry.

In his slow but irresistible rise to power in Syria, his moves were more like those of a careful chess player than of an aggressive amateur at poker. It was undoubtedly because of him that in the 1970s Syria became a true regional power in the Near East, whereas until then only Egypt and Israel could honour themselves with such a title. In certain respects he represented in the practice of international relations a new style of power in the Arab World. It was perhaps this that worried his Arab peers who came to believe that nothing in future could be done in the Near East without his agreement. In any case, everything in his personality made him an opponent of Sadat.

Far from bringing the Syrian–Egyptian dispute to an end, the October 1973 war only made it worse. For one thing the Syrians reproached the Egyptians, first, for not fully exploiting their advantage in the first few days of military operations, thus allowing the Israeli army to concentrate on the Syrian front and rapidly stop the Syrian break-through, and second, for being too quick to accept a cease-fire on 22 October 1973. Although operations were turning in Israel's favour, the Syrians felt that with their Iraqi reinforcements, they could have held on and even launched a counter-attack.

In the negotiations that followed, the Syrians again saw the Egyptian haste as a sign of weakness in a global settlement of the Arab–Israeli conflict, which the Israelis were exploiting to split the Arab diplomatic front more effectively. Syrian fears were only too well founded. On 18 January 1974, Egypt by itself signed a military disengagement with Israel. In addition, the Egyptian President rarely took the trouble to consult his Syrian ally before making one of his spectacular decisions. The Arab oil embargo, though more symbolic than effective, was lifted under Egyptian pressure before there was any Syrian–Israeli disengagement. It was only on 31 May 1974, after furious battles on Mount Hermon overlooking the Golan Heights that Israel and Syria signed a military disengagement agreement, much less generous for Syria than that of 18 January for Egypt. It was thus already clear that a tendency was developing, at international level, to exclude Syria, which continued to have good relations with the Soviet Union from the settlement of the Arab–Israeli dispute.

A surfeit of love for the West

This tendency was confirmed on 1 September 1975 when Egypt signed an agreement with Israel bearing on Sinai under which 'the conflict existing between these two countries in the Near East will not be solved by military force but by peaceful means'.[14] The first seeds of an Israeli–Egyptian peace had been sown in the Near East. The visit to Jerusalem two years later and the Camp David Agreements of 1978 and 1979 were no more than the logical repercussions of this action. In order to reach the Sinai Agreement, the Egyptian President made an unilateral gesture, as usual, and without any *quid pro quo*, by opening in June 1975 the Suez Canal and starting to rebuild the destroyed canal towns. This was in effect an unequivocal signal to Israel that Egypt no longer intended to fight, and just when Israel was blocking progress in the negotiations with Egypt, the most important Arab military power. Syria was thus well and truly dropped by Egypt.

At the same time, the unconditionally pro-Western forces in the Near East, Saudi Arabia, Egypt, Morocco and Sudan, seemed to want to go it by themselves. King Faisal had been assassinated in March 1975, only a few weeks after an official visit to Damascus. With King Khalid's accession, the new strong man of the Kingdom was Prince Fahd, now Crown Prince, whose pro-Western feelings knew no bounds. An axis soon formed between the above countries, which seemed more concerned with driving the Soviet Union out of the Middle East and Africa than with finding a global solution to the Palestinian conflict. Thus, in 1977, without batting an eyelid, Egypt sent considerable military assistance to Zaire, which was being threatened by the Shaba rebellion, and Moroccan troops were airlifted by France, while the Israeli army continued to go for the Lebanon.

Morocco is an important member of the Arab world's pro-Western lobby. It was King Hasan who, in 1977, sponsored secret meetings in Rabat between the Israeli Minister of Foreign Affairs, Moshe Dayan, and Egyptian representatives, and again Morocco which, with Western support, set off the conflict in the Spanish Sahara, which its troops occupied in concert with Mauritania after the Spanish evacuation at the end of 1975. Algeria inevitably reacted by supporting and promoting the rebellion of the Western Saharan tribes demanding self-determination.

Everything was going badly in 1976 in the Arab part of Africa. In August, Egypt and Libya were on the point of a general armed conflict, with Sadat calling President Gadaffi 'the madman of Libya'. Exposed to vigorous Egyptian and Moroccan hostility, Libya leant more heavily on the Soviet Union and drew closer to Algeria.

This same out-and-out 'Westernism' eventually pushed Syria, isolated and despairing of any balanced solution to the Arab–Israeli conflict, into a co-operation and friendship treaty with the Soviet Union in 1980. At the same time, internal opposition in Syria had taken on dramatic proportions; acts of terrorism committed by Islamic fundamentalist organizations were becoming ever more frequent and the foundations of the Syrian regime seemed to be weakening.

In reality, the Arab Rejection Front, set up after Sadat's visit to Jerusalem and consisting of Algeria, Libya, Syria, South Yemen and the PLO, had existed virtually since 1975. It was partly a reaction against the excessive attitude of those Arab countries officially united in an unconditionally pro-Western lobby and which wanted to see all traces of Soviet influence eliminated from the Near East. These countries disapproved of the formation of a Palestinian State so long as the Resistance enjoyed the support of the Soviet Union and certain of its movements adhered to Marxist ideology in one form or another.

From this point of view, the Lebanese civil war merely highlighted the political tensions of the whole of Arab society, generated by the excessive ideological commitments of the political elites, which seemed to consider the active support of one or other of the two super-powers a major ingredient of political success. Syria under Hafez al-Assad sought to avoid any such total alignment or, for that matter, a commitment to any strict ideological position. In his foreign relations, the Syrian President was above all a prudent and pragmatic man. It is probably his see-sawing and balancing acts that finally antagonized the contradictory and impassioned political forces of the Arab Near East, in their Manichean political world where cultural incoherence had wrought so much havoc. He acted differently on his domestic front where his previously very positive image was now definitely tarnished by the increasingly serious violence and repression which the Syrian army unleashed in Lebanon against the Christian militias, and inside Syria, against a formidable religious fundamentalism.[15] Like most Arab Heads of State, the Syrian President's image was also tarnished by the considerable shrinking of his power base over the years, by the violent suppression of all forms of opposition and by corruption in the ruling bureaucracy in the administration, the party and the armed force.

Syria under Hafez al-Assad was further discredited at the beginning of the 1980s by its continued occupation of Lebanon, which involved constant trouble, particularly in the north Lebanese capital, Tripoli, but which did not save Lebanon from Israeli attacks. The full extent of the Syrian failure became evident when Israel invaded Lebanon in 1982.

Bad calculations by the Arab Left

Syria's Lebanese policy engendered so much criticism because it created indignation among the ideological forces of the Left without winning favour with the Right. In fact it seemed as if in 1975–6 the revolutionary Left in Lebanon, born of the alliance of Lebanese radical parties and Palestinian resistance movements, had not understood the balance of power in the Arab world and Syria's role in it. At that time, the Arab Left in Lebanon, still believing that revolution and enthusiastic 'mass' action was valid, as in the 1960s, imagined that the 'reactionary' Arab regimes, ready to sell Palestine for a smile from the West, would collapse on the announcement of a seizure of power in Lebanon and that if the Syrian regime dared to oppose the victory of the revolution in Lebanon, it too would immediately collapse.

Besides indicating political naivety, this involved seeing people as abstractions, visualized for the needs of the cause as revolutionary masses in perpetual spontaneous mobilization. And this at a time when the economic and social consequences of the tyranny of oil and a deep disillusionment over Arab unity, modernity and progress had either left the Arabs totally indifferent politically or had driven them into deeply reactionary religious fundamentalism. This was also to misjudge the nature of power in the Near East where, behind modern ideological quarrels lay regional, tribal and sectarian allegiances which were still very much alive. A facade of modernism hiding ignorance of the real facts contributed to the failure of the Arab Left.

To this ignorance was added a political opportunism which took the form of pandering to religious, sectarian and tribal allegiances as a means of self-defence or of counter-attack. Thus the ideologically radical and secular movements purporting to defend the Islamic masses, evidently had an understanding with the fundamentalist movements trying to destabilize Syria and which saw the Christian face of Lebanon as an aberration. But the government in Syria was also denounced because the Syrian President, along with many of the civilian and military cadres of the Baath party, were Alawis, as underprivileged and oppressed a minority as ever existed in the course of history.

The Arab Left's perception of the political realities in Lebanon has always suffered from the cultural misperceptions of Arab society. In fact, even when Egypt was dealing directly with Israel and signing the first peace agreement in 1975, and when the Gulf's oil and financial power were being put back into the hands of the West, it was the Near East's small Maronite minority that the Arab Left marked out for 'popular' condemnation as having been responsible for the Arab defeat against Israel. The accusation was especially poignant since from the middle of the nineteenth century some of the greatest figures of Arabism had arisen from among the Maronites.

But when the Left began to speak of class struggle, with the Maronites as the 'bourgeoisie' and the Islamic masses as the 'proletariat', their analysis became utterly grotesque, while simply ignoring the feudal system functioning among the Druze and the Shia and the considerable fortunes in real estate among the Sunnis. It counted for nothing that the Maronite feudal system had dwindled away with the events of the eighteenth century, that the great majority of Maronites were of poor rural origin, that their urban petite bourgeoisie was of relatively recent creation, that their numbers included a large part of the working class and unionized employees, finally, that many rich Maronites did not owe their wealth to exploiting the Islamic masses but to their emigration to the four corners of the world and especially to Africa, Latin America and Australia.

The absence of a proper perception of reality was here, once again, total. It was manifested again during the summer of 1976 from which time on Syria unequivocally blocked the military movements of the Lebanese–Palestinian Left. President Assad was then roundly denounced on the grounds that he belonged to a minority group. Yet a large number of leaders on the Lebanese Left, headed by Kamal Jumblatt, were also from minorities, not to mention the leaders of the Palestinian Rejection movements, particularly George Habash.[16] It was disconcerting that Kamal Jumblatt, who until then had seemed to mix tradition and modern culture so perfectly, could to such an extent have fallen victim to those same misperceptions which had ruined so many beautiful dreams in the Near East.

It was actually this mixture of tradition and modernity that made Jumblatt such a fascinating character. He himself was probably attached to neither, being a fervent follower of Hindu wisdom who frequently returned to India to achieve new stages of initiation. But there is no doubt that his behaviour during these dramatic years was characterized by a conflicting juxtaposition of tradition and modernity: tradition when, although for the most part generous and grand seigneur, he was overwhelmed by an inexorable desire for historical revenge against the Maronite political elite who in the previous century had reduced the power of his family and of many other aristocratic Druze clans; modernity when, with evident sincerity and unshakeable conviction, he called for social democracy for Lebanon and the Arab world, where social justice, secularism and freedom would enable Arab society to come into cultural phase with modern conditions.

His great mistake, however, was to reveal himself too fully to the Syrian President, who, with his silences, was so good at extracting confidences. He did this during a discussion with the former lasting close on nine hours on 27 March 1976, in the hope of winning him over to his point of view. In two famous speeches, one in April, the other, more vehement, in July, the Syrian President denounced a war which, under the guise of revolution, aimed to bring down the Arab Christians, thus passing himself off as the defender of equality among all Arabs, irrespective of religion. To ingratiate himself with Islam in revolt in Syria, Hafez al-Assad also denounced Jumblatt and the Lebanese National Movement's secularism as contrary to the spirit and letter of orthodox Islam. It cannot, however, be forgotten that in 1973 Assad himself, as the heir to a secular Syria, had had to face a wave of fundamentalist protest over a new and highly secular constitution which did not even mention that Islam was the State religion. But in 1976 religious fundamentalism submerged the Middle East, on the Right as well as on the Left, and the fundamentalist movements came to be utilized by contradictory political forces. To avoid alienating them still further, Assad then tried hard to appear respectful of the strictest Islamic orthodoxy.

A thousand and one plots in Lebanon

Vicious political confrontations in which the minorities were the protagonists stirred up Arab opinion in 1976. There was much talk of Israel and the United States hatching an international plot to Balkanize the Near East into a number of mini-States, carved up to correspond with the map of religious beliefs. In this way, the turbulent revolutionary Arab nationalist feeling threatening Israel's future and unsettling to the West would once and for all be destroyed. However, according to the supporters of this thesis it was not precluded that Moscow would derive advantage from such an operation, for it could always secure for itself special clientele from out of the mosaic of different religions.

Everybody talked about the disintegration of Lebanon in terms of a plot and not least the feuding parties themselves. What the plot was depended on ideological leanings, but each accused the others of being a party to the conspiracy. The Left spoke a lot of a plot to eliminate the Palestinian Resistance, to abstract Lebanon from its Arab environment and to maintain the ascendancy of one community, the Maronites, over all the others, in which context, the right-wing Christian militias were accused of 'isolationism'. This was a term invented during the Mandate by those Christians calling for a united Greater Syria, geographically incorporating Lebanon and Palestine, to describe their co-religionists desiring a Christian Little Lebanon. The Right denounced an Islamic crypto-communist plot financed by Moscow to get rid of Eastern Christians, attached by the bond of religion to the capitalist West.

On both sides another and less implausible theory was propounded, namely that the Palestinians were to be settled permanently in Lebanon. This would in fact have amounted to the Palestinian State which Israel would not hear of at any price and which many Arab governments feared would provide a new channel for Soviet influence in the Middle East. The Christian Right was all the more eager to support this view as it felt abandoned by the Western powers which, throughout the crisis, seemed to give a sympathetic ear to 'Palestinian–Progressive' arguments.

Another argument much in favour with Right-tending Christians concerned about Syria's age-old territorial ambitions in Lebanon, according to which the 1975–6 events merely represented the peak of a clever de-stabilization of Lebanon practised by Syria to annex the country, or at least those of its regions which had previously been attached to Syrian provinces, notably under the 1861 regime.

The supporters of this thesis put forward two main arguments. The first was that the Muslims of Lebanon had never accepted the Lebanese identity emerging from the French mandate, as proved by their involvement in Arab nationalist movements advocating Arab unity, particularly Nasserism and the Baath party. The second was that Syria, independent since 1945, had always refused to establish classic diplomatic relations with Lebanon. Arguing from the close bonds of fraternity linking the two peoples and the proximity of the two capitals, only 120 kilometres apart, the Syrian authorities had always turned a deaf ear to Lebanese requests to open embassies.

In reality, Syria had always disquieted Lebanon. Its size (300,000 square kilometres against Lebanon's 10,400), its population (8 million on the threshold of the 1980s against 3 million in Lebanon) and its successive regimes, turbulent ultra-Left and pan-Arab in language, had always greatly frightened the club of traditional notables and big businessmen governing Lebanon.

The Syrians on their side were never quite at ease on their Lebanese flank. Sensitive nationalists who felt their country pulled in different directions because of its geographical position and the complexity of its populations, the Syrian leaders, living in chronic political instability, often regarded Lebanon as a centre of hostile 'plots'. Lebanon, aligned with the West, open to all movements, with a free press, welcoming political refugees without distinction and a big centre of regional espionage was not less disquieted by Syria than vice versa.

Even in the matter of community, there was a noticeable antipathy, sometimes quite strong between Syrians and Lebanese Christians, at least the new Maronite bourgeoisie represented by the Phalangist party. The former have always been conscious of their Arabness and convinced that their ethnic roots lie in a Greater Syria which imperialism had artifically divided. Although the latter had often played an eminent role in the renaissance of Arab learning and, at times, in the ideology of Arabness, they had over the years acquired a feeling of distance from the source of their regional ethnicity.

On the Left as on the Right, the road to the Near East passes through Damascus

In the matter of Syria's role in events in Lebanon in 1975–6, the principal motivation did not seem to be to annex territory, but to gain political and military control. As the only country to shelter an effective and increasingly important Palestinian armed resistance and enjoying furthermore a doubly strategic position in relation to Syrian–Israeli cease-fire lines in South Lebanon and the Beqa'a Valley, Lebanon had acquired in Syrian eyes a key position by the end of the 1973 war.

The importance of that position merely increased as the Lebanese State became weaker under the weight of internal tensions. When in 1975 it became obvious that, in its move towards a separate peace with Israel, Egypt was definitely about to abandon its Syrian ally and that the Lebanese State was on the verge of breaking up, Syrian intervention proved inevitable. Palestinian – Lebanese 'revolutionary' chaos was in effect an open door into the unknown which neither Syria nor the main Arab political forces at work during that period could allow themselves to leave without a doorkeeper at a time when so many efforts were being deployed to settle the Arab–Israeli conflict.

Initially (before January 1976), Syria's intervention was through Saika, a Palestinian organization of Baathist persuasion that had been growing in strength, and rather more on the Palestinian – Progressive side, since a weakening of the Palestinian Resistance in Lebanon and a victory of the Lebanese Right, which now belonged to the pro-Western Arab lobby, would have considerably weakened Syria's position in any global negotiations over the Arab–Israeli dispute. In January 1976, the three brigades of the Palestinian Liberation Army integrated into the Syrian army entered Lebanon without being too clear at that juncture the meaning of this gesture.

Nonetheless, Syria was already working for political stabilization. It was under the Syrian umbrella that in February 1976 the Lebanese President presented a constitutional reform of a highly conservative character which confirmed the allocation of the three highest positions in the State between the three main communities and made only marginal adjustments in the balance between Christian and Muslim communities. Henceforth, things would never be the same again between Damascus and the Palestinian–Lebanese revolutionary alliance.

Then followed the second phase of events (March–November 1976) in which Syria, faced with the complete disintegration of the Lebanese army and military progress on the part of the Palestinian–Lebanese alliance, sent in more and more regular Syrian units.[17] The latter placed themselves between the opposing sides, once and for all blocking the military advance of the Left which had already received a considerable check from Right-wing militias in the spring of 1976 when an attack on a mountainous region held by the Right failed.[18] The months of May and June saw bloody confrontations between the forces of the Left and the Syrian-controlled Saika. On 22 June, Christian militias laid siege to the Palestinian camp of Tel al-Zaatar, a stronghold of Rejection organizations, enclaved in the Christian zone, which fell on 12 August.

Curiously, it was during this period that the Arab League's attempt to mediate, which had failed in 1975, finally materialized, and led to the dispatch of the first contingents of 'green helmets'.[19] Likewise, after a period of very bad relations since the September 1975 agreement on Sinai, a reconciliation between Egypt and Syria was effected at a conference in Riyadh in Saudi Arabia on 23 and 24 June between the Prime Ministers of Egypt and Syria, the Crown Prince of Saudi Arabia and the Kuwaiti Minister of Foreign Affairs.

The situation was moving towards stabilization. Nevertheless there were thousands more victims before the Syrian solution to the Lebanese crisis was eventually confirmed and legalized. This took place in October in Riyadh, at a limited Arab summit of Lebanon, Saudi Arabia, Egypt, Kuwait and the PLO and enlarged some days later in Cairo to include the whole of the Arab League. It was now possible for Syria, under cover of the Arab League to move regular units into the whole of Lebanon.

Religious fundamentalism in the service of the West

But events were heating up in Syria also, with rumblings in the opposition, on the Right in the form of a recrudescence of terrorist activities by the fundamentalists, on the Left in virulent denunciation of Syrian action in Lebanon. Damascus itself had a dose of Palestinian terrorism when a commando took hostages at the Hotel Semiramis in the city centre on 26 and 27 September, causing several casualties. The government reacted brutally by publicly hanging members of the commando. In October, Palestinian commandos attacked Syrian embassies in Rome and Islamabad (Pakistan). On the international front, Syria had also to face Soviet displeasure, openly expressed in *Pravda* in September. The United States, on the other hand, though at first hesitant over Syrian action in Lebanon, seemed to accept it, while ensuring that the Syrians understood the importance of the 'red line' established by the Israelis in the south.

There was a considerable anxiety elsewhere in the Middle East too, especially in the Gulf countries, where there was a considerable Palestinian diaspora. To counter mass-based religious fundamentalism and the ultra-Leftism of radical ideologies, Saudi Arabia turned on its own zeal in a brand of State religious fundamentalism and put pressure on its neighbours to do likewise, particularly Kuwait and the United Arab Emirates, where a rather easy-going way of life prevailed (availability of alcohol, mixing of sexes in public places, secular education, night life, working women, etc.). In August 1976 the Kuwaiti Parliament was dissolved[20] and the country's mainly pro-Palestinian press was called to order.

In Egypt, President Sadat did everything to encourage fundamentalism, especially in the universities, where orthodox movements were gaining ground at the expense of the Left and of the Nasserites, who, until then, had reigned supreme in the active opposition to Sadatism. He also encouraged Islamization of Egyptian legislation, thus angering the Christian Copt minority and shocking the country, which since Muhammad Ali had largely adopted a secular way of life. It is hardly surprising that at a time of difficult getting together with the West, when so much had to be conceded to Israel, these blatantly pro-Western and anti-Soviet governments should regard State religious fundamentalism as the best way of simultaneously paralyzing domestic opposition both on the Right and on the Left.

Stabilization: ephemeral unity while waiting for Jimmy Carter

What actually restored calm in Lebanon, once the Left was brought to heel, was the prospect of fruitful negotiations following the election of Jimmy Carter to the American Presidency in November 1976. This was also the main factor in bringing Sadat and Assad closer together for a while. In the American capital, liberal ideas on the Middle East (developed in a report by an important American foundation, the Brookings Institute) were gaining ground and influencing leading opinion. The report expressed the clear need for a more balanced American policy on the Near East which took account of legitimate Arab aspirations and, first and foremost, of the Palestinian right to self-determination in the territories conquered by Israel in 1967. Breaking away from the Kissinger policy of pushing the Soviet Union out of the Near East, the report urged Soviet participation in any global settlement of the Arab–Israeli conflict. To the great dismay of the Israelis,[21] President Carter endorsed most of the report's conclusions.

The provisional stabilization of the situation in the Near East, reinforced by the Riyadh and Cairo summits, culminated in a Syrian–Egyptian reconciliation in the worst possible Arab political tradition. The two Presidents, who psychologically and politically had nothing whatever in common, met in Cairo from 18 to 21 December 1976 to lay another 'historical milestone' with a view to uniting the two countries. A unified political command was thus created between the two States, together with a series of point committees to study means of accelerating unity in all fields (constitutional and legislative, security and defence, diplomacy, information and the economy).

The really significant feature of this meeting was the joint Sadat–Assad request to the United States and the Soviet Union to convene the Geneva Conference (of which the two powers were co-presidents) before the end of March 1977 to speed up a global settlement of the Near Eastern situation. The rest was more a smokescreen designed to mask the gulf between Egypt and Syria than another serious and disinterested attempt to unite the two countries, a sort of confidence trick which had no effect on Arab public opinion, enabling each country to blame the other in the event of failure or of a sudden worsening of relations between them. In 1975, Syria had made a similar agreement with Jordan in the context of efforts to create a common front comprising Syria, Jordan, the PLO and Lebanon, which, in view of the Egyptian desertion, would have the weight to negotiate the best terms for a settlement of the Palestinian question. Other unity agreements, which came to nothing, were also made with Iraq in 1978 after Sadat's visit to Jerusalem and with Libya in 1980. Though rational in theory, these moves were unrealistic because of the individualism of the governments in question. Besides, their flagrant political packaging had from the beginning removed all their credibility in the eyes of a public opinion these Heads of State insisted on treating as childish.

Schism, when you descend upon us

So ended a particularly bloody episode in the history of the Near East, costing more in human life than the Arab–Israeli war of October 1973, of which in certain respects it was merely a continuation. The stabilization achieved at the end of 1976 was in any case only temporary; a year later, in November 1977, Sadat left for Jerusalem on what some perceived as a peace mission, others as a disgrace. For the Israelis, it was proof that sustained and pigheaded intransigence paid off.

In reality, the fighting in Lebanon solved nothing in essence. The Palestinian Rejection organizations were of course weakened, but they continued to have powerful protectors, notably Iraq and Libya, endowed by oil with considerable financial means. Between Iraq and Syria, however, the merciless struggle between the two parties, brother enemies, continued. To the dispute over ideological legitimacy was added a serious economic quarrel. The Syrian dam built on the Euphrates deprived the Iraqis of part of the waters and catastrophically increased the salinity of Iraqi soils. After the Iraqi nationalization of the oil companies, Syria, for its part, was denied payment by Iraq of a steep increase in transit dues for Iraqi oil being sent to the Mediterranean. The pipeline linking the Iraqi oil wells to the Syrian port of Baniyas was closed. In retaliation, and with Turkey's agreement, Iraq had a pipeline installed in record time to carry its oil to the port of Iskanderun.

Throughout 1977, serious fighting in the Palestinian settlements in Lebanon broke out between the Rejection groups and the more moderate movements. In addition, there were serious clashes in the extreme south of Lebanon between Palestinians and Right-wing Lebanese militias led by Israeli-controlled Lebanese officers. Since these operations were to determine who exercised control over the border towns, there was a considerable amount at stake. As mentioned earlier, these often deadly battles ended in an all-out war between Israelis and Palestinians in the spring of 1978, in which the former invaded and for several weeks occupied South Lebanon. Shortly afterwards, the situation in Beirut between Syrian forces and right-wing militias degenerated. The alliance between Syria and the Maronites, increasingly subject to tight control by the Phalangist party, seemed to have broken down. It was the Israelis who now set themselves up as protectors of the Christians.

Israel was perhaps already preparing to return Sinai to Egypt in stages, but nonetheless extracted considerable political and bargaining advantages for itself in Lebanon.[22] On the international stage, Syrians and Palestinians were again overshadowed when the Camp David Agreements, offering a real and separate peace between Egypt and Israel, focused world attention and soon created a new and dangerous schism among the Arabs. In 1978, a summit of Arab Heads of State in Baghdad under the leadership of the Iraqi President, Saddam Hussein, decided to exclude Egypt from the Arab community.

We have now to examine exactly what it is about Israeli power that enables it to reduce the Near East to fragments. The episodes recounted earlier which culminated in the destruction of Lebanon show that the Arab Near East, so rich in history, oil, and in complex political personages, lost its social and national cohesion and economically became increasingly fragile. As an extremely pluralist society no central power had ever succeeded in making homogeneous and which was now destroyed by oil, the beautiful tarnished vessel that was Arab Near East was suddenly cracked all over. The Israeli hammer, perhaps only of wood, managed to smash everything, and no force in the West seemed willing or able to prevent its repeated blows. Narcissistic even in its remorse, Western Christendom remains fascinated by the State of Israel, strange product of its own historical violence.

7 From the First Zionist Congress to the Camp David Agreements: 1897–1978

Israeli cowboys, Palestinian Indians

To write of Israel and of the political and ideological movement which presided over its creation, Zionism, is always a dangerous undertaking. The terrifying shadow of the Jewish victims of the Nazi madness is forever present, dissuading those whose vision of the Jewish problem in any way fails to conform to the accepted intellectual view on the matter. Because of the immemorial persecution culminating in genocide to which they have been subjected the Jews consider that they alone have the right to talk about Palestine and the way it has been shaped by Jewish settlers as a Jewish State. Non-Jews, in their view, have no right to imagine a situation for Palestine as bi-national, secular Arab – Jewish states are quite different from what it actually is. Nonetheless, since the birth of the Zionist movement at the end of the last century, some Jewish personalities have tried, though without much success. Even when the suggestions came such people as Dr Chaim Weizmann, the first President of the State of Israel, or Dr Nahum Goldman, President of the World Jewish Congress for many years, they did not have very much influence, for the reason that any recognition of the presence and origins of the Palestinian Arabs, or any attempt to work towards a compromise, automatically undermines the force of the Zionist movement by introducing into it moral scruples and notions of justice. It also means reacting against the very heavy historical burden of anti-Semitism, of which the racist exclusivism of the Jewish immigrants in Palestine throughout the twentieth century is a direct result.

The irony of it is that those immigrants who should have been the most sensitive to justice and moral considerations, the socialist leaders of the Zionist movement, are the same who, in the name of their ideals, rejected all contact with the Arab population. Refusing the exploitation of man by man and glorifying work and the 'Jewish people's' return to the land, these leaders strictly forbade their followers to employ any Arab labourers in a country with a largely peasant indigenous population. And as for feudal or religious dignitaries, what compromise could then socialists have with them? Although there were some contacts with Arab leaders between 1918 and 1948, notably and practically exclusively by Weizmann and Goldman, these never bore fruit. For the warrior-farmers, so well personified in the personality of David Ben-Gurion, the real founder of the State of Israel, never let themselves be diverted from their principal objective, 'A Palestine as Jewish as England is English'.

The Israeli 'epic' is well known and there is no need to repeat it here. In the immense movement of cultural, religious and literary 'voyeurism' unleashed by the trauma of the Nazi practices, nothing has been left aside that touches on Jewish existence, and therefore, by the same token, on the State of Israel. For a long time Israel was the Zorro of the Near East, inciting mass enthusiasm in the West, but its image was somewhat tarnished by the 1967 war. For there was no getting away from the fact that, after all, these poor 'Indians' of the Arab Near East, decimated by the vigorous and good 'cowboys' from overseas, had a right to their 'reserve'. The Israelis' first response to this slight swing in the West was to call it 'the shame of oil', the West's adoration for barrels of oil. Then there was 1973, when the Indian tribes showed that after all they could still fight and do damage. Finally, there was the great Sioux chief, Sadat, who smoked the pipe of peace in the heart of the cowboys' camp, thereby showing that a compromise was indeed possible. With technical aid from America, the highest authority on 'reserves' for Indians, at Camp David a 'reserve' for Palestinians was envisaged which the latter had the bad taste to reject.

Presented like this in comic strip form, the story *would* be comic if the truth were not so tragic and blood did not continue to flow quite so freely. Perhaps the most distressing aspect is the knowledge that there is nothing definite on the horizon that might end the frightful story of Israeli cowboys and Palestinian Indians. The deep wound Israel has inflicted on the Arab Near East is the result of logics doomed never to meet in the present framework of the conflict.

Nonetheless, the points of possible agreement have multiplied over the last few years, but remain conspicuously fragile and threatened by deteriorating situations and atrocious events. In reality, time is in nobody's favour, neither for the Arabs nor for the Israelis and their supporters in the Diaspora, nor even for the Western powers of the 'free world', all of whom are bound in a triangular relationship in which mounting tensions could at any time swamp whatever possibilities for appeasement remain.

A triangular relationship condemned to contradiction

It is therefore important to study this relationship, all the more so as here more than anywhere else it is a question of contradictory ideological and cultural perceptions that simply intensify the geo-political clashes at the heart of the triangular conflict in which the Arabs, the West, and Israel, with the Jewish communities of the Diaspora, are locked in explosive and unhealthy contact. The Arab–Israeli conflict has been created more from an accumulation of historical, religious and cultural misunderstandings than from any other cause. Its true dimension can be grasped only by looking beyond the distorting prisms that have given rise to and still sustain these misunderstandings.

A solution to the conflict can come only through recognizing the power of the ideological and cultural forces maintaining those distorted perceptions of reality (cause of the conflict's permanence) and thus of the necessity to reduce them. It is only in this way that the elements which normalize the situation can emerge. There is no lack of calm and lucid intellects clearly pointing the way to reason and compromise at the three points of the triangle. But their voices are lost in the general uproar and frenzy. The irresponsibility of the media is also an obstacle to a solution, for all manipulators of ideology, information and culture project their own fantasies into the triangle of the Arab–Israeli conflict.

It must be admitted that the situation lends itself to this. To the average Westerner, there is nothing more morbidly exciting than watching Arabs and Jews, traditional targets of European cultural and religious racism, fighting to the death like gladiators for the greater amusement of a crowd in search of some out-of-the-ordinary sport. To the average Arab, who is also a Muslim, the Israeli invasion and conquest of Jerusalem, in the name of Judaism and with the massive support of Christianity, can only be seen as a return by the 'Infidels' either to throw the Arabs back into the ancestral deserts or to accomplish some new imperialist abomination. Among this people, which formerly produced so many historians, memories of the Crusades could not be erased and still less of modern colonialism, and in any case, the invasion of Palestine was there to revive them. Finally, for the Jews, whether believers or not, it was sheer intoxication, exaltation, to regain their lost past and with it the Bible, 'Nation', 'democracy', as well as conquest, colonization and direct or indirect domination over Christian or Muslim 'gentiles' after so many centuries of marginalization, suffering and even extermination.

The biggest question in the Arab–Israeli conflict is indeed whether Jerusalem is to be a symbol of war or of peace. Can this sacred birthplace of the three great monotheistic religions (and the violence that sanctity can engender when it is a cover for the political order) eventually emerge into modernity? Can it make the transition from the order of the sacred in which it has been confined by Zionist Jewry to the spiritual, pluralist and therefore secular order of contemporary values? Can it also cease to symbolize the dichotomy between development and underdevelopment? It can hardly be contested that the low standard of living and low level of integration into a modern technological economy of the Palestinians, Egyptians, Syrians and Jordanians who surround the Israelis puts them in the underdeveloped category, whereas their enemy neighbours are well on the road to development, even if their situation is highly risky.[1]

It is difficult to see how the basic misunderstandings could have been avoided. In the history of Palestine, as with other important historical events in the Near East since Muhammed Ali, the Arabs had barely enough time to catch on before the business was settled. And for that matter, the particular business of Palestine was a transaction in the particularly weighty historical issue of the relationship between Jewry and Western Christendom to which the Arabs were never a party. The persecuted Jews of Europe had always been assured of a refuge among the Arabs, especially among the Umayyades of Spain and then in the Muslim empires up to and including the Ottoman. There were even occasions when Islamic governments protected them from persecution by Eastern Christianity, still alive on Islamic soil but no less anti-Semite than the Western variety. For the needs of a cause it is not difficult to blacken the picture of traditional Islamic protection of Jewish communities and there are propagandists for Israel who do just this. But by and large, Jewish historians have done justice to Islam in this domain.

It was not without reason that in their pathetic quest for a refuge for victims of Slav pogroms, the early leaders of the Zionist movement for a while pinned their hopes on the benevolence of the last Ottoman Sultan as far as Palestine was concerned, as well as on Sinai and Uganda. For them the matter was urgent. The Slav pogroms were occurring at an alarming rate, and at the end of the century the Dreyfus affair in France raised doubts about the extent of Jewish assimilation in Western Europe, which until then had seemed so assured. But the Ottoman Sultan's position, later also that of Palestinian and Arab leaders, was absolutely clear: he would agree to individual immigration, even in consider- able numbers, but not to collective colonization with the aim of building a State. Only King Faisal, son of Sherif Hussein, King of the Hijaz, who ruled for a while over Syria (1919) before becoming King of Iraq, went further and at the Peace Conference in 1919 signed an agreement with Chaim Weizmann recognizing the validity of the famous Balfour Declaration (1917), which gave the Jews a 'National Home' in Palestine. This agreement was conditioned by European recognition of Arab independence from Ottoman rule but now threatened by the colonialist designs of the West.

1917: a colonial death sentence for the Palestinian people

We may stop a minute to take a look at this Balfour Declaration, a remarkable example of racist esotericism, which already contained the whole Palestine tragedy, but the intricacies of which only a few historians of the period are familiar with. It suffices here to recall that, with this text, a government, that of Great Britain, disposed of a land, Palestine, over which it exercised no sovereignty in law or practice, for the benefit of a religious community, the Jews, who lived almost exclusively outside that land.

Despite efforts by the Zionist movement, at the beginning of the century Palestine's Jewish community, including those of pure Palestinian stock, numbered 60,000, representing only 9 per cent of the country's population and a minute proportion of the total Jewish population of the world. And yet, marvel of marvels, the

Declaration, claiming to 'respect' legal rights and equity, referred to the Arabs, 91 per cent of the population, simply as 'the non-Jewish' communities in Palestine', whose 'civil and religious rights' should not be prejudiced! There was not a word in the text on the political rights of those strange 'non-Jewish communities', the Palestinian people, already denied a name but now deprived of political rights and thus also of any chance of collective existence.

In a similar vein of misplaced asymmetry, the text stipulated that 'the rights and political status enjoyed by the Jews in any other country' should not be prejudiced. A futurist text if there ever was one, the Declaration is imprinted in Arab memory as a monumental perversion annually mourned. Seen from the opposite point of view, for the Jews it was the crowning of the immemorial attempt to re-constitute an identity snuffed out of existence by the brutality of history.

For the Arabs, the entire question had in fact got off to a bad start, especially since the text of Britain's mandate over Palestine included creation of the Jewish National Home envisaged by the Declaration. The Mandate itself was a breach of contract between Britons and Arabs, because Hussein, King of the Hijaz, had set off the Arab armed revolt against the Ottoman Empire in 1916 in exchange for a formal promise of Arab independence by Britain. Instead, and in addition to the Balfour Declaration, in that same year, the Sykes–Picot Agreement (named after the British and French officials concerned) shared out the Near East: Palestine and Iraq were for perfidious Albion, and the Lebanon and Syria for the Republic of the Rights of Man in full colonial euphoria. The Kurds and Armenians, to whom 'civilizing' Europe had promised independence and also armed against the Ottomans, were incidentally left to pay the price themselves and abandoned by the Allied armies, to be cut to pieces by Ataturk's troops. This, however, was only after they had jauntily massacred one another for possession of territories which would in any case escape them, to be shared out between Turkey, Persia and British-controlled Iraq.

It is better not to linger too long over these painful blots on the West's colonial history. The creation of the State of Israel, alas, followed in the wake and consequently carries the stigma of that history in the eyes of the victims of colonial intrigue. But dyed-in-the-wool Zionists, who in the cause of Jewish survival brush aside moral scruples and considerations of equity, see nothing in the origins of Zionism to make them blush. They remain especially impervious to the indignation of anti-Zionist Jews and their repeated accusations that the Zionist movement's fantastic ener- gies have served more to colonize Palestine than to aid Jewish survival, particularly during the terrible years of Nazism.

There is no doubt that Nazi madness added plenty of grist to the Zionist mill, which can only exist and be kept going because of anti-Semitism. There was also something morbid about the weakness that led certain Zionist leaders into making macabre deals with the Nazis in exchange for a little emigration to Palestine every now and again. It of course remains an open question whether the Zionist movement could have done more to prevent the savage blood-letting of those years of horror and madness if it had been less concerned with Palestine and more with effective aid to the tortured communities of Germany and Eastern Europe, either directly or through very much greater pressure on the leaders of the democratic countries.

But these were Western concerns, from which the Near Eastern Arab was somewhat removed. For him, Palestine had changed so quickly between 1919 and 1947 that, in little more than a quarter of a century, it became a delayed-action infernal machine planted by the colonial West which blew up in his face. Even if in 1947 the damaging effects of the 'deal' between Jewry and Western Christianity still appeared limited to Arab eyes, the situation very quickly became more serious, with the crushing victory of 1948, in which all the Arab armies were defeated, raising the total conquered Palestinian territory to 80 per cent, whereas the United Nations had stipulated a share of only 57 per cent; with the Suez war in 1956 when Israel invaded Sinai, in connivance with the dying colonialism of France and England trying to 'punish' Nasser for nationalizing the Suez Canal; and culminating in the 1967 war in which, under the impassive eyes of the West, Israel finished conquering Palestine and occupied Sinai and the Syrian Golan Heights. For twenty years the Arabs had watched the relentless rise of Israeli militarism and expansionism, with the complicity of the Western Christian powers supporting Zionism with money and arms.

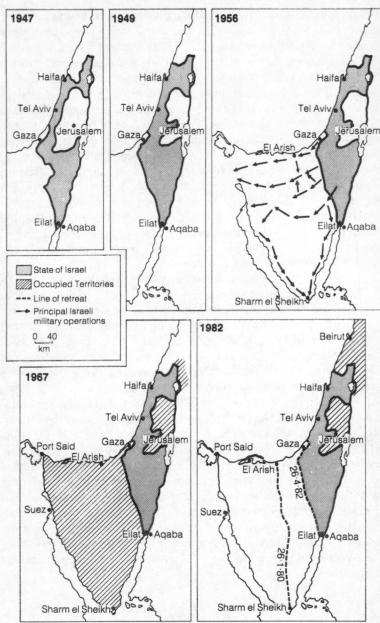

ISRAEL'S BORDERS 1947-1982

The anti-Semitism in reverse of the West

The Jewish problem had severely traumatized the Western conscience. The suffering and injustice inflicted on those remote Arabs, barely touched it all. Unfortunately, it took the terrible massacre at the 1972 Olympic Games in Munich and a series of Palestinian terrorist operations in Europe before Palestine's unhappy plight began to be realized by Western opinion.

The suffering of the Jews, however, on the other hand, cut into the heart of European history, its full impact brought home after the 1939–45 war when the Nazi horrors finally came to light. Under the shock, Europe recognized this genocide as but the culmination of age-old persecutions. The guilt then unleashed, combining with centuries of anti-Jewish racism, produced blind support for the Zionist movement. Indiscriminate moral or physical persecution turned into all-out adulation. Blind support for the Zionist movement thus became really a form of inverted anti-Semitism: always in a category apart, the Jewishness previously despised was now above criticism. At least this was the message a number of moderately Zionist, cool-headed Jews, not to mention the anti-Zionist Jews, wished to put across. But to no avail in the torrent of 'Zionophilia' which for long swept aside everything in its path.

A great assortment of Western cultural and ideological currents were drawn into this torrent. For one thing the biblical heritage of the various Protestant churches in the Anglo-Saxon world which thrilled to the prospect of a return to the 'Promised Land', first sign of the last things. Then that of Western European socialist circles which for long regarded Zionism as a product of social democracy. The Israeli Labour party, which ruled Israel uninterruptedly from 1948 until 1977, is a member of the 'Club' of European social democrats. Finally, the applause of Right-wing and extreme Right-wing circles for 'super-star' Israel's exploits against the pro-Soviet Arab 'natives' and for whom Judaism, even if still secretly or even openly despised, at least served since the creation of Israel to protect Western Christian civilizations from Islamic or Islamic-communist 'barbarism'.

Added to these was another historical heritage of Christian Europe: fear of Islam and the memory of invasions in which Arabs in Spain on its western flank and Turks in Austria on its eastern flank had made Europe tremble. Not to be omitted from this miscellany was the Algerian war and its sequels, especially the return to France of the traumatized '*pied-noirs*'.

It was thus hardly surprising that pro-Israeli cultural and political pressure groups should appear in the West, as much at ease as fish in water. This was especially evident in the United States where political lobbying is a perfectly acceptable part of everyday life and serves as a profession to numerous firms and personalities in all walks of life. Arabs are often staggered by this phenomenon, which they sometimes describe in rather anti-Semitic terms as the international omnipotence of Judaism or Zionism. This clearly reflects a failure to appreciate the full breadth and complexity of the relationship in the West between Christians and Jews.

Throughout these years of misfortune for the Near East, everything combined to prevent the liberal West from exercising balanced and rational judgement and so arriving at a policy that might have made things go quite differently. The attitude of the big Western powers to the Near East well expresses this general lack of understanding. Instead of quelling the fervour of Zionism in the interests of all three points of the triangle, they allowed it a free hand in excess. Obsessed with the Soviet Union and an increase in its presence in the Near East, region of high strategic importance internationally, they were blind, and particularly the United States, to what was really happening in Arab society. Hence the old dream of Harry S. Truman, pursued by Dwight Eisenhower, taken up again by Richard Nixon, once again brought onto the agenda by Ronald Reagan, of bringing Jews and Arabs in a Holy Alliance against the Soviet presence in the Middle East, but without a global settlement of the Palestinian and Arab–Israeli disputes. Or again the dream of reaching an agreement from which the Soviet Union would be excluded, forgetting that Moscow is only 3000 kilometres from Beirut, but Washington 11,000 kilometres away. In any dispassionate consideration of the geopolitical interests of the great powers, those of the USSR, in what to them is practically a border area, are so obvious that it is very shortsighted to insist on ignoring them.[2]

It should be said that for a long time the Arabs, for their part, were unable to provide any obvious base of support for the West, traumatized by its historical memories on the one hand and by the cold war on the other and incapable of understanding the intricacies of the Arabs' changing socio-cultural world. To mutual cultural incomprehension was added absence of geopolitical understanding. The misunderstandings that arose during the Nasserist period have already been discussed in some detail at the beginning of this book, as have the Arab messages to the West on the occasion of the October war. When, in the 1970s, the West began to realize that there had been a change of scene on the Arab stage and that oil would tie the Near East to itself once more, there was a great flurry of activity among pro-Western Arab political forces, as well as a certain naive idealism among some leaders, the result of which was to abort what might have turned into a constructive dialogue.

It was now that Lebanon started to fall apart and Sadat made his spectacular gesture of going to Jerusalem, thereby breaking the Arab solidarity that had only recently formed around the events in Lebanon. Thus he who in fact possessed the guns, the tanks, the substantial army, was the one to brandish the olive branch rather than the rifle thereby making things easy for the enemy of yesterday. In his anxiety to fasten the Egyptian boat alongside the American ship, the Egyptian President upset the delicate balance between the Arab powers and allowed Israel to tighten its grip, the even greater pressure making the Palestinian wound bleed copiously once more with Lebanon henceforth paying the price.

The Camp David Agreements

In the sad tale of the Camp David Agreements, establishing a framework for peace in the Near East, a new unequal treaty tied Egypt, the pivot of the Near East, to the West via Israel, and, graver still, made the Agreements merely an updated version of the Balfour Declaration. Egypt and Israel together disposed of the remains of Palestine, i.e. the West Bank and Gaza, while inviting a third non-Palestine government, Jordan, to share in future negotiations on the juridical status of these territories – a status which the Agreements left undetermined for a period of five years, thus enabling the Israelis to maintain their claims to sovereignty over the West Bank and Gaza.

As for the Israelis, Palestinian autonomy means administrative autonomy, the Agreements provided only for 'an autonomous authority', the text even specifying 'administrative council' in brackets. There was nothing that even approximated to the beginnings of a collective sovereignty exercised by a people. Menachem Begin even got Jimmy Carter to clarify, in a letter appended to the Agreements, that for the Israeli government the expression 'West Bank' was 'interpreted and understood' as 'Judaea and Samaria', the biblical terms on which Israel founded its legal claim. In the same letter, the American President declared that he had duly noted that the expressions 'Palestinians' and 'Palestinian people' 'are and will be interpreted' by the Israeli party 'as Palestinian Arabs'. The nuance was important, for it maintained and sanctioned the Zionist fiction that there was no Palestinian people as such, in other words none competent collectively to express an autonomous political will.

It is curious that no Western lawyers have used their talents to analyse the vagaries of these Agreements, as much a masterpiece of legal and moral perversity as the Balfour Declaration. The enthusiasm engendered in Western opinion by the Israeli – Egyptian accolade as well as the persistence of its psychological attitudes over the Arab–Israeli issue again probably explain the absence of reason and equity.

Admittedly, and also in a letter addressed to President Carter and appended to the Agreements, President Sadat took care to set out his position on the Arab section of Jerusalem. As is well known this section, which the Israelis had not been able to conquer in 1948, was placed under Israeli sovereignty by a law of the Knesset, the Israeli Parliament, shortly after its conquest during the June 1967 war. Sadat therefore reaffirmed Arab rights to this part of the Holy City already taken over by the Israelis 'forever', as the official declarations put it. On the other hand, not a word from the Egyptian side, in the letters appended to the Agreements, on the nature of the 'full self-determination of the West Bank and of the Gaza Strip', voided of all content and mentioned once and once only in the entire text of the Agreements, whereas the 'definitive status' of the territories belonging to the Palestinian population was to be 'negotiated' between Egypt, Israel, Jordan and the territories' elected representatives.

On the Arab front, President Sadat's initiatives immediately threw political circles into a state of turmoil. Several weeks after the Egyptian leader had sacrificed himself in Israeli Jerusalem on the alter of love for the West, Arab Heads of State met in November 1978 in Baghdad, capital of the Rejection Front, to decide amidst much pomp 'not to recognize' the Camp David

Agreements or their 'results' and 'to reject all their consequences, political, economic, legal or other'. This was a repeat performance of the 1967 Khartoum summit, for here too no sanctions were imposed on the West. Some months later, in March 1979, shortly after the peace treaty between Egypt and Israel had been signed at the White House in Washington, economic and political sanctions were imposed on Egypt at a meeting of Arab Ministers of Foreign Affairs, again held in Baghdad.

There was one pathetic event in these historic moments during the Baghdad summit. A delegation was sent to Cairo to try and dissuade President Sadat from continuing along the path opened up by the Camp David Agreements by offering him aid to the tune of 5 billion dollars a year. But the delegation was hurriedly shown the door at Cairo Airport itself and Sadat made it known through the press that Egypt was not for sale. The 'oil social security', which had been so marvellously effective in Khartoum, had not worked here; the offer came too late for this Egyptian nationalist who loved the West and hated the Soviet Union. He had already decided that, to cure Egypt's terrible poverty, it would be better to go directly to the Western doctor, source of all that wealth, rather than to have it treated in small doses by the paramedical petrol pump attendants of Arab oil.

Thus the reconciliation between Syria and Egypt, which had concluded the first big round of Lebanese troubles at the time of Jimmy Carter's election in November 1976, proved itself short-lived. President Sadat, who was in too much of a hurry to bring the Arab–Israeli conflict to an end, quickly grew irritated by his Syrian equivalent's caution and by the PLO's inability to commit themselves, which reflected the tensions between the Palestinian movement's moderate and Rejection groups. By the beginning of 1977, however, the PLO was obviously in favour of negotiation, American goodwill being now evident. In March, at the 13th Palestinian National Council, the Resistance movement's various factions were reconciled to each other and accepted the principle of creating a Palestinian State on any territory evacuated by Israel.

This, was then the first time that an American administration had been so open to Arab problems. Carter actually spoke of a Palestinian 'national home' and of a total Israeli withdrawal from the occupied territories, which made life difficult for Israeli intransigence. 'You are more stubborn than the Arabs and are putting obstacles in the way of peace,' he said to Moshe Dayan, then

Minister of Foreign Affairs, on a visit to Washington, in September 1977.[3] Referring to Carter's attitude during that stormy meeting, Moshe Dayan, who repeated his words, went on to say: 'Those on our side of the table saw cold hostility in his blue eyes. His voice was quiet but the language was strong, and at times his face flushed with anger.'[4] These scenes became quite common in American–Israeli relations of that period.

The Egyptian President in any case was playing a double game since, as from September 1977, contacts were established with the Israelis behind the Syrians' back with the Moroccan King as intermediary. He was evidently in a hurry because, despite his policy of liberalization and opening up to the West, Egypt's economic situation was none too good. In January 1977 he had had to face three days of rioting in Cairo, following an increase in the price of bread and other vital footstuffs decreed under pressure from the IMF. Politically, the situation was no better. Although Sadat blamed Marxist and Nasserist groups for the January riots, it was the fundamentalist extreme Right that really hit the government hard. In July, some militants from the Al-Takfir wa-al-Hijra group kidnapped and then murdered a former Minister of Religious Affairs, Sheikh Hussein al-Zahabi.

On 1 October, the American administration broke the Kissinger tradition and embarked on a new strategy by signing a joint declaration with the Soviet Union on the Near East. This infuriated Israel, for it reinforced the Syrian and Palestinian position in the negotiations that were due to open in Geneva. Sadat, whose pet hate was the Soviet Union, was equally displeased by the gesture. Some days later, on 26 October, he suspended payment of his debts to the Soviet Union.

To cut short the interminable discussions prior to the opening of the Geneva Conference – discussions about procedure which also reflected the difference between Syrians and Palestinians on the one hand, and Israelis and Egyptians on the other – Sadat decided to knock down the psychological barriers separating Israelis and Arabs and offered to go to Jerusalem. Though his memoirs gave a rather confused account of this decision, they show clearly that he felt a strong need to finish with the problem to end Israeli intransigence and to settle an affair that had already cost too much. Thus, as he said, 'we ought to find a completely new approach that would bypass all formalities and procedural technicalities by breaking down the barrier of mutual distrust.

Only in this way can we hope to . . . get out of the deadlock of the past.[5] his idea for speeding up the start of the Geneva Conference was a meeting in Jerusalem of the leaders of the five great powers and all the Arab parties concerned, but was soon discouraged by the difficulties such a project entailed.

He then chose the quickest and most spectacular option: a visit by himself to Jerusalem. Thus, out on the tightrope without a safety net and prepared to pay whatever price success demanded, he was to find his balance on the high-wire of concessions becoming more and more unsure. Faced with the hostility of his Arab partners and with mounting opposition, his political fate became tied to the 'success' of his initiative, whatever its quality. The Americans, who no longer had to contend with a united Arab front but, on the contrary, a still over-powerful Israeli lobby in the United States itself, took the line of least resistance, especially as Jimmy Carter was facing serious problems on all home fronts and his popularity was waning. A big foreign policy success was indispensable. What better than to have Begin and Sadat embracing one another at the White House and duly signing a peace treaty under his patronage? The enthusiasm this reconciliation aroused in the West prevented any serious attention to the ambiguities of what had been accomplished and the doubtful nature of the new balance of power created in the Near East. In the confusion, Israeli intransigence easily found a way of satisfying all that its fantasies and desire for territorial expansion demanded.

The peace treaty between Egypt and Israel, signed in March 1979, was not less perverse than the framework for a peace agreement in the Near East, signed in September 1978, which, to the Israelis' great joy, created the Palestinian Bantustan that nobody wanted. The treaty in effect imposed on Egypt total military neutrality *vis-à-vis* Israel in all circumstances, without any Israeli *quid pro quo* other than handing back Sinai in stages. On the other hand, it strictly limited Egypt's military sovereignty over the territories recovered in order to exclude the least military threat to Israel. Worse still, in a separate memorandum the United States underwrote these restrictions on Egyptian sovereignty and undertook to support all 'appropriate action' by Israel in the event of a violation of the treaty.

In keeping with the heights of juridical perversity characterizing the Palestinian tragedy since 1917, in an annexure to the treaty, Jimmy Carter in 1979 once again declared that he had been informed that the expression 'West Bank' was understood by the Government of Israel to mean 'Judaea and Samaria'. He noted this in the margin of a joint letter addressed to him by Sadat and Begin concerning measures taken to implement the September 1978 outline of the Agreements. To all this were added America's obligations to Israel, including military and oil supplies and economic aid to recompense Israel for its 'sacrifice' in the matter of security by returning a quasi-demilitarized Sinai under the legal control of the great powers to an Egypt rendered militarily inoffensive.

A return to the rejections and the schisms

A good part of the Arab political elite was certainly favourable to the West and for one reason or another many Heads of State were even more than favourable. But a treaty that so unequally tied the biggest Arab country to the Jewish colonist State, in Arab eyes merely a despoiler and a destroyer, was more than even the most pro-Western Head of State could accept. This was why the Hashemite monarchy, the Saudi monarchy and the Sherifian monarchy of Morocco, which had encouraged the first direct contacts between Egyptian and Israeli officials, abstained from supporting the Israeli–Egyptian peace and were present at the meeting in Baghdad at which Egypt was ceremonially condemned.

These Near Eastern pillars of the West were certainly not present at the other Heads of State summit held a year earlier in Tripoli in Libya, at which the Arab Rejection Front was officially and institutionally set up, the so-called Front of steadfastness and confrontation.[6] This summit assembled Libya, Algeria, South Yemen, Syria and the PLO. Iraq took part half-heartedly and refused to join in the final communiqué, yet another sign of its leaning towards the pro-Western States, already evident from its rapprochements with the various monarchies and with the Gulf Emirates. Iraq never attended subsequent Front meetings and prepared to take on the role of polarizer and common denominator for the Arabs.

Iraq's fiery Vice-President, Saddam Hussein, hoped to bring together what remained of the Arabs after Egypt's defection, with Iraq as leader. Egypt being now ostracized by the Near East, Iraq, backed by its oil, by the success of a grandiose development policy and by the republican and secular modernity of its regime, as well as by its strategic position in the centre of the Persian Gulf, was ideally placed to assume such a position.

The Baghdad summit was a step in Iraq's rise in the Arab world, a rise fitting into the even more irresistible logic of the tyranny of oil. Baghdad was increasingly wooed by the West, whereas relations with the Soviet Union deteriorated and the Iraqi Communist party, which had always played a prominent role in local political life, was increasingly suppressed. Suddenly, isolation began to work against Syria, whose trump cards, so carefully acquired over the last few years, were consequently devalued. After the Egyptian secession, Iraq's abrupt rise on the international stage, in close conjunction with Saudi Arabia, once more marginalized Syria and, in its wake, the PLO. The West thus had the satisfaction of succeeding in swallowing up Egypt, propping up Saudi Arabia and most of the Peninsula countries and seeing Iraq, now that it had become an oil power, move closer to itself.

The PLO and Syria, with part of its Golan region still occupied, could wait, and still more so could South Lebanon, where savage fighting had been going on since 1977. Things were going too well in the Near and Middle East to occasion any anxiety, and in the matter of oil Syria was of no major interest, for it produced only 7 to 8 million tons in any case with too heavy a sulphur content. Lebanon had been thrown to the beasts, to be torn asunder in Arab fratricide, and if the Palestinians became too boisterous, the Israeli soldiery could be relied on to deal with them. This last was exactly illustrated by the invasion of Lebanon in June 1982. Decidedly, as far as the Near East was concerned, the purblindness of the over-mighty West knew no limits.

Fatality seemed to have dominion over the Arab land. Deserted for centuries by the great prophets, abandoned at the beginning of the twentieth-century by great empires responsible for its days of glory and which had protected it from the unruliness of its people, the Arab Near East dried up and crumbled under the impact of the political and economic disturbances shaking it, and of the powerful Israeli grip in which it was held.

After colonialism, followed by de-colonization which Nasser, unhappy Pharaoh of modern times personified so well, the unprecedented violence of the flood of oil drowned the thirsty land it should have irrigated. The grip of Israel became more and more painful. The Arabs' unhealthy oil wealth merely provided the balm for a wound that continued to suppurate.

The Camp David Agreements and the Israeli–Egyptian peace treaty were far from being a lasting means of loosening Israel's hold on the Near East. Contrary to appearances, these legal texts, backed by the most powerful country, the United States, fitted into the pattern of Zionist activism in the Near East since the beginning of the century, a drive that nothing seemed able to stop, in a region in which society was sicker than ever, and in which the centres of power secreted only centrifugal tendencies and schisms.

Peace: an 'end' to the Jewish people or normalizing Israel?

Israel's image in the eyes of the world has certainly become tarnished over the past ten years – particularly following the invasion of Lebanon in 1982 – and the West has come to recognize the existence of a Palestinian problem. Likewise, the image of the Arabs is no longer as negative as it once was. It is not, however, oil that has been responsible for this still rather limited shift in opinion. On the contrary, Arab oil wealth has tended to increase endemic anti-Arab racism, whether in the form of resentment over what is perceived as economic dependence and a drastic reduction in standards of material well-being or in images of sheikhs and emirs invading the French Riviera or buying up the Manhattan tower in the La Defense complex in Paris.

The shift in opinion was actually caused by the dynamism with which the Palestinians, despite all their setbacks showed that they really existed. Furthermore, the Sadat gesture undoubtedly served to modify the 'knife between the teeth' image of the Arabs so deeply engraved in the Western mind. Unfortunately, Arab opposition to the 'peace' between Egypt and Israel remains poorly understood in a Western socio-cultural climate still largely conditioned by the factors described in this chapter. Hence, the view of President Sadat as a man of peace isolated in the Arab world, a view that does not take the trouble to realize the explosive character of this not so honourable 'peace' and to put it into a historical perspective.

Although the then Israeli Prime Minister, Menachem Begin, antagonized many with his arrogance and stubbornness, he was also seen as a man of 'peace', who had obtained the Nobel Prize.

The criticism of him tended to concern the form rather than the content. From the point of view of legitimizing Zionism, Begin was perhaps something of a hindrance and his extreme Right terrorist past in the Zionist movement itself did not exactly help his public image: nonetheless, in essentials he always belonged to the purest Zionist orthodoxy. It is not widely recognized that to give in to even the smallest demand expressed collectively by the Palestinian people is tantamount to removing the foundation stone of the edifice built up by the Zionist movement by the strength of its arm over the course of this century. For Galilee and the Negev are as Palestinian as Gaza or the famous West Bank of Jordan, a geographical designation which, as Begin took great care to specify (in the texts appended to the outline of the Agreements and to the peace treaty signed with Egypt), had to be 'interpreted and understood' as 'Judaea and Samaria'. Without the Bible, there would have been no Zionism, or at least no ideological basis for such a very weak legal claim. To yield today over 'Judaea and Samaria' is perhaps tomorrow to open the way to Palestinian rights over Galilee, Haifa, Acre, etc., regions and towns that were still completely Arab in 1948. And what would this then imply for Jerusalem!

By the same token the possibility of a Palestinian State is still rejected, as well as any negotiation with the PLO, the potential Palestinian government, whose legitimacy and representativeness on the Palestinian and Arab level are indisputable. The slightest Israeli weakness in this area would signify recognition of the existence of a people driven from their soil and therefore of a wrong needing to be put right. This would mean admitting that they had a right to return or to compensation, a right moreover sanctioned by numerous United Nations resolutions, now forgotten and hidden under the thick layer of the dust of Israel's disdain and the West's passive complicity. It would also mean opening the door again to questioning the very foundation of the Zionist movement, namely, the non-existence of a Palestinian people; at most there were 'Palestinian Arabs', to use the Israeli terminology, whom the other Arabs, as Israeli saw it, had refused to absorb.

The relationship in this domain has become implacably dialectical. To recognize the existence of a Palestinian people who had lived in Palestine until 1948 is to undermine Zionism's deepest foundations, or at least to break its momentum, demoralize it, and therefore allow the Palestinian movement to develop its own momentum. The ferocity of the Begin government's war against the PLO in the Lebanon in 1982, with the massive destruction and loss of Lebanese and Palestinian civilian lives it occasioned, can be seen only in this context.

It is symptomatic that the Israeli Labour party did not dissociate itself from the actions of a government formed from a coalition of various religious parties. In the matter of any recognition of the Palestinians, there is in fact little that separates the Israeli Left from the Right. Though less 'backward-looking' than the religious parties, and thus less 'biblical', the Labour party has nonetheless always inflexibly refused to recognize the rights of the Palestinian people. This party, which was in power until 1977, was as uncompromising over territories as the religious Right. Though adopting an even harder line on Sinai, it might perhaps have given up bits of the West Bank of Jordan, but only to Jordan, which it contacted several times after the 1967 war in the hope of reaching an understanding.

This stubborn insistence on dealing with Jordan, which resurfaced in the Camp David Agreements when that country was included as a negotiating party on any future statutes for the Palestinian territories occupied in 1967, and this without even Jordan's agreement, is explained by Israel's phobia about the existence of the Palestinians. The religious Right, incarnated in Mehachem Begin, had of course agreed, through the Camp David Agreements, to return Sinai to Egypt in progressive stages ending in April 1982. In so doing, it would be returning a largely demilitarized territory to an Egypt that not only recognized and legitimized the Zionist conquest, but was itself militarily and politically neutralized under the direct guarantee from the United States. In return, Israel was enabled to maintain its claim to sovereignty over the rest of historical Palestine conquered in 1967, and this with the blessing of the principal Arab power, Egypt.

In orthodox Zionist eyes, this was a perfect solution, consolidating the conquest militarily and at the level of ideological and legal legitimacy without any concessions to Palestinian rights, which since 1967 had, however, acquired new force and obtained international recognition.

In these conditions, it is hardly surprising that in terms of actual territory this Palestinian legitimacy remained without a single square kilometre of Palestine in which it could be exercised. For this reason, it was able to express its strength only by building up its military potential in Lebanon, particularly in the south, thanks to Syrian and Soviet goodwill, and through successful efforts by the Palestinian political elite to keep up the movement's morale and autonomy in decision. It was this potential that, among other things, Israel destroyed during its murderous invasion of Lebanon in 1982. For years the West stood by watching impassively this tragedy unfold, in which, both because of the political and military powerlessness of Arab society in the Near East and because the Western powers accorded a tacit legitimacy to Israeli intransigence, a people were denied exercise of rights recognized and affirmed by the international community.

Many right thinking people, even within Israeli society, warned of the explosiveness of this situation, but their voices were overwhelmed by the permanent cultural, religious and geopolitical factors at work at the heart of the Arab–Israeli conflict. The cultural and religious factors were those that mattered within Western society, distorting as they did its perception of the geopolitical realities at stake in any serious and therefore fair solution to the conflict. These factors indeed rise up from the depth of the Western psyche and consequently their evolution can only be slow. What is at stake is the whole nature of Jewish existence and its relationship with the non-Jewish view of Judaism. Even within Jewish thought, there is extensive debate on whether the destiny of Jewry is 'unique' or 'universal'[7] and, to a lesser extent, within the Zionist movement itself because of the importance of the State of Israel for Jewish existence.

Many people agree with Arthur Koestler that at the level both of religion and of the State, Judaism needs to lose its specificity, which no longer serves any real purpose, especially since the creation of the State of Israel. For Koestler Jewish 'separatism' needlessly perpetuates 'the Jewish question' and becomes a source of racism and anti-Semitism.[8] This is the view of liberal Jews, both within and without the Zionist movement. According to them, setting up the State of Israel was a necessity brought about by the Nazi persecutions, the scale of which undid the gradual assimilation of Jews into Christian societies. But for all that, Israel should not become a special kind of State seeking unnecessary conquests devoid of all legitimacy and demanding blind allegiance from every Jewish community in the world. For the liberals of Judaism, Israel and the Zionist movement have already accomplished their mission. They now need to normalize it by allowing the Jews of the Diaspora to assimilate themselves, if that is what they wish, and by accommodating the Arab world so that Israel can live in peace with its neighbours and become a State 'like any other'.

This liberal perspective for Jewish existence is evidently disturbing to many. An important French sociologist, himself liberal, once took up the theme in an essay with the somewhat evocative and disquieting title of 'End of the Jewish People?'[9] With a normalized State freed of its encirclement complex and linked into the socio-cultural life of the Near East, and with many Diaspora Jews tending to assimilate themselves and constitute simply a religious denomination like others, what then would remain of Judaism and its epic history? A destiny thus arrived at would amount to auto-liquidation of Jewish existence in all its historic specificity.

Orthodox Zionism can only reject such a perspective. Holding that anti-Semitism runs deep in the consciousness of the Christian and Islamic world, it sees Nazism capable of being reproduced in any form and place without exception. Bringing all the Jews of the Diaspora together in Palestine is therefore a long-term historical necessity and so far only the first foundations have been laid. After the first Arab–Israeli war of 1948, which made the creation of the State possible, colonizing territories occupied in 1967 is a sacred duty and the communities of the Diaspora are under an obligation to give moral, political and financial support to those who have undertaken the task in Israel.

For this kind of Zionism, it is dangerously unwise to hold liberal and optimistic views of Jewish existence, as the history of anti-Semitism has amply demonstrated. Such views definitely weaken the force of Zionism and therefore of the State of Israel which owes its existence and legitimacy to it. From this point of view, the relationship with the surrounding Arab world must also remain unequal, assuring the permanence of Israel's superior power. As a new ghetto transplanted from Warsaw into Palestine, from Eastern Europe into the Near East, Israel must remain an impregnable bastion in constant expansion so that one day the great design of bringing all the communities of the Diaspora out of the mirage of possible assimilation and back into the fold as the lost sheep might be realized. Any compromise on this position would merely open the door to the gradual disappearence of Zionism, and in time of the State of Israel.

In fact, to accept assimilation as a reasonable perspective and thus to recognize that Nazism is an accident of history, is another way of completely reopening the Palestinian dossier and legitimizing Yasser Arafat's dream of a democratic and secular Palestine in which Jews and Arabs, Muslims and Christians would form a single people. Zionist moderates think that the essentials of the programme have already been achieved and that extremism would only lead to catastrophe. They estimate that it is necessary to negotiate with the PLO and return the West Bank and Gaza, thus enabling a Palestinian State to emerge. For them, time is against Israel and options possible today may no longer be available tomorrow. But the weakness of Arab society and Western society's casual attitude towards 'Jewish existence' smother these wise voices and enable orthodox Zionism to continue in its bold design of acquiring legitimacy for all that has already been accomplished.

There are evidently causes at work that neither common sense nor reason succeed in perceiving in the day-to-day events. Only time will bring a solution. The Arab–Israeli conflict is so complex, with its triangular relationship between the Arab Near East, the Christian West and Jewry, that even the most scrupulous historian would be hard put to provide a forecast. But this must not be allowed to deter men of goodwill, unbiased by passion and prejudice, from working towards ensuring that the history which the future must ineluctably weave is the product, not of passion and prejudice, but of good sense and reason. Here the Christian West carried a heavy responsibility. Its views on Judaism will undoubtedly be of determining significance in any future solution to the Arab–Israeli conflict and to the future of Jewish communities throughout the world.

8 The invasion of Lebanon: 1982

Circumstances

From the viewpoint of a historian, it is still too early to evaluate
the invasion of Lebanon and the Israeli army's siege of Beirut in
June 1982. These events were certainly important enough to cause
considerable upheavals, but at this stage it is difficult to appreciate
exactly what these are likely to be.

Within the context of the forces that we have seen at work so
far in the Arab Near East, the new Arab–Israeli war – which was
actually the first Palestinian–Israeli war – only confirmed the
break-up of Arab solidarity on the one hand and on the other the
strengthening of unbridled Zionist military power which the West
still refuses to curb. There is no doubt that for Israel all this lent
itself to a new bid for power. For this reason, no one could see
a Zionist as orthodox as Begin missing the opportunity to achieve
by force what Israeli propaganda and international mood were
no longer able to accomplish: the completed obliteration of a
Palestinian existence that had been near-totally destroyed in the
period between the establishment of the Israeli State in 1948 and
international recognition of the PLO in 1974.

Let us first turn to the regional situation. At the Fez summit in
Morocco, in January 1982, Arab countries once again showed
their lack of unity. A plan prepared by Saudi Arabia, called the
Fahd Plan after the Saudi Crown Prince, was torpedoed at the
last minute by the so-called Front of Steadfastness – Libya, Syria,
South Yemen and Algeria. The PLO actually favoured the plan,
but nonetheless felt obliged also to withhold its support. The
Fahd Plan really only intended to show Arab goodwill once more
towards the West, and this by recognizing Israel through accepting
the United Nations resolution guaranteeing the right of all States
in the region to live in peace within secure boundaries. In addition
to this recognition, the Plan mentioned the Palestinian people's

legitimate rights which the United Nations Security Council resolutions had until then left on one side. Hardly begun, the summit was adjourned to an unspecified date in the future.

Already deeply divided over the attitude to adopt towards the West, the Arab countries were no less so over the Iraq-Iran war, which was beginning to pose a threat to the stability of the conservative regimes in the Arabian Peninsula. The war had begun in an atmosphere of euphoria in September 1980, with Iraqi troops invading Arabistan (Khuzestan) and other Iranian border provinces in order to put an end to the threats of political destabilization which Khomeinist Iran was uttering towards its neighbours in the Gulf, as well as to border clashes between Iraqi and Iranian troops. In the spring of 1982, disaster faced Iraq when, at the end of May, it had to withdraw all its troops from Iranian territory and prepare for an Iranian counter-offensive. In this conflict Iran received active support, including military aid, from Syria and Libya. For the Syrian regime, the fall of the Iraqi Baath would at last bring about the victory so actively sought by each of the two 'brother' parties which had been quarelling for so long over the hegomonic legitimacy of 'militant' and 'revolutionary' Arabness. At a stroke, Syria could become the fundamental factor in the balance of power in the Arabian Peninsula, despite its lack of oil and of financial means. The United States would no longer be able to ignore it and the oil monarchies of the Gulf would finally be forced to make regular and substantial contributions to the Syrian exchequer.

Hostility towards the Iraqi regime was so great that in April 1982, when the Iraqi offensive gave up the ghost, Syria closed the pipeline that took Iraqi oil through its territory to the Mediterranean, thus depriving Iraq, whose economic potential was already suffering badly, of precious financial resources. At the same moment, the world was staggered to learn that Israel had supplied military equipment to Iran.

The schism provoked by the break between Egypt and the other Arab countries, following the Camp David Agreements, had already considerably weakened the Arab Near East politically and militarily. From now on, the total breach between Syria and Iraq, as well as the military paralysis of the latter in the futile war with Iran, served only to give the Israeli army a free hand in the whole of the Near East. Already during the summer of 1981 the Israeli army had shown that it intended to profit from this by the air raid it launched with complete impunity on the Tamuz nuclear power station in Iraq, as well as a particularly deadly raid on Beirut, accompanied by actions of blind violence all over South Lebanon.[1] In the absence of even minimal military solidarity between Iraq and Syria, and with the Egyptian army neutralized by the Camp David Agreements, the Israeli army, over-equipped by the United States, became master of the Near East. As a consequence, everything that the Arab countries had accomplished diplomatically, economically and militarily since the beginning of the 1970s to overcome the 1967 defeat and the deadlocks of the Khartoum summit, to settle the Palestinian problem and to meet the West on an equal footing, was wiped out.

It was just this that was demonstrated by the pitiable sight of Beirut, the most important political and cultural capital in the Arab world, besieged, starved, tortured and pitilessly destroyed by the Hebrew State's all-powerful artillery and air force, above the heads of hundreds and thousands of unarmed civilians. The relentless determination to wipe out the PLO under the pretexts of fighting terrorism and of 'peace in Galilee' beneath the impassive gaze of the entire world, and of the Arab regimes, was also the last act in the drama of the failure of anti-imperialist Arab nationalism. In this respect, the invasion of Lebanon completed what the defeat of 1967 had not totally achieved, that is to say, perhaps the final crushing of Nasserism, of which the PLO and its allies in the Lebanese National Movement encircled in West Beirut were perhaps the last manifestation.

The end of Nasserism

It must be said that Nasserism, which expired in Beirut in the summer of 1982, had been unable to arouse much sympathy among the Lebanese population, let alone at an international level. Set up as a State within a State and itself subjected to Syrian control over Lebanon, over the previous years the PLO had been concerned only with maintaining its hold over the Lebanese population in the areas in which it had implanted itself, i.e. in the south and in West Beirut. Caught between the Syrian anvil and the Israeli hammer, the Palestinian Resistance organizations had actually been imperceptibly led into a position of being able to justify themselves solely by their armed presence in Lebanon and by the same token irrevocably bogged down as hostages of one party or the other. The Resistance movements were thus increasingly cut off from what ought to have been their proper bases, the West Bank of Jordan and the Gaza area, where the populations, especially in the former, were engaged in resisting the all-out colonization and seizure of land and water carried out by the Israelis in violation of all international law.

Internationally, the PLO's position had remained the same since the big victories of 1974. In then rejecting the option of creating a Palestinian government,[2] the Palestinian Resistance condemned itself to a limited foreign representation, without any of the advantages of a State. A totally unfavourable military position in relation to Israel, as well as the West's disenchantment with Third World causes, could not help but further limit the PLO's international influence.

As for the Left-wing Lebanese movements, these had in any case been discredited for a long time in the eyes of the Lebanese people. The anarchic way in which they managed the areas under their control, their total dependence on their Syrian and Palestinian protectors, as well as their continual internal wrangles, expressed through repeated street and neighbourhood fighting between rival militias, all ended in discrediting the ideologies and political symbols that these movements had adopted since 1976, namely revolution, Arab unity, socialism and anti-imperialism. Since 1980 West Beirut had become an enclosed field of violence and insecurity, in which car bombings, assassinations, dynamite attacks, kidnappings and constant street battles between rival organizations took place for motives utterly futile or at least totally alien to the population's concerns. This was the case, for example, of the series of murderous bombings and fighting reflecting Iraqi–Syrian tensions which were unleashed by the launching of the Iraq–Iran war; or again the bombing attacks against the French diplomatic presence. On the other hand, East Beirut and the Christian areas held by Right-wing militias, which had been united since 1980 under Bashir Gemayel's command, seemed more and more like oases of peace and prosperity. Admittedly, pluralism, either in opinions or behaviour, had practically disappeared from the Christian regions, but to the population the loss was compensated for by the order and security that ruled there. It was therefore with a certain degree of envy that the populations of the 'Progressive-Islamic' areas viewed the benefits of the Phalangist order.

In carrying out its invasion of Lebanon, Israel knew well that it was picking more than ripe fruit. Exhausted by the anarchy and violence that the Palestinian–Syrian presence had brought to Lebanon since the famous Cairo Agreements in 1969, and especially since 1975, the Lebanese people were ready to accept anything so long as it re-established security and order. Israel and the United States appeared as the only countries able to bring Lebanon out of its state of agony, the Palestinian Revolution and the Arab States having demonstrated their destabilizing role, and, above all, their powerlessness.

It is true that faced with Israel's intransigence and brutality during the siege of the capital, the people of West Beirut closed ranks, defended their city worthily and then in a last superhuman effort gave the Palestinian fighters a grand send-off. Much as the Egyptians had responded to Nasser in 1967 after the crushing June defeat, and again on his death in 1970, by bearing him in triumph though he was defeated and leaving his country in ruin after the futile war of attrition on the Suez Canal, the people of West Beirut, unfortunate companions of the dying fires of the Arab 'revolution', offered the world a last fleeting show of solidarity and resistance to the powerful Israeli–American war machine. Then followed the short and striking epic of Bashir Gemayel, a Lebanese mixture of Nasser and Sadat who dreamt not only of glory for his country but of a totally restored friendship with the West.

The twenty-two days of Bashir Gemayel

The deeds of Bashir Gemayel are mentioned here because they are a good illustration of the kind of tragedy that has beset the Near East since 1956. In a meteoric career, this young man of thirty-four, Lebanon's symbol of Christian 'irredentism' and of pro-Western Right extremism, condemned by the whole Arab Left for his collaboration with Israel, became in a few days the charismatic leader of an orphaned people who had suffered for years from the painful contradictions of the Near East. Elected President in a military barracks under the menace of Israeli tanks on 23 August as soon as the Palestinians had been evicted from Beirut, in twenty days managed to win over the hearts of all the Lebanese communities. In his daily television appearances, in simple and direct language far removed from the erudite and pompous formulae of classical Arabic, Bashir spoke of his dream of a strong united people, and administration free of corruption, a society in which promotions went by merit rather than wealth or family and religious allegiance and of a country that foreigners would respect because at last it would have a strong army and a powerful diplomacy.

Enchanted, the people of West Beirut, who only the day before had been tearfully saluting the departure of an attainable Revolution, saw before them at last a young, proud and fiery Lebanese hero. The possibility of effacing all the humiliations to which a traditionally powerless, if not emasculated, political regime had subjected the Lebanese people suddenly shone on the horizon. And, likewise, the young Head of State's violent, partisan image, earned during the troubled years from 1975 to 1980, began to soften. On good terms with Israelis and Americans, close to Saudi Arabia, heroic anti-hero of Arab ultra-Leftism, Bashir Gemayel now appeared as the charismatic saviour the whole nation had so long awaited.

As if to confirm this providential event, when Menachem Begin summoned him to Israel at the beginning of September, the new President stood up to his former ally and resisted pressure to sign a peace treaty there and then. His popularity soared in consequence. When he was assassinated on 14 September, nine days before officially taking up his post, he was mourned by the country. Many, even on the Christian side, refused to believe he had gone. The young President was killed when a dynamite bomb (the kind the various secret services rife on Lebanese soil specialize in) destroyed the building in which he was holding a final meeting with party lieutenants. Some swore to have seen him leaving the building alive after the explosion, but widespread public rumour held that Israel had killed an ally over whom it thought it had absolute control but who the moment he attained his objective turned out to be far from docile.

In the twenty-two days of his meteoric rise to fame, Bashir Gemayel had perhaps missed changing the course of Lebanese history; but like Kamal Jumblatt and then Iman Musa al-Sadr, this no less unusual figure disappeared, leaving his people once again in search of a leader.

Far from creating a constitutional vacuum, the loss of the young President once more caused the Lebanese people to close ranks. Israel fully exploited his death by entering West Beirut, after the multinational peace-keeping forces (hurriedly pulled out on 13 September) had cleared all its approaches of mines, and provoking the Sabra and Chatila massacres: the Lebanese remained unmoved, refusing to lay themselves open to manipulation. On 21 September, two days before the expiry of the outgoing President's mandate and by a near unanimous vote of the Deputies present, the Parliament elected the assassinated President's older brother, Amin Gemayel. Thus Phalangist supremacy was established in Lebanon, symbolizing a restoration of order and a return to the Western fold.

The inevitable swing to the West

The rise to power of the Lebanese Right which the Israeli invasion had brought about with such lightning rapidity was in fact only a new state in the swing towards the West taking place in the Near East since 1967 and described in these chapters. We have seen the change in the political and ideological character of the region and noticed the Arab political elite's ineluctable swing towards the liberal West, to which it had always been attracted since the time of Muhammad Ali. But if this tendency had retained a certain subtlety and an air of dignity in 1973, this was no longer the case in 1982, when all the Near Eastern Arab governments turned to the United States in the hope that it would stop the Israeli war machine that was relentlessly destroying Lebanon. Between Faisal's majestically decreeing the partial oil embargo in 1973 and King Fahd's[3] repeated telephone calls to President Reagan to obtain reconnection of the water supply the Israeli army had cut off in Beirut, which was dying of thirst, the Arabs completely lost all dignity and replaced it with total clientelage *vis-à-vis* American power.

Furthermore in the summer of 1982, the Foreign Ministers of Saudi Arabia and of Syria, pillar of the Front of Steadfastness, met the American President on behalf of the Arab League, at the same time as the Arab press was denouncing the Soviet Union's 'passivity' towards events in Lebanon. The Soviet Union, whose Arab policy had not had much of a chance after the battering it received from Sadat's Eygpt, as well as after the unpredictability of Hafez al-Assad's Syria and the change in direction of Saddam Hussein's Iraq, could well protest that if no Arab country cared to commit itself to going to the aid of besieged Beirut, it could not very well be more royalist than the King. The short battle between Israeli and Syrian armies that took place in the Beqa'a during the invasion and during which batteries of Soviet-produced missiles were destroyed and more than 70 Syrian MIGS shot down, once again raised the question of the crushing superiority of American-Israeli armament over that of the Soviet Union. In this respect it was the situation created by the 1967 war all over again.

The Israeli war aim was obviously to turn the clock back so as to reduce the Near East to the state of powerlessness it had been in immediately after the 1967 defeat. By liquidating the PLO and its whole politico-military infrastructure, Israel aimed above all at bringing the collective expression of Palestinian nationalism to a complete halt as it had done in 1948. The Israeli Defence Minister, General Sharon, did not even attempt to conceal his objectives. As far as he was concerned, the whole aim of invading Lebanon and destroying the PLO was to settle the problem of the West Bank and of Gaza to Israel's best advantage, i.e. by annexation, an option far from excluded by the Camp David Agreements.[4] By attaining these objectives, Israel also aimed to show that it was the principal political and military power of the region. General Sharon did not shrink from declaring that the Israeli army's effective range extended as far as Pakistan. As in 1967, Israeli and American interests did not show any great divergence. The United States had never had any sympathy for the PLO, with its revolutionary discourse and its ties with radical and Left-wing European movements and with anti-imperialist regimes in the Third World. The all-encompassing cold war ideology of Ronald Reagan meant his team had to try and destroy a movement seen as an important link in the chain of international communist 'subversion'. Reference to Beirut as a centre of international terrorism thus became a common theme used by the United States and Israel to justify shelling the western half of the Lebanese capital. Saudi Arabia, ultra-conservative ideologically, could hardly fail to sympathize with such an attitude and therefore felt no compulsion to impose any symbolic oil or financial pressure on the United States, which in no circumstances did it wish to oppose.

Violence in the Near East and its perception by international opinion

Twelve years earlier, under Nixon, the American bombings of Hanoi and of Vietcong sanctuaries in Cambodia had no objective other than to reduce communist 'terrorism'. Massive and repeated protests in the United States and in the main capitals of Europe had then made a powerful contribution to stopping the American war machine. The shelling of Beirut in 1982 of course caused a certain emotion in the world, but nothing compared to that provoked by American action in the Indo-Chinese Peninsula at the beginning of the 1970s. In ten years, international political feelings had clearly changed and it was the Lebanese and the Palestinians of South Lebanon and West Beirut who paid the price of this turn about in international ideological circumstances. This can perhaps be attributed partly to the hardly brilliant results of the Vietnam war but also to the militarist and expansionist policies of the Soviet Union. Protests against the Soviet invasion of Afghanistan and against the military coup in Poland concentrated the attention of the Western intelligentsia to a much greater degree than the destruction of West Beirut. The horrors of the siege of Beirut engendered mostly pointless arguments which either trivialized death in Beirut, or, on the contrary, gave it a particular resonance by invoking Warsaw, Stalingrad or Oradour as if the collective death of unarmed civilians could have different degrees of horror, depending on the victims' religion, or on historical circumstances or on ideological convictions. Decidedly, as far as the Near East was concerned, everything had become corrupted, even the simplest moral judgement about the deaths of innocent people.

As if to confirm this state of affairs, a spate of terrorist assassinations took place in France, of which one, in the rue des Rosiers in the middle of the Jewish quarter of Paris deflected the sense of events exactly when West Beirut was agonizing. Thus France paid dearly for its attempt to reconcile its friendship for Israel with its defence of the rights of the Palestinian people, on whose behalf it had tried in vain at the end of June 1982 to stop the Israeli war machine, a French resolution in the Security Council being vetoed by the Americans.

Israeli brutality was in fact stopped by the United States only after seventy days of siege. Unlike the French efforts, the Habib

Plan, named after the American who had been mediating in Beirut since the beginning of the Israeli invasion, did not envisage an Israeli retreat from Lebanon, or even from the outskirts of Beirut. The Plan was in fact concerned only with the evacuation of armed Palestinians and Syrian troops from Beirut. There was not a word in it about Israel's occupation of two-thirds of Lebanese territory. Compared with the Habib Plan, the famous Security Council Resolution 242, voted in November 1967, condemning the principle of acquiring territories by force and demanding withdrawal of Israeli forces from occupied territories, seemed very harsh on Israel, though already displaying a disquieting laxity regarding the Palestinian case.

In the event, the Lebanese authorities appeared as unconcerned as the other Arab countries by this major defect in the Habib Plan. Their silence seemed to approve the Israeli surgical operation which caused a diaspora of the combatants and cadres of the PLO into several Arab countries. It was this shortcoming that enabled Israel to enter West Beirut the day after Bashir Gemayel's death to carry out a systematic combing of the already traumatized town. It also allowed the Israelis to carry out unopposed the traditional policy of occupiers of Lebanon, namely to divide and rule by playing one community off against the other. In central Lebanon, in the Shuf, Israel organized inter-denominational conflicts, alternately inciting Druze and Maronites to kill each through their local militias. Consequently, the legal Lebanese authorities found it impossible to maintain law and order. In the south Major Haddad was more than ever Israel's man who, the Israelis insisted, should be reinstated in the official Lebanese army, along with his men. Israel's invasion of Lebanon removed the Palestinian armed presence in the south and in Beirut and thereby destroyed for the time being the parties and militias of the Lebanese Left. But, on the other hand, it also created no less formidable problems. From now on, Israel held officially those pledges in Lebanon which in practice it had already been enjoying since 1975 and which in the dynamics of its position in the Near East it could not fail to make use of.

Amidst all this mess, only the carnage in Sabra and Chatila unequivocally aroused the emotions of the world. This time the dose had actually been too strong. Not content with razing the Palestinian camps and imprisoning in most deplorable conditions 8000 Palestinians and Lebanese suspected of belonging to resistance movements, Israel actually incited certain elements among the Right-wing militias directly under its control into perpetrating the infamy of Sabra and Chatila. Even in Israel, the tarnishing of the country's image overseas, whence Zionism derives all its support, moved a certain section of public opinion into demonstrating its disapproval in the streets of Tel Aviv. The show of indignation was, however, selective. However atrocious the Sabra and Chatila massacres, they were still only part of the continuing violence which was a direct result of the conquest of Palestine. From Deir Yassini[5] in 1948 to Sabra and Chatila in 1982, and adding the total destruction of Suez Canal towns during the war of attrition between Egypt and Israel, as well as all the collective violence inflicted by the Israeli army since 1968 on the Lebanese civilian population sheltering the Palestinian Resistance, one and the same violence has beaten down the Arab neighbours of the State of Israel. Recognizing this linkage obviously means re-opening the whole dossier of politico-military Zionism. Western opinion is not yet ready for this.[6] The easy answer was to respond indignantly to that particularly embarrassing 'mistake' and to shift all the blame onto Begin and Sharon, who were in any case not much to the liking of international opinion.

The Reagan Plan and the Fahd Plan: a new impossible equation

Paradoxically, the Arab countries reacted to Sabra and Chatila with indifference. Arab society was actually exhausted. To the hammer blows of the powerful Israeli war machine, which had already neutralized Egypt and had now overrun Lebanon was added the anguish of the Iraqi-Iranian war which weighed heavily on all the countries of the Arabian Peninsula. The spectre of Shiite religious fundamentalism and its armies, which were beginning to thrust into Iraqi territory, had a strong paralyzing effect. This came on top of a particularly bad oil situation and a severe stock market crash in Kuwait, result of the confusions and speculations of its badly managed oil wealth. As for the countries of the so-called Front of steadfastness, they were in complete disarray. The Syrian army had been beaten in only a few days. Libya's main interest was in playing the great African power, but the Organization of African Unity (OAU) summit held in Tripoli in the summer of that year, 1982, had lamentably failed. And finally, Algeria had sunk into the drabness of a regime that was failing to discover an identity.

Too many disappointments since 1956 had led Arab society into total political immobility. The revolutionary fanfare that had accompanied the nationalization of the Suez Canal was so obviously over by the summer of 1982 that all the Arab Heads of State welcomed the Reagan Plan with an enormous sigh of relief. Nevertheless, the Plan, which the American President announced on 1 September, did nothing more than put the Palestinian question back fifteen years. It was actually Jordan that was invited, within the framework set out both by Resolution 242 of the Security Council and the Camp David Agreements, to negotiate with Israel to recover the Palestinian territories occupied in 1967. Under these circumstances, the PLO could at best hope to become part of the Jordanian-led team of Palestinian representatives in the negotiations, and this solely on condition that it openly recognized Israel's right to exist. With one stroke of the pen, Arab silence and American strength invalidated everything that the PLO had achieved during the 1970s and particularly the exclusive right to represent Palestine established at the 1974 Rabat summit and its admission to the United Nations as an observer.

However 'reactionary' it might be, the Reagan Plan nevertheless infuriated the Israeli government. The American President made it quite clear in his 1 September speech that if peace could not be achieved by forming an independent Palestinian State in the territories of the West Bank and Gaza it could no more be achieved on the basis of Israeli sovereignty or permanent control over the West Bank and Gaza. This clearly went against all that the Israelis had gained from the Camp David Agreements concerning recognition of their right to sovereignty over the Palestinian territories conquered in 1967.

The Reagan Plan was announced some days before the summit of Arab Heads of State held in Fez, in Morocco, from 6 to 9 September. Vain attempts to convene a summit had been made ever since the invasion of Lebanon, but only resulted in some stormy meetings between a few Foreign Ministers, such as that in Ta'if in Saudi Arabia at the end of June. The Heads of State were really waiting for the Israeli operation in Lebanon to end so that they could establish a minimal platform. This was achieved at Fez, where the previous summit had brought the Fahd Plan to a sudden end. This time, however, the Plan was adopted without any major discussion. Reflecting the main Arab concern of the moment, the summit concentrated on the Iraq–Iran war in order to reaffirm

Arab solidarity with Iraq, a new victory of the 'moderates' over the 'hard-liners' of the Front of steadfastness, more or less open in their sympathy for Iran and who had until then prevented any discussion of the war in Arab official circles.

The Fahd Plan, however, was far from coinciding with the Reagan Plan. It envisaged the creation of a Palestinian State after a transitional period of several months during which the Palestinian people would exercise their right to self-determination under the leadership of the PLO, which would be their 'sole legitimate representative'. From seeming like an enormous concession to Israel in January 1982, some months later, after the Reagan Plan and the invasion of Lebanon, the Fahd Plan provided a last-minute way out for the grand conclave of routed Arab Heads of State. And height of irony, photographs of the summit show these Heads of State holding hands and making the V for victory sign with the other, whereas their adoption of the Fahd Plan gave the green light to the Reagan Plan, which negated the Saudi Plan's main clause, namely the creation of a Palestinian State.

But, like the Fahd Plan, the Reagan Plan was actually only a confidence trick. While expressing an interest in the Palestinian question in principle, it nevertheless failed to initiate any practical step either on the Arab or on the American side towards creating a Palestinian entity. With their customary arrogance, the Israelis were the first to declare that the Reagan Plan should be thrown into the dustbin; for them it contradicted the Camp David Agreements, signed under the aegis of the United States, which left open the question of eventual sovereignty over the West Bank and Gaza. Only the Palestinians and King Hussein of Jordan, whose intervention was sought in the Plan, tried to get something out of it. At the first Palestinian National Council meeting to be held since the PLO's departure from Beirut, which took place in Algiers in February 1983, lively discussions took place over what attitude should be adopted towards the Plan. It was certainly not accepted, but then neither was it rejected. Nobody openly condemned Yasser Arafat for making new contacts with the King of Jordan, aiming at ensuring his participation in the process theoretically opened up by the Reagan Plan; but neither was he congratulated for this. But these were merely Byzantine manoeuvres for as 1983 approached, and only three months after its announcement, the American President's solemn declaration on the Palestinian question was already forgotten. The Israelis would not even hear of it and besides it was now on Lebanon that the full attention of American diplomacy was concentrated, with Reagan trying to pull off a great foreign policy success. Following in the footsteps of his predecessor, Jimmy Carter, he sought to normalize Israeli-Lebanese relations. After Egypt, it was now Lebanon's turn. The rest of the Near East would no doubt follow. Nothing would then stand in the way of American supremacy in the Near East.

Lebanon under the American umbrella and Israeli management

But this tactic seemingly so promising for the United States nevertheless turned into the greatest disaster since the Vietnamese debacle. Hardly eighteen months after the Phalangists had been installed in Lebanon under the vigilant eye of the American government, which had the multinational peace-keeping force brought back to Beirut after the Sabre and Chatila massacres, Lebanon was plunged into chaos and American troops had to beat a hasty retreat, followed immediately by the Italians and some months later by the French. To keep his post, the Lebanese President had no option but to present himself in Damascus and declare his allegiance to President Assad. What then had happened in such a short time to ensure the West, which believed itself so close to total domination of the Near East, and with the tacit consent of almost all the Arab countries, should thus be driven from out of Lebanon, one of its most traditional fiefs since the reign of Emir Fakhreddin.

Once more, unfortunately, both in the West and in the Arab countries, public opinion was struck by an unusual degree of shortsightedness. This was not less so among the Arabs, including large sectors of the Lebanese population, exhausted after seven years of terrible sufferings. A strong wind of optimism began to blow in the East as well as the West about a hopeful end to Lebanese misfortunes, thanks to the Israeli invasion and the cooling down of the Middle East conflict due to the weakening of Syria, the passivity of Moscow and the new American initiative brought about by the Reagan Plan. But the incomprehension was unprecedented that prevailed during the autumn and winter of 1982 and into the first quarter of 1983, among all levels of opinion and of course in governmental circles in the big Western and Arab capitals. The same that had brought so much catastrophe in its wake brought new suffering to Lebanon, which had already suffered so much agony at the hands of Arab and Western negligence and through the pusillanimity of its local leaders.

It was ridiculous to have imagined that Israel, formidable warrior of the near East and, as explained earlier,[6] by its very genesis insensitive to any aspect of morality and international law, could invade Lebanon without destroying the country's fragile balance, already severely weakened by the seven years of open conflict that had followed the war of 1973. Here again, there was evidence of blind support for Zionism, probably all the more virulent after the horror of the Beirut siege had at last provided an occasion to criticize the State of Israel openly, which until then had been unthinkable. But encouraged by several Israeli actions, the upsurge of criticism quickly caused the pendulum to swing back in Israel's favour. Firstly, the Peace Movement's demonstrations in Israel had an impact on public opinion: anxious for their country's image abroad and for its democratic reputation, many Israelis expressed on world television their disapproval of the Sabra and Chatila massacres. Then followed the Kahane Commission's inquiry into the extent of responsibility of Israeli civilian and military leaders for the massacres. Suddenly Israel's name was more than cleared among Western opinion and it was once more praised for its admirable 'democracy'. Begin was merely a rather mystical figure whose advanced age prevented him from following the affairs of his government in detail. The birthday in bad taste of the summer of 1982, where the cake was in the shape of an Israeli Merkawa tank, was forgotten; Sharon was only a stormy firebrand, a military chief without political finesse, whom the Commission mildly censured.

To anyone who knows the area around Sabra and Chatila and the small hillocks overlooking the camps where the Israeli troops stayed throughout the four days of the massacres, or who knows how closely the leaders of the local militia, who were only the executors of the operation, were tied up with the Israeli military apparatus, the findings of the Kahane Commission (which suggested that the Israelis were only indirectly involved in the massacres, and which the whole of the West applauded) can only seem surreal. This is especially so since, at the very moment when the Commission was carrying out its inquiry, this same Israeli army was directly encouraging atrocious massacres between Druze and Christian villages in the Lebanese region of Shuf which, in September 1983, culminated in the whole Christian population of the region being evicted as soon as the Israeli troops withdrew from it. It was clear that no one any longer wanted to point a finger at Israel. As was so often said about Sabra and Chatila, it was merely said that the Lebanese were undoubtedly 'savages' whose entire history was one of massacre.

Isreal also gained in respectability from the success of the Camp David Agreements for Egypt. Had not Israel returned Sinai to Egypt on the date stipulated in the Agreements, even if it had illegally kept back a small square kilometre comprising the village of Tabaa. To think of Israel as annexationist could therefore only be an illusion deriving from Arab hatred of Jews. There was, of course, still the West Bank (and Gaza, from now on always in parentheses), but how could anyone upset Begin, that frail mystical old man who believed so strongly that people's rights should be determined by the Bible rather than by the justice and equality described by Saint Thomas Aquinas, Grotius and Spinoza? At some future date, when the Israeli Labour Party, secular and democratic, came to power, it would finally give back a little bit of the West Bank to King Hussein, as advocated by the Reagan Plan.

This was how Western opinion reasoned at the beginning of 1983, and along with it a good part of Arab opinion, whose incorrigible passion for the West has already been noted. When, under American protection the Lebanese government officially opened negotiations with the Israeli occupying power, no voice or almost none was raised to denounce such an explosive process. On the contrary, it was seen as an almost natural continuation of the Camp David Agreements, the success of which had been proved by the return of Sinai to Egypt with which Israel was from then on at peace. After Egypt would come Lebanon. Then, encouraged by the Reagan Plan, Jordan would be put back in the saddle by the military annihilation of the PLO and by the weakening of its leader. Silently digesting its defeat in Lebanon, and tempted by the prospect of massive financial aid from Saudi Arabia, Syria would come to heel while the Soviet Union (distracted by Afghanistan, Poland, the installation of American missiles in Europe, and the problem of Brezhnev's succession) would not have the time to react. How could there be a refusal of a 'pax Americana' which was so close at hand, or rather, since

1967, within easy reach of the Israeli army's tanks? Admittedly, at the beginning of the Israeli invasion, the United Nations Security Council voted in favour of two resolutions, numbers 508 and 509, demanding the unconditional withdrawal of Israeli forces from Lebanon: denying an invader a bonus is an elementary principle of good sense. These resolutions would end up in the oblivion to which all the others on the Arab–Israeli conflict had been consigned. Another Arab country being at last prepared to sign a peace with Israel, such an opportunity could not be allowed to slip away.

The Israeli-Lebanese Agreement of 17 May: a diplomatic victory for American shortsightedness

In obliging the Lebanese government to sign the agreement of 17 May 1983 with Israel the United States believed it had achieved a great victory in foreign policy. The Americans of course failed to see, in this case as at Camp David, that this peace was neither honourable nor just and therefore unlikely to last, and that on the contrary, as with Egypt, it was a peace imposed on a people worn down by the violence and ravages the Israeli war machine had inflicted upon it. More seriously, the American government failed to perceive the difference between Egypt and Lebanon: the former a large homogeneous country, a state powerful from ancient times and capable of ordering its population; the latter, a small country, open to any wind that blew, whose people though indeed exhausted, remained over-politicized and easily manipulated because of its fears and because of its corrupt military leaders, prisoners of foreign patronage.

The United States also failed to see that by allowing the extreme Right wing of the old-guard Lebanese political Establishment to dominate the country, with the solid backing of the Phalangist party, they were definitely condemning the Lebanon to fall back into instability. As a country of balance and compromise, it could be governed only from the Centre, as the whole of Lebanese political history had proved. There had always been serious upheavals whenever a Lebanese faction had sought to align itself with a foreign power and had practised partisan politics locally. Naturally, after so many years of torment, the Lebanese yearned for peace and order, as Bashir Gemayel's fleeting adventure proved so well. They hoped that his charisma and authority would enable the young President to bring his own troops to heel and get rid of the Israeli influence being directly exercised in their ranks. But with him gone, his party remained more powerful than ever, hardly inclined to internal compromise and directly subject to Israeli diktat.

The most serious aspect was the American government's failure to see what Israel had let it in for in Lebanon. Already certain of its triumph, it remained insensitive to all the signs of the destabilization Israel itself was encouraging. The most obvious indication of this was without question the maintaining of Phalangist militias not only in Christian areas, but also and especially in the Shuf, a mixed Druze-Christian area, where horrible massacres had already occurred in the previous century as a by-product of Anglo-French rivalry in the Near East. The occupying power, Israel, not only let the Phalangist militias, largely under its control, build up tensions, but also encouraged the rearmament on a grand scale of Druze militiamen from the Progressive Socialist party led by Kamal Jumblatt's son. Even in West Beirut, subjected to numerous Phalangist incursions, arms once again poured in, despite the presence of 6000 men from the multinational peace-keeping force and of the Israeli army still encamped on all the outskirts of the town. Soon, the predominantly Shiite southern suburbs turned, like the Shuf, into a powder keg.

In the spring of 1983, while everything was poised for a new flare-up, Lebanese and Israeli diplomatic and military personnel, with great pomp and ceremony and under the approving proud gaze of American diplomats and the absolute silence of Arab governments, negotiated a peace treaty which gave Israel rights of military control over Lebanon and envisaged, through new negotiations, a normalization of relations between the two countries within six months. Indeed a surrealist spectacle: for while it was seemingly peace that was being negotiated, in reality all the elements of war were being slotted into place; a war, furthermore, for which the Lebanese would once again pay the price. Nothing symbolized this better than the shells from the Shuf, an area almost totally occupied by the Israeli army, which came crashing down around Khalde, one of the places where 'peace' negotiations were being held, without the United States showing any signs of being particularly alarmed. Even the dynamiting of their Embassy in Beirut in the same period did not seem to make them look any more closely at what was happening around them. In fact, their only concern was to extract a new Arab–Israeli peace treaty, no matter what, and the American Secretary of State, Schultz, began to ape Dr Kissinger on his shuttles between Beirut and Tel-Aviv, delivering the last of Lebanon's 'reservations' and the indispensable Israeli 'compromises'.

The treaty between Israel and Lebanon was eventually signed on 17 May, But Israeli Machiavellianism and American blindness together again provided the straw that broke the camel's back. In a separate letter reminiscent of the truly reprehensible Camp David procedures for the West Bank, the withdrawal of Israeli troops under the treaty was tied to the simultaneous withdrawal of Syrian troops from Lebanon. This was being 'cunning to a fault', as an Arab proverb would put it and merely repeating the errors of Camp David. While Arab governments were naturally eager to see peace established between Israel and its neighbours, so as to enable them at last to enjoy a trouble-free relationship with the West, they could hardly acknowledge any Israeli right to be the official and legal Board of Control for the affairs of the Near East. Yet this was just what the separate letter did, by putting Syrian military presence in Lebanon, ratified by the Arab League in 1976, on the same footing as Israel's occupation of one more Arab territory.

Syria, so far silent, and even seeming to encourage Lebanon to negotiate with Israel, now came to life and raised its voice high and loud to alert its Arab partners against the new Camp David. The latter did indeed receive the official emissaries sent out by the Lebanese government to explain that the treaty of 17 May was less damaging to Arab interests than that of Camp David, but all felt obliged to express their sympathy with the Syrian refusal to be classed with the Zionist invaders in a United States-sponsored international document. Syria was in an especially good position to speak up at that moment, for the Soviet Union, under the forceful leadership of Yuri Andropov, was re-supplying it with sophisticated military equipment to replace that lost in 1982 during the Israeli attack in the Beqa'a Valley. The Soviet Union, for its part, was going all out with propaganda against the American military presence in Lebanon, aimed at allowing Israel to legalize its Lebanese conquests, that is to say American-Zionist military-imperialist collusion designed to increase the subjugation of the Arabs.

New massacres and a return to 'terrorism'

From then on the pace of things quickened on the Lebanese side. A steady flow of arms from Damascus poured in to the Druze of the Shuf and to the Shiites of the southern suburbs of Beirut, which the Israeli army let through. For its part, the Lebanese government carried on as if nothing had changed, even though heavily armed Phalangist militias on one side and Druze and Shiites on the other were reoccupying territory everywhere. American Sixth Fleet warships in Beirut harbour and Ronald Reagan's booming declarations of intention to see the treaty of 17 May respected misled the Lebanese authorities, though on the question of the treaty they had been abandoned by the most pro-Western of the Arab governments. In September 1983, when the Israeli forces withdrew their troops to South Lebanon, the Shuf region turned into a veritable slaughterhouse. Armed to the teeth by Syria and with logistic connivance from Israel, Druze militiamen annihilated the Phalangist militias in an atrocious carnage which lasted for three days and which forced the whole Christian population of the Shuf to leave the region. At this point, the official Lebanese army intervened through fear of Druze militia descending on the Presidential Palace, where several of the region's main roads converged. There was also the thunder of the guns of the American fleet, for there were 2000 American marines on land who could have been endangered by such a military thrust, interpreted by the Americans as a Syrio-Russian reprisal against their diplomatic victory in the Near East represented by the treaty of 17 May.

The attack on the American and Western presence came on 22 October when bomb-loaded suicide trucks drove into American and French army headquarters and claimed hundreds of victims among the military personnel present. A clumsy reprisal raid by French aircraft on a training camp for Amal Shiite dissidents, pro-Iranian and Syrian controlled, at Baalbek in the Beqa'a Valley, raised tension even further. The Arab–Israeli conflict now came to be presented to world opinion as fanatical Islamic 'terrorism' manipulated by the Soviet Union via Syria against the 'democratic' and 'civilized' West. The issues could hardly have been more clouded: even attempts to resist the Israeli occupation in South Lebanon were treated as 'terrorism'. Having signed a peace treaty with a second Arab State under the aegis of the United States, leader of the free world, democratic and peaceful Israel was being subjected, along with its allies from the West, to attacks of blind Islamic 'fanaticism'. Forgotten more than ever were the West Bank and Palestinian rights, along with the United Nations Security Council Resolution 242 demanding the return of the territories occupied in 1967 and 508 and 509 demanding unconditional withdrawal from South Lebanon. As for the Reagan Plan, the United States itself henceforth had other things on its mind, particularly the prestige of its army and of the diplomacy which was going all out to turn Lebanon, after Egypt into a friend for Israel and an unconditional ally for the West.

To face up to the danger, the United States repeated its classic reflex to the Near Eastern conflict by further strengthening its ties with Israel, to the great consternation of the pro-Western Arab countries headed by Saudi Arabia, which had been counting greatly on American understanding to put an end to Israeli pretensions and to reclaim Syria once and for all from the hands of the Soviet Union. It was at this moment that clear signals went out from Syria to the Western countries but which international opinion merely dismissed as absurd.

How Arafat was besieged in Tripoli, or how the road from Palestine passes through Damascus

It was the Palestinians loyal to Arafat and, once again, all the Lebanese civilians present on the scene who were to bear the brunt of these signals. The spectacle at Tripoli, capital of North Lebanon, was surreal at the end of 1983. Syrian-supported Palestinian rebels, who had broken away from the official PLO leadership, had surrounded the last of Arafat's supporters in Lebanon, now trapped in the town.

Relations between Yasser Arafat and the Syrian government had been steadily deteriorating ever since the PLO had left Beirut. This was actually nothing new. Antagonism between Syria and the al-Fatah movements, led by the head of the PLO, went back a long way, particularly to the confrontations between the Syrian army and the Palestinian movements in Lebanon in 1976. Syria had never fully appreciated the independence and political evasions of the PLO leader. Ever since Egypt decided to go it alone after the 1973 war, Syria's whole foreign policy had been built around establishing a Front (which it would dominate) made up of Lebanon, the PLO and Jordan, thereby giving it an international weight it could not possibly have alone. But the Reagan Plan, which re-established Jordan as spokesman in any negotiation with Israel, and the reconciliation between the PLO and Jordan after the Palestinian movements left Beirut in 1982, threw Syria back into isolation and into the arms of the Soviet Union, thereby eliminating it from any possible settlement in the Near East.

So the Palestinian opposition to Arafat's leadership developed in the Beqa'a areas where Syrian troops were in control. The erosion of the military positions held in these areas by Arafat's followers followed the good old Syrian tradition of half a step forward, three-eighths of a step back. In the autumn, when the PLO leader went to Damascus to try and obtain an end to the rebel opposition with Syrian army logistic support, he was expelled at a few hours' notice. Thus after Beirut had come Damascus; soon it was Tripoli, where the PLO leader put himself at the head of his surrounded but faithful followers and where the astounded world watched a replica of the siege of Beirut, with Israelis replaced by Syrians. In the besieged town, the Palestinians cleaned up all possible pro-Syrian pockets of resistance, with the communists in particular taking the punishment, while a local Islamic militia was deployed in the town as a further defiance of the Syrian government, which regarded Islamic fundamentalism as its main enemy.

International opinion had difficulty following this subtle and cruel game of Near Eastern chess, which only reflected the complexity of the Middle East conflict as played out by the interested parties and mainly by Americans and the Israelis who held most of the pieces, especially since the 1973 war.

The siege of Tripoli at the end of 1983, lasted several weeks, during which Arafat made some memorable television appearances, though somewhat less gloriously than in Beirut, for this time he was being besieged by an Arab power supporting Palestinian rebels. It was lucky that Israel interfered by blockading the port of Tripoli and letting off intermittent bursts of gunfire for several days, for this delayed the departure of the PLO combatants and their leader, which had been negotiated by France, and restored some of his prestige. The French managed at the same time to pull off the spectacular feat of exchanging thousands of

Lebanese and Palestinian prisoners from the camp of Ansar for only a handful of Israelis held by pro-Arafat Palestinians.

As in 1975–6, Syria in 1983 thus demonstrated, by the siege of Tripoli and by encouraging Palestinian dissent, that the road to peace in the Near East must inevitably pass through Damascus. Arafat, henceforth at odds with the Syrian regime, tried to prove the contrary: after leaving Tripoli, he went directly to Egypt where he met Sadat's successor, Housni Mubarak.

This gesture was purely for effect, for Egypt was still excluded from the Arab League and the Camp David Agreements had contributed towards the continuing erosion of Palestinian rights. Spectacular but useless, and too clever by half, the action was basically no different from all the other short-lived and broken alliances so characteristic of Arab political life over the last few decades. Geopolitical reality and the cynicism of States were much stronger than this kind of politicking, of which Arab opinion had grown so weary.

Even closer to the brink

Ten years after the ephemeral Arab spring of 1974, the new year of 1984 opened for the Near East with even blacker prospects. Gone was the oil wealth, for consumption had fallen drastically and prices were dropping; Iran and Nigeria, in particular, were selling off their oil at any old price despite OPEC's efforts to keep prices up and to impose export quotas on its members. In difficult times, an association of poor countries, such as OPEC, has no hope of imposing any kind of discipline on its members. Revolutionary Iran, which had brought about a breathtaking rise in prices in 1979–80 by drastically reducing its exports, was now making them fall by rapidly stepping up exports without consideration of price in order to finance its war effort against Iraq. At the beginning of 1984 a new Iranian offensive from within Iraqi territory had tried to cut the strategic route from Basrah to Baghdad. Acts of sabotage, probably inspired by Iranian fundamentalists, took place in Kuwait against the symbols of the Western presence, while the frail emirate was being shaken by an unprecedented stock market crisis. Wild speculation in the shares of companies engaged in more or less fictitious activities led to financial catastrophe during the course of 1983, which cost the government several billion dollars to disentangle. This was in addition to the enormous amounts of aid that Kuwait, along with Saudi Arabia and other Gulf oil countries, had to supply to Iraq. If Iraq were to be overwhelmed by the Iranian army, it was the Arabian Peninsula countries as a whole which would fall like ripe fruit into the hands of the Khomeinist ideology and its numerous agents.

Everywhere in the Arab world the economic situation was deteriorating because of the international crisis and the abrupt end to oil prosperity. In Morocco and Tunisia, price rises in essential products provoked rioting which was severely put down. In Algeria too, the freeze on growth encouraged the development of fundamentalist religious movements, while in Egypt neither the liberalization of the economy nor the Camp David Agreements had delivered the desired economic results.

The fruits of the semi-victory over Israel of 1973 had also vanished into thin air. Israel, more powerful than ever, occupied a good third of Lebanon, thus progressively encircling Syria and accelerating the illegal colonization of the West Bank. Whether turned in on themselves and their insoluble problems or taking on foreign adventures, Libya in Chad, or Iraq being bogged down in its war with Iran, the Arab States no longer had enough energy to think about Palestine or Lebanon. The Iranian advance constituted a much more immediate danger for the countries of the Peninsula. In Syria, President Assad's uncertain health and the sharpening of factional rivalries within the regime over the succession weakened a country which had nonetheless succeeded in getting the Americans out of Lebanon.

Thus was the stage set for the era of hostages and of terrorism which, in Western eyes, signalled the return of the Middle East to barbarism. The years 1985 and 1986 saw massive terrorist operations in Europe and European and American citizens taken hostage in Lebanon, providing a long and tedious list: from the hijacking of a TWA plane at Beirut in the summer of 1985, which was followed by various hijacks or attempted hijacks, all bloody, to the murderous attacks at Rome and Vienna airports at the end of 1985 and those in Paris and Berlin in 1986, not to mention the hijack of the M.V. *Achille Lauro* in October 1985 and that of an Egyptian plane in Malta in November 1985, resulting in dozens of lives lost, as well as the fantastic attempt to blow up an Israeli plane which led to a campaign of intimidation by the Western powers against Syria.

Perpetrated in the names of quite diverse groups, such as Shiite militant Islam, factions of the PLO whether dissident (like that of Abu Nidal) or not, pan-Syrian or pan-Arab Lebanese Christian radicals, all these operations were just so many violent messages born out of the seized-up Middle Eastern situation which the invasion of Lebanon and the development of the Iraq–Iran war had only served to exacerbate. As usual, Western opinion and governments got the wrong end of the stick. They took no notice at all of the labels brandished on high to justify the operations. For them it was simply a matter of resisting the Oriental 'barbarism' at the heart of the terrorist struggle aimed at destabilizing the Western democracies by undoing the State of Israel.

More was heard than ever of Arab atavistic violence, and of the resurgence of Islamic fanaticism. A Western reprisal, the spectacular American raid on Tripoli in Libya in the spring of 1986, left numerous civilian victims. True, this was no more than the replica of a murderous Israeli raid a few months earlier in the autumn of 1985 on the headquarters of the PLO in Tunis, itself a reprisal for an attack which had cost the lives of three Israelis in Cyprus. Tripoli and Tunis, two Arab capitals geographically far removed from the real suppurating centres of terrorism, Lebanon, Palestine and Iran.

To be sure, at the end of 1986, the American administration declared that Beirut should be put in quarantine and when more American citizens were taken hostage in the Lebanese capital, even bombardment was considered. Beirut airport was in fact closed a few days later, following bombardments by Lebanese Front militias. But soon after, to general stupefaction, the news broke of the scandal of American arms sales to Iran, thanks to the good offices of the State of Israel. Incoherence, then, is found not only in the East, but also in the West; and all the more so because these arms deliveries enabled the Iranian army to begin to break through the defences of Basra, the major port of southern Iraq.

Thus, the invasion of Lebanon and the siege of Beirut, which were supposed to rid the 'civilized' world of the terrorist 'gangrene', succeeded only in creating conditions for a destabilization of the region on an even greater scale. This was all the more facilitated by Iran's increasing assertion of its importance in the region, with plenty of complaisance on the part of the principal regional actors, headed by Israel and Syria and ultimately of the

United States themselves. After 1985, it was on Lebanese territory that this Iranian breakthrough was to be the most spectacular, rounding off the job of disintegrating Lebanon undertaken by the Israeli invasion.

The Party of God (Hizbollah) or the Iranian breakthrough in Lebanon

Under the impassive gaze of the traditional protectors of Lebanon, the Western powers, Israel first provoked the massacres in the Shuf in 1983 and then did the same in South Lebanon, withdrawing in stages during the winter of 1984 and spring 1985 but always maintaining the notorious security line achieved by means of the 1978 invasion. The Israeli army of occupation in Southern Lebanon from 1982 to 1985 in effect allowed, if indeed it did not actually encourage, the development of the Shiite militias and the rearmament of the Palestinians in this area.

Furious at the abrogation of the treaty of 17 May 1983 (which it had in any case itself torpedoed), Israel applied the same policy in South Lebanon as in the Shuf: divide in order to conquer, weaken both adversaries and allies, a scorched earth policy which led to the spilling of so much innocent blood. As Israeli forces withdrew, the same spectacle was witnessed as in the Shuf: massacres and the forced eviction of Christian communities, villages pillaged and burnt, tens of thousands of Christian refugees going wherever the wind blew them. As was the case with the Druze militia in the Shuf, the Shiite militia in South Lebanon became preponderant.

By February 1984, the Shiite militia Amal had already imposed itself as the dominant force in West Beirut, several days before the departure of the multinational force, panic-stricken after the outrages of 23 October 1983. At the same time, in East Beirut, the Christian militia, so hard hit by the events in the Shuf, regained strength. The control of West Beirut by Amal had been made possible following a massive bombardment lasting several days and nights in the southern suburb of Beirut by the Lebanese army responding to provocations. The unusual scale of the artillery barrage led to the disintegration of the Sixth Brigade of the Lebanese army, the Shiite elements of which joined Amal.

With Amal, inevitably, came the Hizbollah, a militia directly financed by the Iranian Embassy in Beirut and sister organization of Islamic Amal in Baalbeck under direct control of the Revolutionary Guard introduced by Syria into the Beqa'a in 1982. But whereas in the Beqa'a the Syrian army controlled the movements of Islamic Amal, in Beirut and South Lebanon where there was no security control at all, the Hizbollah had a free hand and were able to establish lines between the south of the country and the southern suburbs of Beirut where they set up their headquarters.

In just a few months, half the country, everywhere south of the Beirut-Damascus road, which during the preceding decades had been at the hub of secular and socialist Pan-Arab nationalism, was transformed into a quasi-Islamic republic Iranian style, where every day more and more turbans were sported. A communist manhunt soon began, at the same time as the first demands arose for the foundation of an Islamic republic in Lebanon, thus legitimizing the call by the Christian militia for a division of the country along community lines.[7] Under the Islamic thrust of Hizbollah, the secular inclinations of Amal soon gave way. There were more and more kidnappings of Christians living in the west part of the capital, leading to the exodus of thousands of inhabitants to the other sector. Attempts to booby-trap cars increased the insecurity of the Western sector which was emptied of all Western diplomatic and cultural presence as the kidnappings of Western diplomats and journalists continued.[8]

Under various labels connected with Islamic Jihad, the Iranian Embassy in Beirut had found the best way of altering the policy of the Western powers towards Iran. The taking of hostages was an ultra-powerful lever producing spectacular results. France exiled the Iranian opposition to the Khomeini regime from Paris, agreed to discuss its huge financial dispute with the Islamic Republic and paid up an advance instalment of 300 million dollars; discreet deliveries of arms were also made. As for the United States, the Irangate revelations showed the extent of the arms deliveries and of the political contacts working to restore normal relations. Lebanon had thus been Iran's first choice as a springboard just as it had been for the Palestinians several years earlier.

Iran's pressure on the Western countries to quit Lebanon was not limited merely to the taking of hostages. In South Lebanon, during the autumn of 1986, Hizbollah attacked the French contingent of UNIFIL which had been stationed there following the invasion of 1978, thus following on the numerous Israeli attempts to get rid of UNIFIL which, however, had at least had the advantage of alleviating the sufferings of the civilian population in the areas where it had been located.[9] In France, public opinion already inflamed over the fate of the French hostages, demanded withdrawal of the French contingent. The French government applied to the Security Council of the United Nations, demanding that Israel should allow the deployment of UNIFIL according to its original mandate, right up to the border, so that it could efficaciously fulfil its mission. After eight years – better late than never – a Western power had thus officially pointed out that UNIFIL's mission had been well and truly hampered by Israel. The crisis calmed down and France, having regrouped the elements of its contingent in a secure zone, repatriated the greater part of it.

This episode well illustrates how Iran and Israel now call the tune in the destabilization of Lebanon. Moreover, when the Irangate revelations were made, Israeli authorities very clearly formulated advantages of collusion with Iran, the aim being to weaken still further the already rickety Arab countries. Islamic fundamentalism, too, did not seem displeasing to Israel, initially of course because it counteracted the only dangerous Arab claim against the existence of the Hebrew State, namely the secular nationalist cause, but also because it fractured Lebanon more deeply and threatened the other Arab countries. Furthermore, if there were to be sectarian States (Sunni, Shiite, Druze, Alawi and Christian) in the Middle East, how could a Jewish State be left out? Lastly, the development of Islamic terrorism, which hit Western nationals and criss-crossed the sinister operations of Abu Nidal in Europe and the *Achille Lauro* affair, provoked a tension in Western public opinion which was all to the good for Israel.

For Europe and the Middle East, the mess had never been greater. The American–Israeli tandem, by acts of commission or omission, had well and truly made the Middle East a hurricane zone whose furious wind blew over Europe. It is in Lebanon that the bloody chaos continues to be the most spectacular, though the Iraq–Iran war, with arms flowing in from all sides, still produces the greater number of victims.

The thousand and one wars of Lebanon

The retreat of the multinational force in February 1984 followed by the Israeli retreats from the south of the country left Lebanese territory more than ever in the hands of the profusion of militias armed and equipped from abroad which acted as mercenaries in the service of the diverse causes that agitate the Middle East. We have already noted the massacres and forced displacement of the Christian population of the Shuf and in the south. Despite the direct responsibility of Israel in these crimes against humanity, the Christian militias continued to maintain close relations with the Israeli Army and to be well received in western capitals. In the spring of 1985 a *coup d'état* inside the militia brought the openly pro-Israeli elements to the fore; a liaison office was opened in Jerusalem by the Lebanese Forces following the closure of the Israeli liaison office in Beirut after the Lebanese government had declined to ratify the agreement of 17 May 1983.

As regards government, it was that of the militias that was installed by the so-called 'national reconciliation' conferences, held in Geneva and Lausanne in autumn 1983 and spring 1984 respectively, under the double umbrella of Syria and Saudi Arabia. A farce in bad taste, where ancient politicians, of dubious character or ravaged by extreme old age, and violent and cruel young militia leaders discussed how many angels dance on a pin in the padded luxury of grand Swiss hotels, while in Beirut the guns mowed down thousands of innocent victims.[10] East and West Beirut engulfed each other in a veritable deluge of fire and flood, the like of which had not been seen in the capital since 1975–6.

On 30 April 1984 a Cabinet was formed by Rashid Karami, the same leading personage from Tripoli who, as Prime Minister in 1969, had paralyzed the whole of Lebanese political life by refusing to govern but refraining from resigning, thus resulting in the Cairo Agreements, one of the principal causes of the destablization of the country. The Cabinet included the principal militia chiefs or their representatives, thereby making the division of the country into confessional ghettos official; henceforth each militia Minister would use the apparatus of state to consolidate his hold on the territory he had carved out for himself.

This new government, vainly discussing what constitutional reforms were required for each community to have its fair share of power, brought only a very brief respite to the country. Obviously no political force wanted a real dialogue, something in any case impossible as long as power and religious communities are linked. Meanwhile, each militia consolidated its position, with the big manoeuvres of 1985 in mind. From September 1984, there was great tension between Amal and the reconstituted Palestinian movements. By the spring of 1985 it had become a generalized war between Palestinian and Shiite militiamen, this also serving to heighten the tension between Druze and Shiite militiamen. This tension lasted throughout the whole of 1986 and degenerated even further in 1987 when the refugee camp war became harsher and harsher in Beirut, as in Saida and Tyre, with the Amal militiamen blocking food supplies to all the camps.

All this developed into a general war in West Beirut between Druze and Shiite militia, rendering inevitable the entry in March 1987 of Syrian troops into the 'Muslim' sector of the capital in order to relieve a civilian population paralyzed by the terror of so much violence and destruction. The Israeli invasion of Lebanon might just as well have been a machine for throwing time out of gear and turning back the hands of the clock: five years after the siege of Beirut by Israeli troops aimed at clearing out the 'terrorist' ghettos of Lebanon, the same Syrian troops returned to try and put a stop to the violence and terror which had never held sway over the Lebanese capital to such an extent.

Behind the terrible fighting between the Shiite militia Amal and the reconstituted Palestinian movements there was, of course, the shadow of Syria. In July 1985 Syria had, moreover, delivered forty-two tanks to Amal in order to reinforce the military potential of its militia client. But there was also in the fighting a murderous hysteria against the armed Palestinian presence, which cannot fail to recall the hysteria that seized the Phalangist militia in 1976 at the time of the no less murderous siege of the Palestinian camps situated in Christian zones, in particular the notorious Tell al-Za'atar. The supreme horror was that the armed Palestinian presence in Lebanon was able to reconstitute itself against the wishes of Syria after the Israeli invasion, only because Israel and the Christian militias had left plenty of men and arms in the camps to maintain an armed presence. In January 1987, the television stations of the Christian militias even invited Arafat to plead his cause for hours on end on the screen. This was politics of the worst choice, under which the civilian populations, whether Palestinian or Lebanese, Muslim or Christian had unendingly suffered.

The Syrian shadow also lurked behind the violent fighting between rival factions of the Christian militia of the Lebanese Forces in January and then in July 1986. In fact one of the militia chiefs who became famous for the massacres of Sabra and Chatila in September 1982 performed a spectacular about-turn in favour of Syria in September 1985. Received with great pomp in Damascus, he agreed, along with Jumblatt, chief of the Druze militia, and Berri, chief of the Shiite militia, to sign an agreement defining a new allocation of political powers among the communities as well as the establishment of special links between Lebanon and Syria in the military, education and information fields.

The Lebanese held their breath: was this the end of their martyrdom, the solution to the crisis which for more than twelve years had shaken the foundations of a whole society with a rare violence? Alas, no! In January 1986, several days after the agreement was signed, pitched battles broke out in East Beirut and in the Mountain where the Christian militias were predominant, between pro- and anti-Syrian factions of the Christian militia – to the benefit of the latter who initiated the hostilities and emerged victorious. Syria, ordinarily so prudent in its moves, really seemed to be in too much of a hurry to reap the fruits of its policy against the Israeli occupation of Lebanon and the Israeli–Lebanese treaty of 17 May 1983 which it had put an end to. In fact why should the Israelis and the Americans, still powerful on the Lebanese scene, have left Syria a free hand and accepted the establishment of its preponderance over a traditionally pro-Western Lebanon? Nor did the Syrians see that, beyond the immense desire of the civilian populations of all communities for peace, their agreement bestowed on the Christian side the leadership of a militia faction chief not only too young and inexperienced, but in addition with a past that was less than imposing; in the absence of an international consensus on this agreement, the other factions of the Christian militia, the President of the Republic and other scheming politicans of the Maronite community did not hesitate to frustrate the Syrian plan, which had ignored them. For Iran and its Lebanese Hizbollah, moreover, the Damascus agreement would have signalled the end of an influence that was too valuable to be abandoned so easily.

Thus everything combined to bring about the failure of the Syrian plan for the pacification of Lebanon, a plan drawn up at a speed hardly customary for the leaders of that country, recalling American–Israeli haste to have the Israeli–Lebanese treaty of 17 May 1983 adopted. Checkmate, then, in Lebanon: for American–Israelis as well as Russian–Syrians. This bloody game of chess in the Middle East is still being played out on Lebanese soil, every day destroying more innocent civilian lives. For it continues in the Palestinian context as shown by the violent fighting between Shiite militias and the reconstituted Palestinian movements.

The diplomatic and military peregrinations of the PLO

Thrown out of Beirut in August 1982 and out of Tripoli in December 1983, the leader of the PLO, whose headquarters had been moved out to Tunis, had no option but to seek a rapprochement with Egypt and Jordan in the hope of hypothetical negotiations under the aegis of the United States. By the same token, the schisms which had already torn the PLO apart during the 1970s now opened up wider than ever.[11] The maximalist organizations, which had kept their headquarters in Damascus, seceded, denouncing Arafat for his capitulationist line. He had actually signed a joint declaration with the King of Jordan in January 1985 by which the PLO undertook to enter into a process of negotiation with the State of Israel, under the aegis of the United States, within the framework of a Jordanian–Palestinian delegation. The question was whether this declaration would be followed by other declarations by the PLO with a view to accepting Resolutions 242 and 338 of the Security Council of the United Nations and renouncing guerilla operations.[12]

A Palestinian Council held shortly afterwards in Amman was boycotted by the leftist Palestinian organizations. Nevertheless, Yasser Arafat, not content with reinstalling PLO's offices in Amman, strengthened his links with Egypt. Thus once again the hands of the clock were turned back. The PLO's entire Lebanese venture had achieved nothing, beyond creating all that suffering for the Lebanese and Palestinian civilian populations in Lebanon. Forgotten were Black September[13] and the Camp David Agreements which had been so violently denounced by the PLO: here was the leader of the PLO to all intents and purposes imprisoned in a *tête-à-tête* with Jordan and Egypt, two frankly pro-American Arab countries with which the PLO had had nothing to do for years.

But this zigzag of the PLO was to no avail: firstly because 1985, as we have seen, was a year of violent large-scale Palestinian operations on the European scene (hijacking of the *Achille Lauro*, operations at Rome and Vienna, the assassination of three Israelis in Cyprus) which took away some of the credibility from the option of negotiating within a Jordanian–Palestinian framework to which Arafat had committed the PLO; secondly because at the last minute the PLO refused to endorse United Nations Resolutions 242 and 338. This caused great diplomatic embarrassment: the members of the PLO who were part of a Jordanian–Palestinian delegation were to have made a declaration endorsing the Resolutions in London before being received by the British Prime Minister. One member did make the declaration but, to the consternation of the diplomatic sponsors of the visit, the other refused. At the same time, tension mounted between the King of Jordan and the PLO. In January 1986 relations broke down, to the relief of the Israelis whose Parliament had passed a law forbidding all contact between Israeli citizens and members of the PLO.

Evidently peace is not much valued in the Middle East; the collapse of this fragile hope brought with it a perceptible deterioration in the situation in the occupied territories where twenty years of iron-fisted occupation had brought the Palestinian population to its knees. Attacks against settlers or members of the armed forces provoked violent reactions on the part of the authorities and of the Israeli population. But international opinion remained unmoved: terrorism polarized a hostility drawn from the very depths of European anti-Arab and anti-Islamic racism. Probably only the June 1967 war witnessed a like contempt for the whole Arab 'race' in Western opinion. The sabre-rattling by Arab radios had contributed to such mobilization of opinion. This time of course it was a question of violent actions but Europe had forgotten that there had been others in the 1970s, in particular the especial violence at the Olympic Games in Munich.

To help polish up its image and to establish its unity the PLO now only had poor Lebanon. With the energy of despair, everything was staked on a return in force to the Lebanese stage, helped by the benevolent neutrality of Iranian Hizbollah and the active co-operation of the Christian militias. It was the civilian population of the camps who paid the heavy price.

Thus in fact everything combined in 1985 and 1986 to hinder the visibility between West and East. The hostages in Beirut, 'Shiite' militancy and, more generally, the bugbear of Islamic fundamentalism, the Palestinian operations, the attacks in Paris in September 1986 attributed to Marxist and Pan-Arab Lebanese Christians: all this inflamed Western opinion against the 'barbarism' of the East, all the more when oil prices slumped and there was no longer any reason, as there had been after the war of 1973, to take the rights of Arabs in the occupied territories into account for reasons of economic opportunism. Reagan and Thatcher, champions of triumphant neo-conservatism, led an anti-terrorist crusade which replaced the by now very weak inclinations toward finding the way to a real Arab–Israeli peace in the Middle East. The Arab world had thus really gone back in time to 1967.

The time-machine, set into motion by the Israeli invasion of Lebanon in 1982, worked so effectively that soon, at the beginning of 1987, in the context of the total surrealism brought about by the revelations of the Irangate scandal, the Soviet Union made a forceful reappearance in the Middle East, just as in the good old days of the 1960s. Dynamic and dashing, Gorbachev bustled about after the long cold night of Leonid Brezhnev. The Sovet Union was suddenly everywhere: at first at the Palestinian National Council held in Algiers in April 1987 where the schisms came to an end. Arafat was reconciled with Habash and Hawatme, the two slightly faded stars of 1960s Arab ultra-Leftism. Syria had to yield, thus apparently losing the Palestinian card it had so long sought to hold. Somewhat deflated, Hafez Assad went to Moscow to give account of his policy, no longer pleasing to the Russians.

At its Algiers sessions the Palestinian National Council denounced the agreements between Hussein and Arafat of January 1985 already repudiated more than a year earlier by Jordan and condemned the contacts with Egypt, thereby angering the Egyptian government which closed down the offices of the PLO in Cairo. In the space of two years, Palestinian diplomacy had thus made a spectacular diplomatic round trip, going to Cairo and Amman, the most pro-American and anti-Palestinian of Arab capitals, only to return to starting point, without anyone being able to tell what direction the Palestinian movement would take in the future or how its credibility could be re-established. For the time being, it was clear that the Soviet Union was the motive power that had enabled reunification of the movement.

The Soviet Union also became very active in Gulf affairs, lend-ings its flag to Kuwaiti oil tankers attacked by the Iranian fleet, strongly supporting Iraq, apparently pushing Syria towards a reconciliation with the latter and lastly, establishing contacts with the Saudis who for once seemed to be dismayed by the ineptitude of American policy. Within Israel and the World Jewish Congress there were also 'Cries and Whispers' when Shimon Peres, in a

surreal pre-election run-up with the Likud, pleaded for an international conference on the Middle East in which the five permanent members of the Security Council would participate,
including, of course the Soviet Union, and which would give its
patronage to direct Arab–Israeli negotiations. In full rout over
Irangate the American government could not object, thereby
abrogating one of the most sacred principles of its Middle East
policy, namely, keeping the Soviet Union out of the picture.

The fragmented Middle East

Between Suez in 1956 and the invasion of Lebanon in 1982,
the Middle East pursued a chaotic and breathtaking trajectory.
Shattered a thousand times since 1967 by the military, economic
and ideological shocks we have described throughout these pages,
this geographical region was once again the prey to the powers
that be of this world, as at the beginning of the century after the
demise of the Ottoman Empire. Its charismatic leaders gone, its
secular nationalist aspirations dissolved into thin air, its economic
and technological development nowhere in sight, the Arab Middle
East is more fragmented than ever, bogged down in the quagmire
of impossible equations and unmastered time. Transfixed and
immobile, like a Greek chorus, the Arabs are witnessing the
gradual sliding of their society into chaos and anarchy: a future
perpetually harking back to the past or one that seems unable to
come into existence at all.

9 Conclusion

A quarter of a century is a short time in the scale of history. It would be foolhardy to judge or attempt to appraise the burning issues that arose from events in the Arab Near East between the nationalization of the Suez Canal in 1956 and the Camp David Agreements in 1978, not to mention the Israeli–Egyptian peace treaty in 1979 and the invasion of Lebanon in 1982. At the very most one can broadly outline the characteristics of that period and the fundamental questions they raise for the historian or sociologist. But even this is difficult, for the analysis carried out in these chapters is on the whole confined to the surface of events, to their outward aspect in the political order and to their expression in the ideological domain. Our analysis has sought, whenever possible, to base itself on understanding of cultural trends, collective psychological feelings and economic or social upheavals. But a great difficulty persists, namely the realization that, despite everything, Arab society, like many Third World societies, presents a certain opacity to the outside observer, and indeed to one on the inside, and that it permits only a skeletal and caricatured view of the internal dynamics at work in areas inaccessible to observation.

But basically there is nothing surprising about this. At the beginning of the book it was pointed out that Arab society in the Near East lacks a modern political language, that is to say a language organized and institutionalized around the exercise of political freedom, whatever form that may happen to take. The same applies in the cultural or economic field and this explains why the analysis throughout stresses those exceptional moments when a society expresses itself spontaneously in the political or cultural domain. Similarly, it explains the attempt to grasp feelings, moods, their modes of expression and of change. For it must be pointed out that although Arab Near Eastern society has been freed from direct foreign oppression (Turkish and then

European), except for Palestine, which has yet again changed its foreign oppressor, it has hardly been freed from the internal oppression resulting from centuries of despotic traditions.

Whether monarchies or republics, the political regimes in power hunt down their opponents, usually in a ruthless manner,[1] and tightly control the press, schools, universities, publishing and the mosque. Uncertain of the loyalty of their armed forces, they create militias, legions and national guards, while the various security services, which persecute and often torture the population, prosper exceedingly. This is an aspect somewhat neglected in this book in the interest of focusing the analysis more effectively on the main forces behind the complex events of this period. Yet if one thinks of what has most characterized the history of the last quarter of a century, it is this that comes first to mind.

It would be of little interest to conclude with references to the benefits of freedom and liberal democracy or the harmful effects of totalitarianism. What is important is to understand where the roots of oppression lie and to denounce them, and for this reason it seemed pointless to encumber our analysis with descriptions of the dictatorial nature of Arab political regimes. It also makes good sense to say that it is the essence of the practice of freedom that is important and not its form. Consequently, liberal democracy as practised in Western institutions is not necessarily a model to copy or to take over without adaptation. After all, institutionalized freedom is won bit by bit only after a great many unceasing attempts. It is never totally or finally acquired. In this respect, history clearly shows that no revolution anywhere can boast of having ushered in total and lasting freedom.

It would be exceedingly naive to think that Arab society in the Near East, having only rid itself in 1956 of the most glaring aspects of colonialism, could in such a short space of time build a pluralist democracy that would guarantee freedom. The difficulty was all the greater because having arrived at independence in different ways and times, Arabs were torn between the aspiration to unity and their own regional particularities profoundly anchored in their respective histories, even if overlaid by four hundred years of Ottoman domination.

Irresistibly given over to the desire for freedom in the comity of nations, Arab society, or at least its intelligentsia, for long closed its eyes to evidence of internal oppression. Nasserism, despite its indisputable internal tyranny and the terrible quarrels within its apparatus of rule long provided a feeling of liberation for which many at the time were willing to sacrifice the practice of domestic liberty. The intelligentsia was in general an accomplice of the mechanisms of oppression, for Arab intellectuals, especially in the Near East, have always kept close to power, either to flatter it and provide the conceptual framework for its discourse, or to fight it and prepare to take it over. Amid the great political causes which inspired Near Eastern Arab society, Arab unity, socialism, the liberation of Palestine, accelerated development, the recovery of national wealth, the intelligentsia was silent on problems of freedom and tyranny for fear of holding back the 'progress' of history by divisions of secondary importance. The ideology of religious fundamentalism being promoted since 1975 by States on the one hand and by popular religious brotherhoods on the other still mobilizes a number of Arab intellectuals in search of power and revolution.[2] As far as freedom is concerned, it augurs no good at all.

The rest of the intellectuals now mourn the loss of the liberty and the democracy unattained they had so little cherished in their youth. Often living overseas, even when at home they are in any case too marginalized to influence the political life of the regime in power. With political life becoming more and more dictatorial, no place remains for the expression of even mild differences of opinion. Egypt is the one timid exception; it still maintains traditions in public office, independent political figures and a large stratum of intellectuals remaining in the country and performing a certain cultural and social role.

Added to political despotism is the arbitrariness of the bureaucracies. The latter have developed considerably over the past thirty years, absorbing the tens of thousands of university graduates the labour market was unable to use. Incoherent and contradictory rules and nepotism and corruption unremittingly increasing with inflation characterize these bureaucracies, which make life a misery for the citizen, already politically deprived of freedom. Arbitrariness and bureaucratic corruption are the real scourges of Near Eastern society, paralyzing all efforts being made in other respects to ameliorate conditions for the average citizen. This situation is quite wrongly accepted as a permanent fact of social life. History shows, however, that no true development is possible without a bureaucracy, if not dedicated, at least competent and mobilized to act effectively in the main areas of social change.

But the generation of the 1950s and 1960s was far too committed to the external struggle against imperialism and the desire for Arab unity to concern itself with liberty and good administration at home. It was oblivious to the invisible but indissoluble link that exists between social liberty at home and liberation from foreign oppression. Only President Sadat had given it thought for a short while, re-establishing the pluralism of political parties and invoking the rule of law, but he was mainly preoccupied with combating the Nasser inheritance and with trying to please the West. The experiment was short-lived, being at variance from the beginning with the exercise of State-backed religious fundamentalism under pressure from the oil monarchies; it ended some months before his assassination in a large-scale hunt for opponents when over 1500 people were imprisoned in a single wave of arrests.

The 1970s in general were characterized by new assaults on freedom, on the one hand through the rise of religious fundamentalism, on the Right as on the Left, official as well as popular, a by-product of ill-digested oil wealth; on the other, through the whittling away of popular support for the Baath parties in Iraq and Syria, as well as the exercise of absolute personal power in the name of a one party State, once embodying certain political convictions but now atrophied by the cynicism of its leaders, political despotism and the despair of public opinion.

The finishing touches to our picture have unfortunately to be made in a mood of pessimism, for it is necessary to draw attention to the general deterioration of cultural life in Near Eastern society, as well as of the standard of education in universities and schools. With no role in the new oil-rich society, the only choice open to teachers, writers and artists is either to languish in misery and political oppression or to play the mercenary, whether in the service of monarchs, oil magnates, religious fundamentalism, or even the corrupt and discredited sole party. The school and university system, insufficiently equipped and collapsing under the weight of numbers, produced no more than cut-price education in the total absence of any coherent cultural whole.

This explains why Near Eastern society, and we come now to the second feature characterizing its development over the past quarter of a century, seems as if it is disintegrating and can be held together only by an increasingly violent political despotism. We have seen the disintegrating factors at work: the telescoping of epochs and of political sentiments which to a certain extent reflect those which appeared in industrializing society as well as in the mainstream of international political ideologies; a destructive torrent of oil wealth which again tied up the Arab Near East in a relationship of dependence and anomalous economic extroversion to the industrial society of the West; and failure in all the great aspirations: Arab unity, the revolution that delivers from poverty, exploitation and oppression, the liberation of Palestine, integration into the prosperity, power and stability of the neighbouring West. One after the other, all these dreams have been ground into the dust; and yet they were the dreams of all Arab thinkers since the last century, on which all contemporary Arab culture has been nourished. In this respect the political terrorism of the religious fundamentalist movements clearly marks the end of a world, in much the same way as Israel's destruction of Lebanon and its invasion and the siege of West Beirut, the most important centre of Arab political culture.

More than ever deadlocked in impossible equations, at the beginning of the 1980s Arab society was, lamentably, at a standstill. The range of political perception seemed reduced to mere incantatory denunciations of foreign plots. It was this that enabled the Israeli army to carry out its punitive expedition into Lebanon, ending in encirclement and destruction of a substantial part of the capital without any effective reaction from the principal Arab countries.

Saudi Arabia remains set in its policy of exclusively favouring the interests of the big Western capitalist powers. Despite pressure to establish diplomatic relations with the Soviet Union and its allies and despite the evident advantages that would result from this, its foreign policy remains static, thus in the eyes of its leaders assuring the stability of the throne under American protection.

Isolated Syria, on the other hand, has had no option but to continue leaning on the Soviet Union, leaving its relations with the United States at a standstill until some progress in resolving the Arab–Israeli conflict is made. It has become more and more a prisoner to the narrowness of its own power base, to the strict 'protection' it has chosen to give to the Palestinian cause, as well as to its presence in Lebanon, from which total retreat would merely confirm the decline of its regional power.

Though Egypt is slightly less tense at the domestic level since President Sadat's death, the balance of power there nonetheless remains unstable, because of an unequal and therefore precarious peace with Israel and, despite some signs of reconciliation on the horizon, of its official and continuing isolation in the Arab world.

Iraq is immobilized in a costly war with Iran which could have serious consequences for the whole balance of power in the Near East. The Iranian victory of Shiite religious fundamentalism could eventually spark off even faster disintegration, already registered in the course of past events.

As for the Palestinian resistance movements, their armed isolation in South Lebanon trapped them between the Israeli bludgeon, on the one hand, and the exigencies of Syria's equilibrium on the other, not to speak of the growing hostility of the Lebanese population, particularly in the south, exasperated by the destruction, casualties and instability the Israeli-Palestinian confrontation brought to free Lebanon, the only country bordering Israel that had been opened to armed Palestinian action. In keeping with the image of Near Eastern society, of which they were an integral part, the Palestinian movements remained a prey to all the centrifugal forces that afflict the Arab world politically, ideologically and culturally. This was highly detrimental to their line of action and allowed them to become hostages to the Israeli war machine's invasion of June 1982.

A world is being fragmented, or, perhaps one could also say, created. It remains to be seen whether this chaos, which is still simply allowed to subsist, will be able to give birth to a more coherent world, one less alienated from the realities of the late twentieth century. The notion of a cultured discordance with modern reality has frequently been used in this book to explain some of the impossible equations that Arab political society is expected to solve. An inadequate understanding of the complex geopolitical realities is without doubt the chief characteristic of the Arab ruling elites of the 1950s and 1960s. On the extreme Right of the political kaleidescope, this was best symbolized by King Faisal; on the extreme Left by the Syrian regime of the mid-sixties and by the various ultra-Left Palestinian and Lebanese movements.

It should, however, be borne in mind that these disturbed perceptions are also the result, firstly, of the Manichean world of the cold war, and secondly, of the guerrilla warfare in Latin America and the Cultural Revolution in China. But in the Near East the ground was particularly fertile. Historically, the seeds of the Manichean world of good and evil germinated in the region, for Mani was born in Persia at the beginning of the 3rd century A.D. and his doctrine for long flourished in the Near East, North Africa, as far as Mongolia and into the Europe of the Heresies. It is hardly surprising that Near Eastern society, tempted to a metaphysical facility in search of identity and disoriented by the vicissitudes of its own history, should have picked up modern ideologies through a Manichean filter. Those which disappointed it could simply be regarded as evil; Khomeini in Iran, for example, still treats the United States as the great Satan.

For those Arabs obsessed with the unsatisfactory aspect of relations with the West, there is again a strong temptation to yield to the Manichean perception of the geopolitical situation, offered by violent religious fundamentalism as an alternative to the modernizing ideologies of the preceding periods. The 'materialist' West, its civilization, its morals and its imperialism can thus be seen to personify Evil. After having been the object of all that was desired, the West had eluded them.

This cultural dis-synchronization was thus a third characteristic of the development of Arab society during this period. Maintained by despotism, in its turn it came to reinforce it, especially when it arose out of movements of violent protest, as in the case of the terrorism practised by the Islamic brotherhoods.

More experienced and better informed than in the 1950s and 1960s, today's Arab ruling elite could have escaped from this out-of-phase condition had it not become such a central feature of the sytem of political power, as well as of the political life in Arab society, completely cut off from reality at all levels – ideological, economic, cultural and social – hence the bad theatre of all those Summits of Arab League Heads of State, of the Rejection Front, of the Organization of the Islamic Conference, not to speak of all the short-lived attempts at unity made and unmade in the domain of mere words between one or other of the Near Eastern countries, without the least impact on reality. A shadow theatre punctuated by violent acts of terrorism but which is no longer even a bad or pale reflection of real society, from now on hidden from systematic observation.

Tediously predictable in delivery of diverse political and ideological discourse, the Near East is today totally unpredictable, an area where actual events are concerned in a chaos governed by a convergence subsisting between internal despotism and the external forces at work in the region. At the end of the twentieth century the Suez Canal and the oil pipelines that have sprung up everywhere have as much strategic value to the powers that be in this world as the famous Route to India in the previous century, of which the Near East was the principal avenue.

Disliked and manhandled by the over-powerful West in this century as in the last, Near Eastern Arab society can expect nothing from it. It is in the nature of things that the rich and powerful remain selfish. All the imprecations in the world against imperialism and the 'Great Satan' will not change that reality. It is likewise a waste of precious energy to try and induce the West to recognize that its view of the Other is oppressive and reductionist in the secret hope that, in the final analysis, this will lead to liking and respect.[3] Such an attitude is in itself a sign of cultural out-of-phasedness: hatred of a foreign society that fails to respond to the desire to be appreciated confirms the state of dependence and disphasedness of a society relative to reality which is then made without it.

This is perhaps where the real tragedy of the Arab Near East lies, especially since the constant schisms that shake and tear Arab society apart are centred on the relationship with the big powers. The intensity of gaze fixed on the outside world leaves little scope for examining internal evils. In its turn this element forms an integral part of the despotic system that governs Arab society, for a continuing tendency towards schism and factionalism is yet another way of reinforcing the authoritarianism of power. An alienating or alienated relationship with the West, the detonator of the centrifugal tendencies in the Near Eastern society, is the fourth characteristic of the historical period in question that contributes to its stagnation.

The fact remains that the Near East can only be partially understood. It is true that today it seems to give way under the weight of a double despotism that contents itself with merely presiding over a disintegrating world externally that of Israeli military power, internally that of political domains more than ever lacking legitimacy. This sort of management works through a disphasedness cultural characterized by a marked Manicheism and an alienated relationship to the industrialized world. By its very nature, the latter stirs up the centrifugal forces that cause schisms, which in their turn reinforce the authoritarianism of power. But behind this image which Arab society projects of itself there is nothing to indicate with any degree of certainty which of the forces in gestation are most likely to become active in future generations. The cultural degradation presaged by the wretched condition of the educational systems might in fact be compensated for by the expectation of higher economic standards, and thus of modernity, germinating at all levels of society during the historical period reviewed.

In the struggle between modernity and archaic religious particularisms which will undoubtedly continue to characterize the political and cultural life of Near Eastern Arab society, two factors are likely to be decisive: firstly, the attitude of the Arab intelligentsia, that is to say whether it manages to free itself from its fascination with power and its orbit, and whether it acknowledges the connection between internal freedom and freedom from outside oppression; and secondly, the Christian West's attitude to the Arab–Israeli conflict discussed at length in Chapter 7.

But the economic future, particularly in the sphere of oil wealth, will play a determining role. The eventual disappearance of this artificial wealth, with all the internal and external constraints it has imposed on Arab society, will undoubtedly ensure better conditions for the transition from a state of disintegration (with its internal despotism and external alienation) to the creation of a new order in internal freedom and external liberation. Oil has effectively destroyed the Near Eastern economy's productive bases, already weakened by the assault of Western industrial production in the nineteenth century. On the other hand it has raised the standard of living, but without any local productive effort, itself a powerful factor in the area's alienation and dependence.

For some years now, the Arab elites have focused their attention exclusively on commerce, administration, managing oil fortunes in one way or another and acting the intermediary for the big international companies. But since they operate within the orbit of despotic power of the various regimes, their leanings towards a Manichean metaphysics is thereby reinforced, a return to production, to mobilizing society into satisfying its own needs by generating autonomous sources of material subsistence, is liable to drastically change the present historical landscape of the Near East, but as long as the elite concerns itself only with administering oil wealth, a by-product of the industrialization of other societies, there is little chance that the Near East will escape the negative constraints that have been described and which are sources of disintegration and a lack of predictability. These constraints are increasingly capable of producing serious upheavals of origin, both internal, due to explosion of regional tensions and contradictions and external, due to keener conflicts between great power interests.

The persistence of the oil factor, of the Arab–Israeli conflict and of the Iran menace creates fertile ground for this unpredictability, a product of the unfortunate confluence of internal and external factors at play in the history of the Near East.

Appendix: The economic evolution of the Middle East

Historical data and periodization

Socialist state administration in co-operation with the Soviet Union: 1956–70

To have dwelt on the diverse aspects of the Arab Middle Eastern economy in the course of the book would have been to weigh the text down with it; this is particularly true in the case of vigorous political economies established by the modernizing socialist regimes in Egypt, Syria and Iraq under the stimulus of Nasserite ideology and that of the Baath party. On the other hand, it has been absolutely necessary to dwell on the copious socio-economic and political effects of the tidal wave of oil in the Middle East, which for a large part annulled the results of attempts at accelerated and auto-centred development particularly characteristic of the economic policy of the Nasser regime in Egypt and the Baathist regime in Syria between 1966 and 1973.

These policies were in both cases based on the setting up of huge infrastructures. The construction of the giant dams with Soviet aid constituted a basic symbol of economic liberation brought about in a 'socialist' framework. This is the reason intense polemical discussions developed surrounding the dams and their usefulness for the national economy. Just as much in Egypt as in Syria, the dams became the object of virulent criticisms with regard to how they had been built and the inauspicious effects they would necessarily have on the ecological and agricultural equilibrium of the two countries: the disappearance of the Nile silt in Egypt, indispensable for the fertility of the soil; the increase in the salinity of the soil in the Jazira region of Syria, also reducing fertility.

In fact, in order to be able to judge with some objectivity the achievements of the progressive Arab regimes between the mid-1950s and the beginning of the 1970s, it is again necessary to put the economic policies established during this period into historical perspective. The economy of the Arab Middle East developed more or less in the colonial mode from the end of the reign of Muhammad Ali in the middle of the nineteenth century until the middle of the twentieth century. In hock to European societies, the Middle East economy was certainly modernized during this period but in the most strict financial, technical and commercial dependence. The benefits of this modernization primarily profited the European colonies implanted in the Middle East, whose numbers increased considerably between 1850 and 1950, and a limited local elite associated with colonial prosperity.

During the 1930s, a kind of capitalism that was local, industrial, agrarian and commerical began timidly to emerge, notably in Egypt; its development was enhanced by World War II when the needs of the Allied armies and the mobilization of all European resources for the war effort injected it with a new stimulus. A local bourgeoisie thus existed at the beginning of the 1950s; it lived in tight symbiosis with the large landowners and the traditional aristocracy who retained the largest share of local political power. This bourgeoisie was certainly nationalist; but its social base was still too weak, its economic assets insufficient and in consequence its interests too intimately linked with the traditionally dominant forces who had compromised with foreigners for generations. It could not thus itself be at the forefront of the economic and social change Arab society was impatiently awaiting after the acquisition of independence; neither was it in a position to offer the means for socio-economic change aspired to by the officers who took power in Syria in 1949, then in Egypt in 1952 and finally in Iraq in 1958. The capitalist West having been scarcely aware of these aspirations, being too preoccupied with the struggle against communist 'subversion' at a remarkable juncture in the cold war, it was to the Soviet Union that the new military elites turned in order to secure for themselves the means of promoting rapid economic development.

This orientation was at first rather contrary to the ideology of the military elites who were for the most part great admirers of the society and technology of the capitalist West and in addition mistrustful of Marxism. But the growing support given by the Western powers to the State of Israel and their refusal to supply weapons to Arab countries pushed the Middle East into the arms of the Soviet Union. The United States had of course in 1956 demanded the retreat of the French, English and Israeli troops who had tried to invade Egypt, but it seems they were too late. The nationalist fever triggered off by the nationalization of the Suez Canal, followed by the tripartite aggression, pushed the principal countries of the Arab Middle East into a 'socialist' climate favourable to the spread of nationalization. The local bourgeoisies and the landed aristocracy reacted very badly to the first measures of agrarian reform and the development of the public sector. President Nasser, who introduced these first reforms in Syria as well for the benefit of the Syrian-Egyptian union achieved in 1958, accused the bourgeoisie of connivance with 'feudalism' for which they sabotaged the union in 1961. From then on, the tendency towards establishment of state control of the economy became irresistible in Egypt; it then became dominant in Syria from 1963 and especially from 1966 as the Baathist military consolidated its power. The development of economic co-operation with the Soviet Union was a natural complement to this. The trend would be reversed from the beginning of the 1970s, in favour of the general political changes which have been broadly analyzed (Chapters 2 and 4).

The evaluation of the state-controlled period presents contrasting aspects; here it is possible to describe only the general tendencies. It is incontestibly in the socio-cultural field that the most striking achievements were made at first: generalization of education, free access to the state scholastic system, development of university education which had until then been the privilege of the elite; democratization of medical care by the extension of free public medicine; increase in opportunities for stable employment and thus for social promotion by the considerable development of the industrial and administrative public sector; generalization of female education and the massive integration of women into active life are also, in this context, an important element in the raising of standards of living in families where from then on several salaries would swell the domestic budget, giving access to modes of consumption previously forbidden to large strata of the urban lower middle class.

The general economic development was unfortunately not sufficient to justify these important improvements in standards of living, much more costly as the rate of demographic growth sharply increased everywhere (more than 3 per cent a year on average). Socio-educational infrastructures had never in fact been able to develop at a sufficient pace, neither qualitatively nor quantitatively, to ensure free cover for the needs of the population. This led not only to the permanence of the phenomenon of illiteracy but also to a general decline in the standard of education and an overburdening of medical infrastructures. To this must be added, in the case of Egypt, the gross insufficiency of urban infrastructures and their decay in the face of accelerated urbanization, the result of an irresistible rural exodus. This exodus also affected Syria and Iraq.

In fact in none of the three countries did agrarian reforms and the great hydraulic works succeed in resolving the misery of the peasantry. The co-operative networks established to help peasants who had had land allocated to them only profited the well-to-do agricultural strata. Lacking means, the poor peasants, agricultural workers, share-croppers or small landowners were forced to give up exploiting the portions of land allocated to them by the implementation of agrarian reform. The allocations had been very slow everywhere, as had the extension of the networks of hydraulic irrigation.

All these obstructions to 'modernization' were of course put on the account of state socialism and co-operation with the Soviet Union. This facilitated the swing during the subsequent period towards a more receptive approach to western capitalism, the loosening of state control and the encouragement of the local private sector.

However, the evaluation has other aspects which are positive. In Egypt, the years 1960–5 saw an important rise in industrialization under the stimulus of the state; the country even managed to export industrial products to Africa in not insignificant quantities while at the same time supplying a local market avid to consume and where foreign products had disappeared. The rate of economic growth attained by Egypt during this period was consistently 6–7 per cent per annum, a remarkable achievement for an economy which had until then been narrowly dependent on the international demand for cotton and on the level of prices for this raw material on the world markets. The accomplishment of work on the High Dam at Aswan meant that there were significant quantities of electricity to fuel this industrial effort and to electrify the countryside, an important element where standard of living is concerned. This economic 'take-off' was first halted by the war in Yemen, where from 1963 Egypt supported the republican forces against the royalists who were propped up by Saudi Arabia, and then by the defeat in 1967 and especially the War of Attrition which led Egypt against Israel in the Suez Canal Zone and cost Egypt dearly in economic destruction due to Israeli reprisals.

In Syria the party of 'leftist' officers who seized power in 1966 brought about a remarkable feat in the domain of infrastructures: development of the ports of Latakia and Tartus, notable renovation and extension of the railway network, until then extremely primitive, unification of isolated zones by the extension of the road network in parallel with the railways; construction of an international airport at Damascus; starting construction of the high dam on the Euphrates; development of the meagre oil resources of the country and construction of a refinery which today allows Syria to produce 10 million tons of oil. In Iraq too, as in Syria, thanks to Russian co-operation, the country managed to double its oil production despite the boycott of big oil companies since the laws of General Kassem in 1961 which annulled non-exploited oil concessions. It was also during the regime of Nasser that there began in Egypt an active policy of prospecting for oil, but this time with the assistance of the American companies, a policy which today gives Egypt a production of 20 million tons.

It is in fact difficult to form a judgement of the results of this period; the experiments were either too short or brutally thwarted by the military evolution and general politics of the Middle East and the omnipotence of oil which dominated the period starting in the early 1970s. One remains struck, however, by the vulnerability of the Nasserite economic renaissance; but as was the case with Muhammad Ali in the last century, it seems that it was an untimely military expansion outside Egypt (the war in Yemen) and then the false calculations in the confrontation with Israel which caused the collapse of the industrial base which served as a support for the whole policy of economic and social development, auto-centred and state-controlled. In order to appreciate the achievements of this administration, its limitations must be recognized; they are those of the socio-political horizon of the leaders of the period, analyzed in detail in the course of this work.

Administration by oil revenue in co-operation with the capitalist West: 1970–80

The socio-economic administration of the Arab Middle East by finance from the oil sector, which replaced socialist state-controlled administration, scarcely seems to have been any happier. It has been broadly outlined in the course of this work, so less will be said of it here. To its credit, the extraordinary rise in the levels of consumption throughout the Arab Middle East must be pointed out; this rise was financed by aid from the oil-exporting countries to the countries known as the 'battlefield' (Syria, Egypt, Jordan) whose territories were occupied in 1967, but also by the considerable remittances from migrants from these countries who had gone to work in the oil-producing nations. The relaxation of import and exchange controls, as well as the liberalization of emigration laws, if not actual encouragement as was the case in Egypt, allowed the free circulation of money and consumer goods. The so-called 'open door' policy has been mentioned several times, renowned especially in Sadat's Egypt but operating in Syria too.

On the other hand, the negative aspects of this period are innumerable. In the first place, there was inflation which spread swiftly and widely from the Peninsula to the other countries. In countries used to long stability of price levels, the social upheavals were considerable. The solution lay in savage waves of emigration to the oil-exporting countries where fabulous dvelopment projects made possible by the quadrupling of the price of oil at the end of 1973 offered all sorts of opportunities from unskilled labour to high administrative posts and involving all the fiddles and all the miracles which lead to rapid wealth. All at once, Egypt, Syria, Lebanon and Jordan were emptied of their best trained personnel: teachers, civil servants, doctors, university professors, lawyers, contractors, engineers, bankers . . . a haemorrhage laden with consequences in these already traditionally maladministered countries.

Secondly, the open door to foreign capital and companies meant that local real-estate speculation was unleashed. At first it was the newly rich from the oil-producing countries who could at last buy or build in Damascus or Cairo, prestigious capitals for these men from the desert, luxury appartments or blocks to let; but also the foreign companies saw a market extraordinary for its dense population open up again to them, in addition to the underpopulated market of the Peninsula where everything was still to be done. Colossal local fortunes were thus made selling apartments and offices to purchasers for whom no price was too high. The result was a formidable housing crisis which still affects the middle and lower classes today.

Inflation, emigration to the Peninsula, the massive presence of foreign companies and those newly rich from oil: too many bubble schemes were created, too many immoral speculations, too much easy money and corruption in countries where the average income of a poor farmer, a petty official and a middle-ranking employee ranged between $100 and $250 a month. The only survivors in these social strata were workers in the private sector, especially skilled ones: emigration to the Gulf in this socio-professional category was such that those who stayed behind saw their salaries climb rapidly because of the very strong local demand, in building in particular.

The rage to consume spread like a contagious disease throughout the whole of Arab society. The countries of the Peninsula were an enormous show-case, a giant supermarket for all the products and gadgets of Western and Japanese consumerism; the migrants sent home the latest Japanese and German electronic equipment. After the austerity of the preceding period, the appetite for consumer goods seemed inexhaustible; it still exists today. The counterpart was obviously the decline of local industry which was unable to compete either in quality or quantity with foreign industry and which was often paralyzed by the lack of competent and honest managers because of emigration and, in the case of Egypt, because of the deterioration of relations with the Soviet Union. Also, in many instances, the decline of agriculture assumed dramatic proportions on the Arab-world scale: food production covered no more than 50 per cent of consumer needs whereas 20 years earlier Arab agricultural production had had met more than 80 per cent of food requirements.

In fact, if the oil sector and the financial flow it releases were to be taken away from the national product statistics of the Middle East, a lowering of national production could be seen in many cases. In effect, almost everywhere, the agricultural and industrial sectors have seen their contribution to the national product reduced as that of the mining and services sector increases, solely as an off-shoot of oil prosperity. The oil sector apart, the national *per capita* income throughout the Arab world has risen on average less than in other Third World countries, notably Latin America and Asia. Among gross domestic products in the Arab world, those of the oil-producing countries represented 75 per cent of the total in 1979; the processing industries only represented 8.1 per cent of national products in the Arab countries (with a maximum of 16 per cent in Egypt) and the whole of Arab processing industry only represented 0.2 per cent of world industry. The oil sector apart, the average *per capita* income in all the Arab countries in 1979 did not exceed 1000 dollars per annum as against 8000–14,000 dollars for the industrialist capitalist countries (except Ireland, Italy and Great Britain where the product *per capita* was 4210, 5250 and 6320 dollars respectively). If the oil sector is included, the total Arab national revenues in 1979 represented 301 billion dollars which was less than a third of that of Japan (1019 billion dollars) for a population a third bigger, a little more than half that of France (531 billion dollars) for a population three times bigger; in fact it scarcely exceeded the Italian national revenue (298 billion dollars).[1]

Oil has incontestably allowed a rise in standards of living, but very unequally; against that, it has blocked true economic development based on well-founded industrialization and efficient agricultural modernization. It has also created a formidable external dependency which has rendered the economy of the Middle East more vulnerable than ever.

The second oil shock in 1979–80, originating in the Iranian Revolution, will contribute to maintaining the artificial prosperity of the Middle East for a few years. At 30–34 dollars a barrel, oil was more than ever a money machine so powerful that no government could see the need for adjustment to keep afloat non-oil sectors of the economy.

The upheaval in the oil market and the crisis of Arab economies: 1980–6

The level reached by crude oil prices during the first two years of the eighties was to bring about a complete reversal of price trend. This reversal was helped by various factors: a sharp reduction in the energy consumption of the industrialized countries; the deliberate policy of Saudi Arabia, by far the largest OPEC producer, of stopping the trend in price increases, by overglutting the market with oil, thus helping the Western countries to redress their huge trade deficit with OPEC countries and at the same time allowing the Kingdom to re-establish its position as the largest world oil exporter and the decisive force inside OPEC; the policy of other oil exporters of increasing indebtedness (Mexico, Algeria, Nigeria, Venezuela) or to finance their war needs (Iran and Iraq).

Thus by 1984 it was clear that the oil market was already reversing in favour of the buyers (industrialized countries) and by the end of 1985 the price of crude oil began to crumble dramatically to reach 8–10 dollar level in early 1986. This crumbling of the price, together with a sharp decline of the United States dollar *vis-à-vis* other industrialized currencies, turned all the oil-exporting countries into naked beggars. Except for the Gulf Kingdoms and Emirates who enjoyed large amounts of foreign exchange reserves, all other oil-exporting countries were declaring bankruptcy in servicing their foreign debt, as Mexico already had in 1982, while other Arab countries, heavily subsidized up to now by aid from oil-exporting countries, began also to stop servicing their foreign debt (Egypt, Morocco, Sudan).

OPEC, which had terrorized the industrialized world in the seventies, was now being viewed as a 'paper tiger', unable even to smooth the decline of the oil price, so dramatically sharp that it was now an embarrassment for the world economy. As if to add shame to disaster, no consensus could be reached inside OPEC to determine an export ceiling to be allocated between member countries in order to stop the oil glut.

The policy of Saudi Arabia on one hand and the sharp differences within OPEC, due in particular to the Iraq–Iran war, paralyzed the proper functioning of OPEC. Only through United States pressure and a change of oil minister in Saudi Arabia could OPEC come to some minimal agreement during the second half of 1986 and stabilize the oil market at the level of 18 dollars a barrel by abiding by allocation of export quotas.

In the meantime, the Arab economies were all under stress. Even in countries like Saudi Arabia and Kuwait dramatic budget cuts were made to match the decline in oil receipts, which in turn caused many workshops to close, thus affecting the level of remittances of Arab immigrant workers in the Arabian Peninsula. Economic hardship was aggravated elsewhere in the Arab world by a severe draught (Sudan and Morocco in particular) and an escalation of food imports, in addition to the severe medicine imposed by the FMI and the World Bank wherever countries could not repay their foreign debts. Even in Lebanon, which had so well resisted years of war destruction and internal strife, the decline of the Lebanese pound signalled the end of the resilience of the Lebanese economy based on its intense relations with the other Arab economies.

The economic crises of 1984–6 provided a proof that 'capitalism' that had looked so nice in the seventies after the 'socialism' of the sixties, was another trick from the 'devil' to weaken Arab societies. More than ever, Western systems would appear to be a war machine directed against the masses of the East: this feeling would open wide the doors inside the lower strata of the population to the credibility of a 'Muslim economic system', embodied in Muslim fundamentalist creed, which could help in salvaging whatever could be saved from the economic disasters caused by both capitalism and socialism in Arab society. 'Militant' Islam of the Khomeini variety will not only have a political and ideological cause against the West, but also an economic dimension to cope with economic hardship and social distress caused first by the sharp increase in oil prices (1975–83) and then their sudden fall (1984–6).

Notes

Introduction

1 Muslim Arabs represent scarcely a quarter of the total number of Muslims (approximately 150 million out of 600 million).
2 Among the reforms of Ataturk in Turkey at the beginning of this century was the rejection of the Arabic alphabet in favour of the Latin alphabet in order to mark the desire to belong to the world of the western Mediterranean.
3 It is not possible to be precise about the numbers of adherents in the different minority communities; where figures exist, more often than not they are passionately contested by one minority or another. Those advanced here are approximate 'golden mean' estimates, but no statistical exactitude is claimed.
4 Not to be confused with an even more celebrated work by al-Shahrastani (1086–1153), *Al-milal wa-al-nihal*, which also describes the diverse Jewish and Christian sects, as well as other belief systems which are difficult to classify, such as the Sabaean.
5 In the non-Arab Middle East, in Turkey, the same phenomenon is observed.
6 M. Gilsenan, *Saint and Sufi in Modern Egypt. An Essay in the Sociology of Religion*, Oxford University Press, 1973.
7 An Islamic review published in London, apparently financed by the Arab oil-producing countries, whose anxieties concerning modernism will be analyzed later in this book, devoted one of its recent issues to congratulating itself on the disappearance of the secular heritage of Ataturk (*Arabia, the Islamic World Review*, November 1981, no. 3; theme on the cover under the title, 'The crumbling edifice of Kemalism'), an absurdity arrived at by state fundamentalism attempting to compensate for excessive laxity of attitude towards the harmful aspects of Western politics in the Middle East, as is discussed in Chapter 6.

Chapter 1   From 1956 to the death of Nasser

1 These terms are borrowed from the titles of two excellent books in French by the Egyptian novelist Albert Cossery: *Mendiants et Orgueilleux* (Paris, Le Livre de Poche, 1977); *La Violence et la Derision* (Paris, Jean-Cyrille Godefroy, 1981).
2 Abdel Nasser was actually the second President of republican Egypt. His predecessor, General Neguib (1953–4), however, had so little

impact on events that it is unquestionably Nasser who appears as the real leader of the victorious Republic that ousted the monarchy. (On Neguib, see p. 43.)

3 *A le recherche d'une identité* (Paris, Fayard, 1978).

4 The Hegira is the day when the Prophet Muhammad left Mecca to settle in Medina, in the year 622 AD.

5 F. Braudel, *La Mediterranée et le monde mediterranéen a l'époque de Philippe II* (2 vols., Paris, A. Colin, 1966, 2nd edition).

6 Organization of Petroleum Exporting Countries.

7 See Chapter 5, OPEC or the PLO.

8 The Meiji Emperor (1868–1912) broke up feudal Japan, brought his country out of its underdevelopment and in a few years transformed it, successfully, into a great industrial power.

9 A term used in Islamic countries to refer to specialists in religious knowledge who carry out various functions in society, including teaching, declaring the law and preaching in mosques.

10 In Braudel, *La Mediterranée*.

11 Lawrence Durrell's *Alexandria Quartet* describes the richness of Alexandria's cultural and ethnic life.

12 Notably the short reign of Abbas (1849–1954), a grandson of Muhammad Ali, who abandoned secular modernism in favour of a return to Islamic fundamentalism.

13 E. Said, *Orientalism* (New York, Pantheon Books, 1978).

14 For example, R. Garaudy, *L'Islam habite notre avenir* (Paris, Seuil, 1981).

15 These reforms published in the form of an imperial decree were called *Tanzimat*; the word *tanzim* meaning 'regulation, arrangement'. They mainly stipulate equality between Muslims and non-Muslims and the abolition of revenue farming.

16 D. S. Landes, *Bankers and Pashas: International Finance and Economic Imperialism in Egypt* (London, Heinemann, 1958).

17 Conference of non-aligned countries from three continents (Africa, Asia and America) also attended by delegates from the popular movements.

18 Born in Cairo in 1912, he became famous especially for a trilogy of novels, the titles of which were borrowed from street names in working-class areas, and which tell the story of an Egyptian family confronted by the upheavals of twentieth-century Egyptian society.

19 M. Abou Chedid Nasr, 'L'idéologie nationale arabe dans le discours de Gamal Abdel Nasser, 1952–1970', Ph.D. thesis, Paris, Sorbonne, 1979.

20 Chapter 6 on Lebanon describes the complexities of religious and tribal diversity.

Chapter 2 From the Khartoum summit to the October war

1 Lutfi al-Khuli, in 1975.

2 On State religious fundamentalism encouraged by the oil monarchies, see Chapter 6.

3 A term for the Christians of Egypt who for the most part are not in communion with Rome and form their own Coptic Church, headed by a Patriarch. The Coptic Church is Monophysite, holding that Christ has only one nature, the divine.

4 The totally theoretical embargo decided on 7 June by seven oil-producing States (Iraq, Algeria, Kuwait, Saudi Arabia, Libya, Bahrain and Qatar) on oil supplies to Great Britain and the United States, Israel's main supporters, was consequently 'lifted' at the Khartoum summit.

5 For further details on the economic development of the Near East see Chapters 3 and 4.

6 Sadat's policy towards Israel as well as the Camp David Peace Agreements will be examined in Chapters 6 and 7.

7 On 30 May 1972, an operation claimed by the Popular Front for the Liberation of Palestine (PFLP), and carried out by the Red Star Army, whose ties with the United Red Army were not, however, established.

8 Sunnis, or followers of the Sunna, the sayings and deeds of the Prophet Muhammad, form the more orthodox branch of Islam. Eighty per cent of Muslims are Sunnis, then come the Shias and the Ismailis, and, with less clear connections with Islam because of their esoteric and syncretist doctrines, the Alawis and Druzes.

9 Dr Noureddin Atassi, Head of State; Dr Yussuf Zuayyen, Head of Government; and Dr Ibrahim Makhos, Minister of Foreign Affairs.

10 The PFLP leaders George Habash and Wahdih Haddad are Christians; Michel Aflaq, one of the founders of Baath, is Christian; the team of Syrian officers that took over control of the party during the 1960s were first and foremost Alawis, and secondarily Ismailis and Druzes. Khalid Begdash, leader of the Syrian Communist party, is of Kurdish origin; his counterpart in the Lebanese Communist party, George Hawi, is Christian, as is Naief Hawatmeh, leader of the Democratic Front for the Liberation of Palestine (DFLP); and finally Kamal Jumblatt, a dominant figure in the Lebanese National Movement and leader of the Socialist party assassinated in 1977, was Druze.

11 From 1963 to 1968 Iraq was governed by Abdel Salam Arif, and after his death in a helicopter accident in April 1966 by his brother Abdel Ashman. In 1968, Ahmad Hassan al-Bakr and Saddam Hussein jointly took power, which the latter still holds.

12 Liberation movement of the Western Sahara and Rio de Oro.

13 Gadaffi in fact intercepted a commercial airline carrying putschist officers from London and Khartoum, which was flying over the Mediterranean close to Libyan airspace, and handed them over to the Sudanese Head of State, who sent them before a firing squad.

14 First President of independent Algeria, overthrown by a military coup led by Colonel Boumedienne on 19 June 1965.

15 Liberation Front of occupied South Yemen.

16 National Liberation Front.

Chapter 3   The rise of the tyranny of oil

1   Standard Oil of New Jersey (American), Royal Dutch Shell (Anglo-Dutch), British Petroleum (English), Gulf (American), Texas (American), Standard Oil of California (American), and Socony-Mobil (American).

2   Algeria, Saudi Arabia, United Arab Emirates, Ecuador, Indonesia, Gabon, Kuwait, Iraq, Libya, Nigeria, Qatar, Venezuela and Iran.

3   This refers to the Club of Rome whose first 'Meadows' report was published in 1978 under the suggestive title of *Halte a la Croissance?* (Paris, Fayard).

4   Details of this oil embargo and its real impact are found in Chapter 4, p. 111.

5   The second oil pipeline that crosses Syria runs from Iraq.

6   Cyrus II, the Great, was Great King of Meoles and the Persians from 558 to 528 BC.

7   For details on this subject see Chapters 4 and 5.

8   *Ibn Seoud ou la naissance d'un royaume, Le Roi Saud ou l'Orient a l'heure des releves, Faycal, le roi d'Arabie* (Paris, Albin Michel).

9   From the word *mahdi* which means 'Messiah', returning to earth to re-establish the rule of God; the movement's founder, Muhammad Ahmad Ibn Abdullah (1843–85), was known by the title of *mahdi.*

10   Derived from the name of the movement's founder, Sidi Muhammad al-Sanusi (1787–1859).

11   In 1933, Standard Oil of California negotiated an oil concession of 900,000 km², extended to 1,160,000 km² in 1939. The first discoveries of oil in marketable quantities went up from 500,000 barrels per day (b/d) in 1949 to 1.2 million in 1960, 8.2 million in 1974 and 10.5 million in 1980.

12   President of the Indonesian Republic (1945–66), ousted by General Suharto's *coup d'état.*

13   The bank's capital is held in 'Islamic dinars', but since a dinar is equal to one unit of the Special Drawing Rights (SDR) created in 1969 by the International Monetary Fund, it is thus only a question of labelling.

14   See Chapter 7, p. 194.

15   It was while the forces of law and order were breaking up a demonstration against the introduction of television into the kingdom that the brother of the king's assassin was killed.

16   A religious militia created by King Abdel Aziz Ibn Saud at the beginning of the century to create respect in the kingdom for Wahhabi religious practices.

17   Evidence of such affinities was witnessed in Kissinger's anxiety on his first trip to Saudi Arabia:
    During the flight from Amman to Riyadh [say his biographers], Kissinger kept appearing in the press compartment and exchanging pleasantries, apparently to relieve his own anxiety over what reception awaited him in Faisal's kingdom, where anti-Semitism was rampant. At one moment he pointed to three journalists whom he knew to be Jews and stiffly announced to them: 'You three will get off the plane last'. At another moment, he half joked:

'Only the Wasps (White Anglo-Saxon Protestants) can disembark here.' His eyes ran over the group. 'Are there no Wasps among you?' Several hands went up. 'Well,' he decided, 'you will get off first.' There were some nervous laughs. (M. and B. Kalb, *Kissinger, ses origines, sa formation, son ascension, son apogee* (Paris, R. Laffont, 1975), p. 491.)

18 There are different versions of this anti-Semitic pamphlet, but all accuse the Jews of an international conspiracy to dominate the world. By subtly mixing anti-Semitism with nostalgia for the past and a dislike of change, the pamphlets accuse Jews and freemasonry of fomenting violent revolutions all over the world and of changing ideas and morals. According to this version, the Bolshevik Revolution, like the French Revolution, would merely be the product of a world-wide Jewish conspiracy.

19 See Chapter 2, p. 68.

20 In November 1979, in the middle of the pilgrimage season, a group of Muslim extremists took armed possession of the Mosque of Mecca. It took several days and help from the French gendarmerie to dislodge them and to extinguish the start of a rebellion.

Chapter 4   One war, two epochs

1 The Plan for the partition of Palestine gave the Jewish community 14,500 km², out of a total area of 26,323 km², i.e. 57 per cent of the Palestinian territory. By conquest, Israel expanded its State in 1948–9 to 20,850 km², i.e. 80 per cent. Yet in 1948, the Jewish community set up in Palestine under the British mandate represented exactly 30 per cent of the population (only 7 per cent around 1920), and possessed less than 6 per cent of the lands. In the war of 1967, Israel completed the conquest of Palestine by occupying the West Bank of Jordan and the Gaza Strip and, in addition, also occupied the Sinai Peninsula and the Golan Heights in Syria.

2 This refers to the famous Cairo agreements signed in November 1969, in the Egyptian capital, under the aegis of President Nasser, between the PLO and the Lebanese army. (See Chapter 6, p. 158; note 11, p. 266.)

3 'A fool, a clown, a buffoon who goes on stage every day' was how Henry Kissinger spoke of Sadat to Golda Meir, head of the Israeli government (M. Golan, *The Secret Conversations of Henry Kissinger* (New York, Quadrangle/The Times Book Company, 1976), p. 114).

4 The figure put out by the international press and Israeli sources. General Shazli, Chief of Staff of the Eyptian army at the time, gives a figure of 7752 (in a book on the October 1973 war, *The Crossing of Suez* (London, Third World Centre, 1980, p. 113)).

5 A resolution passed on 22 November 1976 and calling for Israel's withdrawal from the occupied territories without, however, mentioning the existence of the Palestinians, except indirectly by referring to 'a just solution to the refugee problem'.

6 With the famous rider, 'an elite people, self-assured and domi-

neering', which de Gaulle used to refer to Israel at a press conference on 28 November 1967.

7 John M. Blair, *The Control of Oil* (London, Macmillan, 1977), p. 207.

8 Grouped in OAPEC (Organization of Arab Petroleum Producing Countries) comprising Algeria, Saudi Arabia, Bahrain, United Arab Emirates, Egypt, Iraq, Kuwait, Libya, Qatar and Syria; not to be confused with OPEC.

9 Saudi Arabia and the United Arab Emirates immediately announced a reduction of 10 per cent of their production. Certain countries thought of banning exports to the United States and to the Netherlands, one European country that hardly made any attempt to hide its sympathies towards Israel. In fact, all these decisions were confused and nobody really knows to what extent they were implemented.

10 See Chapter 3, p. 78–9.

11 Revenues of the consortium of American oil companies operating in Saudi Arabia rose from 1.1 billion dollars in 1972 to 3.2 billion dollars in 1973. In the first quarter of 1974, Texaco increased its profits by 123 per cent, Shell by 178 per cent and BP by 277 per cent.

12 Alert in the American army consists of five degrees in descending order. It was widely said that this dramatic gesture was designed to distract American opinion's attention away from the famous Watergate scandal which was in development and which some months later led to Nixon's resignation.

13 Figures taken from the memoirs of General Shazli, Egyptian Chief of Staff during the October war. Unlikely to be suspected of anti-Sovietism, especially since he was fired by President Sadat as a punishment for Israel's victorious attack of the Desevoir, he went over to the opposition to Sadat's regime in 1978 (*The Crossing of Suez*, pp. 186–7). Another point made by General Shazli was that from 30 October the Soviet Union and the United States supplied by sea respectively 63,000 tons to Egypt and Syria and 33,210 tons to Israel (*ibid.*, p. 187). Since at that time nothing had yet been done to bring about peace or more simply even a reasonably permanent armistice, the super-powers therefore had to rearm their clients.

14 Nevertheless, fighting continued on the Golan Heights (see Chapter 5, p. 122).

15 *Business Week*, 13 January 1975.

16 Edition of 7 October 1974.

17 Arab geographical vocabulary distinguishes between the Mashriq, or East, to describe the Near and Middle East region, and the Maghrib, or West, to describe North Africa. Boumedienne is thus considered by Arabs to be from the West.

Chapter 5   OPEC or the PLO?

1   Speech delivered at the inauguration of the Second International Fair in Algiers, 4 September 1965, nine years before the United Nations Special Assembly.

2   It is true that the majority obtained for that Resolution (72 votes for, 35 against and 32 abstentions) was clearly weaker than that of 14 October 1974 in which the PLO was invited to take part in the Assembly's debates.

3   See Chapter 7.

4   Speech of 20 December 1977.

5   See Chapters 3 and 4.

6   Solemn declaration adopted by the Summit over this issue, 6 March 1975.

7   See Chapter 2.

8   See Chapter 4.

9   See Chapter 6.

10   The title of a well-known work that has become a classic of journalistic literature on petro-dollars. (Michael Field, *A Hundred Million Dollars a Day: Inside the World of Middle East Money* (London Sidgwick & Jackson).

11   This excellent expression is taken from the novelist Doris Lessing (*The Golden Notebook*, London, Michael Joseph, 1972).

12   Until the middle of the 1960s the Arab world was a net exporter of foodstuffs. In 1980 it imported more than half of the foodstuffs it consumed.

13   'We knew how we became Arabs in Israeli prisons; we knew how we became Palestinians in Arab prisons' (trans. from French). (Mahmoud Darwiche, Palestinian poet.)

Chapter 6   The disintegration of the Lebanon

1   In the case of Lebanon, it is, however, necessary to mention the troubles of 1958, result of the great popular wave of Nasserist Pan-Arabism which swept the whole of the Near East shaking the Jordanian throne, overthrowing the Iraqi monarchy, and bringing about the Syrian-Egyptian Union. This amounted to a mini civil war, accompanied by the landing of American marines in Beirut, more symbolic than with really warlike intentions, and to which a reforming general, Fuad Chehab, put an end. Elected President of the Republic in July 1958, he thwarted an attempted *coup d'état* on 31 December 1961 led by a group of officers belonging to the PPS (Syrian Nationalist Party), whose aim was to achieve the unity of Greater Syria (including Lebanon and Palestine).

2   Dominique Chevallier, *La Societé du Mont-Liban a l'epoque de la revolution industrielle en Europe* (Paris, Geuthner, 1971), p. 291.

3   See chapter 1, p. 41.

4   The Damascus massacres were stopped through the intervention of

the Algerian Emir Abdel Qader, exiled by France in the Syrian capital.

5 On the reforms, see Chapter 1, p. 40–1.

6 Chevallier, *La Societé du Mont Liban*, p. 249. A similar remark was made by a Lebanese reforming philosopher writing at the beginning of this century about reforms in the Ottoman Empire under pressure from Young Turk officers:

The nation has not participated substantially in change . . . The fact is our revolution has until now been military, the change that it effected being confined to the form of power, while our attitudes have not in any way been changed by it, and it has hardly touched our sciences, our industries and our commerce. (Shibli Schmayyel, cited by R. Khoury, *Contemporary Arab Thought: The Influence of the French Revolution on Its Social and Political Orientations* (in Arabic) (Beirut, Dar Al-Makshuf, 1973), p. 134.

7 Musa al-Sadr was a remarkable but contradictory personality since after having contributed towards the over-heating of the Lebanese social climate, he worked without respite for political appeasement. His strange destiny ended in Libya in 1978, where he disappeared during an official visit, no reason being forthcoming as to why the Libyan authorities should have removed him so brutally. Deeply missed by the Shias of Lebanon, the iman's disappearance has led to plane hijackings, so far without bloodshed, as a form of protest.

8 The reforms effected by General Chehab during his six years as Head of State (1958–64) only concerned the economic field, leaving the basic structure of the political system practically intact, and even reinforcing its communal aspects at the administrative level.

9 Maronites had the Presidency of the Republic and the command of the army, in addition to several high administrative posts. The Sunnis had the Presidency of the Council of Ministers and the control of the police force; the Shiites, the Presidency of the Chamber of Deputies, the Greek Orthodox Christians, the vice-Presidency of the Council of Ministers, the Druze were the ignored in these allocations; the Chief of Staff of the army traditionally belonged to the Druze community.

10 One might think here of the 'pieds-noirs' or 'petit-blanc' culture of Algeria. However, there can be no resemblance between the French colonists in Algeria and the Maronites whose historical articulation into Near Eastern society is authenticated for over a thousand years without any discontinuity.

11 This refers to the Cairo agreements in 1969 by the Commanding General of the Lebanese army and the leader of the PLO, ratified by the Lebanese Parliament, which legalized the provision of arms and operational bases in South Lebanon for the Resistance movements, a concession no Arab State ever accorded Palestinian refugees, whose camps and political activities were kept under strict surveillance. The agreements were in fact signed after a first clash between the Lebanese army and the Palestinian movements, which provoked a six-month ministerial crisis. The Maronite leaders correctly affirm that it was under pressure from the Sunni

community, which holds the Presidency of the Council, that they were led into making this exhorbitant concession which gave the Israelis a 'legal' pretext for their reprisals. In fact, in 1969 to yield was the easy way out which put off the day of reckoning, but made everything considerably worse.

12   *Pour le Liban* (interviews recorded by Philippe Lapousterle), Stock, Paris, 1978, pp. 247 ff.

13   The leader of this group of officers was Major Saad Haddad who was to be heard of again during the Israeli invasion of Lebanon in the summer of 1982 (see Chapter 8).

14   Article One of the Agreement.

15   In the spring of 1982, the Syrian army went as far as to raze to the ground the old town of Hama, a stronghold of the Muslim Brotherhood, which had called for general insurrection in Hama and in the other big Syrian towns. The number of victims among the town population was between 10,000 and 30,000.

16   On this point, see Chapter 2, p. 61.

17   A fantastic episode in this civil war was the attempted *coup d'état* of a Sunni Lebanese army general in March 1976, who demanded the dismissal of the President of the Republic. Thanks to the Palestinian co-operation, the author of this attempt, who could barely muster up a hundred men, succeeded in reading his communiqués over Lebanese television. The movement, which apparently enjoyed Saudi support, aroused the hostility of Syria and the perplexity of the Right-wing parties, and only accelerated the disintegration of the army.

18   It is true that the Palestinian logistics indispensable to the success of such an attack seem to have been deliberately withheld, the Resistance controlled by Arafat preferring not to disperse its troops too much at a time when it had already become clear that Syria no longer followed the logic of the Lebanese Movement's alliance with the PLO.

19   Contingents from various Arab countries hurried to Lebanon under the aegis of the Arab League (see above, p. 67).

20   It did not function again until 1981.

21   See Chapter 7.

22   In 1982, it was no longer content with such pledges; hence the invasion of two-thirds of Lebanese territory and the dramatic siege of Beirut (see Chapter 8).

Chapter 7   From the first Zionist congress to the Camp David Agreements

1   'Obsidional' was how a remarkable French Professor of Political Economy in the Faculty of Law at the University of Beirut, who has since died, elegantly referred to the Israeli economy. With equally incisive vision, he spoke of the 'double foreign grip of oil and Israeli capitalism' on the Arab economy. E. Teilhac, *Economie politique*

pour les Arabes (Annals of the Faculty of Law and Economic Sciences of Beirut, Paris, LGDJ, 1960).

2   One should remember that in 1948 the Soviet Union fervently supported the creation of Israel and that Czechoslavakia was an important supplier of arms to the Zionist movement. In the eyes of the Soviet Union at that time, the creation of Israel, under the aegis of a Jewish socialism, in the middle of an Arab Near East dominated by 'feudal' monarchies or 'reactionary' bourgeoisies allied to colonialism, could result in an important 'revolutionary' base. The rise of Arab 'national' bourgeoisies, then the installation of 'progressive' governments on the one hand, and Israel's close alliance with the Western powers on the other, evidently pushed the Soviet Union more and more into supporting the Arab States and keeping its distance from Israel.

3   M. Dayán, *Breakthrough* (London, Weidenfeld & Nicolson, 1981), p. 60.

4   *Ibid.*, p. 60.

5   Anwar Sadat, *In Search of an Identity* (London, Collins, 1978), pp. 303–4.

6   This refers to the usual translation by the international press of the Arab name for the Front. But the Arabic term *tassadi*, translated as *confrontation*, actually reflects the idea of resisting something, of placing an obstacle in its way, which does not exactly correspond to the notion of confrontation.

7   Terms used in the title of a work by a recently deceased Jewish philosopher and historian, J. L. Talmon, *Israel among the Nations* (London, 1970).

8   See, in particular, *La Quête de l'absolu* (Paris, Calmann-Levy, 1981), pp. 274 ff.

9   George Friedmann, 'Fin du peuple juif' (Paris, Gallimard, collection *Idées*, 1965).

Chapter 8   The invasion of Lebanon

1   See Chapter 6.

2   See Chapter 5.

3   Crown Prince Fahd succeeded his half-brother King Khalid who died in June 1982.

4   See the analysis of the Camp David Agreements in Chapter 7, pp. 191–6.

5   The name of a Palestinian village in which militias from Irgun, a Zionist extremist movement led by Menachem Begin, indiscriminately massacred women, children and old people during the 1948 war. In the Palestinian and Arab memory, the name of Deir Massin has become a symbol of the terror practised by Zionism in the conquest of Palestine.

6   See Chapter 7.

7   We should remember that the communist elements had been driven

from the zones held by the Christian militias as early as 1976 and had found refuge in the zones controlled by 'Palestinian progressives'.

8   In October 1985, even three Soviet diplomats were kidnapped, of whom one was executed. The Druze militiamen of the Progressive Social party, with very strong links with the USSR, quickly managed to have the other two freed.

9   Among others, we should remember the kidnapping of twenty 'blue caps' in June 1985 by the militia known as the Army of South Lebanon, financed and officered by Israel, a kidnapping that was officially covered up by the Israeli authorities.

10 An example of this pointless chatter was the hours spent discussing the nature of Lebanon's Arab identity. For a country which in the course of the last century produced the finest masterpieces of Arabic literature, thanks notably to writers from Christian communities and especially the Maronites, the degree of lunatic perversity which reigns in Lebanese political dialogue is obvious!

11 These schisms are described in Chapter 5 of *OPEP ou PLO: 1974–1975*, in particular on pp. 146–52.

12 These Resolutions concern restoration of the territories occupied by Israel in 1967 in return for recognition of Israel by the Arab countries, but do not recognize the Palestinian right to an independent State. Hence the PLO's reticence to accept these two particular Resolutions without explicit General Assembly Resolutions recognizing that right.

13 The events in September 1970 when the Palestinian organizations in Jordan were violently ejected from the country. See Chapter 2, p. 59.

Conclusion

1   This hunting down of opponents has become so widespread in recent years that it has spread into foreign countries, particularly to the large European capitals where assassinations of Arab political figures in exile have become almost commonplace.

2   On state religious fundamentalism, see Chapters 3 and 6.

3   On this point see Introduction.

Appendix: The economic evolution of the Middle East

1   The data here are taken from an important study by the Arab Fund for Economic and Social Development, 'Study of the performance of the Arab nation with reference to development in the 1970s and prospects for the 1980s' (text in Arabic) and from *World Development Report*, World Bank, 1981.

Suggestions for Further Reading

This list is a guide to relevant publications available in English

History, Culture and Religion

Abu-Lughod, Lila, *Veiled Sentiments; Honor and Poetry in a Beduin Society* (Cairo: The American University Press, paperback 1986).

Ajami, Fouad, *The Vanished Imam: Musa al Sadr and the Shia of Lebanon* (Ithaca NY and London: Cornell UP, 1986).

Arjamani, Yahya and Ricks, Thomas, M., *The Middle East: Past and Present*, 2nd edn (Englewood Cliffs, NJ: Prentice Hall, 1986).

Dessouki, Ali E. Hillal (ed.) *Islamic Resurgence in the Arab World* (New York: Praeger, 1982).

Enayat, Hamid, *Modern Islamic Political Thought* (London: Macmillan, paperback 1982).

Epstein, Isadore, *Judaism* (Harmondsworth: Penguin, paperback 1959).

Gilsenan, Michael, *Recognising Islam: Religion and Society in the Modern Arab World* (New York: Pantheon, 1982, published with different sub-title, London: Croom Helm, 1982).

Hodgson, Marshall, *The Venture of Islam: Conscience and History in a World Civilisation*, 3 vols (Chicago: Chicago UP, paperback 1974).

Hourani, Albert H., *Arabic Thought in the Liberal Age, 1798–1939* (London Oxford UP, 1962, later paperback reprint).

Kepel, Gilles, *The Prophet and the Pharaoh* (London: Al-Saqi, 1985), trans. from French.

Laroui, A., *The Crisis of the Arab Intellectuals* (Berkeley: University of California Press, 1976).

Mansfield, Peter, *The Arabs*, 4th edn (Harmondsworth: Penguin, 1980).

Rahman, Fazlur, *Islam* (London: Weidenfeld and Nicolson, 1966).

Ruthvin, Malise, *Islam in the World* (Harmondsworth Penguin, paperback 1985).

Said, Edward, *Orientalism* (London: Routledge and Kegan Paul, 1978).

Shaw, S. J. and Shaw, E. K., *History of the Ottoman Empire and Modern Turkey*, 2 vols (Cambridge: Cambridge UP, paperback 1982).

Watt, W. Montgomery, *Muhammad: Prophet and Statesman* (London: Oxford UP, 1961, paperback 1984).

Contemporary Politics

The Arab States
Ajami, Fouad, *The Arab Predicament* (Cambridge: Cambridge UP, 1981).

Anderson, Lisa, *The State and Social Transformation in Tunisia and Libya, 1830–1980* (Princeton NJ: Princeton UP, 1986).

Batatu, Hanna, *The Old Social Classes and the Revolutionary Movements of Iraq* (Princeton NJ: Princeton UP, 1978; later paperback in 2 vols).

Dawisha, Adeed and Zartman, I. William (eds) *Beyond Coercion: The Durability of the Arab State* (London: Croom Helm, 1988).

Entelis, J., *Algeria: The Revolution Institutionalised* (Boulder, Colorado: Westview, and London: Croom Helm, 1986).

Holden, David and Johns, Richard, *The House of Saud* (London: Pan, paperback 1981).

Hudson, Michael, *Arab Politics: The Search for Legitimacy* (New Haven: Yale UP, paperback 1977).

Khalidi, Walid, *Conflict and Violence of Lebanon* (Cambridge, Mass.: Harvard UP, 1979).

Moore, Clement Henry, *Politics in North Africa* (Boston: Little Brown, 1970).

Piscatori, James P., *Islam in the Political Process* (Cambridge: Cambridge UP, paperback 1983).

Randal, Jonathan, *The Tragedy of Lebanon* (London: Chatto and Windus, paperback 1983).

Sluglett, Marion Farouk and Sluglett, Peter, *Iraq since 1958: From Revolution to Dictatorship* (London: Routledge and Kegan Paul, 1987).

Shaw, John A. and Long, David E., *Saudi Arabian Modernisation: The Impact of Change on Stability* (New York: Praeger, 1982).

Van Dam, Nikalaos, *The Struggle for Power in Syria*, 2nd edn (London: Croom Helm, 1981).

Waterbury, John, *The Egypt of Nasser and Sadat* (Princeton NJ: Princeton UP, 1983).

Zahlan, Rosemary Said, *The Making of the Modern Gulf States* (London: Hutchinson, 1988).

Israel and the Palestinians

Arian, Ahser, *The Elections in Israel 1981* (Tel Aviv: Ramot Publishing, 1983).

Arian, Asher and Shamir, Michael, *The Elections in Israel 1984* (Tel Aviv: Ramot Publishing, 1986)

Benvenisti, Meron, *The West Bank Data Project: A Survey of Israel's Policies* (Washington DC: The American Enterprise Institute, paperback 1984).

Cobban, Helena, *The Palestine Liberation Organisation* (Cambridge: Cambridge UP, 1984).

Gresch, Alain, *the PLO: The Struggle Within* (London: Zed Press, 1983), trans. from French.

Laqueur, Walter, *A History of Zionism* (London: Weidenfeld and Nicolson, 1972).

Lucas, Noah, *The Modern History of Israel* (London: Weidenfeld and Nicolson, 1974).

Ma'os, Moshe, *Palestinian Leadership on the West Bank* (London: Frank Cass, 1984).

Peretz, D. *The Government and Politics of Israel* (Boulder: Westview, and Folkestone: Dawson, 1979).

Peri, Yoram, *Between Battles and Ballots: Israel Military in Politics* (Cambridge: Cambridge UP, 1983).

Safran, Nadaf, Israel, *The Embattled Ally* (Cambridge, Mass. and London: The Bellnap Press of Harvard University, 1978).

Scholch, Alexander, *Palestinians over the Green Line: Studies in the Relationships between Palestinians on Both Sides of the 1949 Armistice Line since 1967* (London: Ithaca Press, 1983).

Iran

Abrahamahiah, Ervand, *Iran between two Revolutions* (Princeton NJ: Princeton UP, 1983).

Bakhash, Shawl, *The reign of the Ayatollahs: Iran and the Islamic Revolution* (London: I. B. Tauris, 1985).

Benard, Cheryl and Khalilzad, Zalmay, '*The Government of God*': *Iran's Islamic Republic* (New York: Columbia UP, 1984).

Mollahedeh, Roy *The Mantle of the Prophet: Religion and Politics in Iran* (New York: Simon and Schuster, 1985).

Zabih, Sepehr, *Iran since the Revolution* (London: Croom Helm, 1982).

Arab Nationalism and Intra-Arab Politics

Amin, Samir, *The Arab Nation* (London: Zed Press, 1978), trans. from French.

Dessouki, Ali E. Hillal and Korany, Baghat (eds), *The Foreign Policies of the Arab States* (Boulder, Colorado: Westview, 1984).

Gomaa, Ahmed M., *The Foundation of the League of Arab States* (London: Longman, 1977).

Haim, Sylvia G. (ed.). *Arab Nationalism: An Anthology* (Berkeley: University of California Press, paperback 1974).

Kerr, Malcolm H., *The Arab Cold War, 1958–1967*, 2nd edn (London: Oxford UP, 1967).

McLaurin, R. D. *et al.* (eds.), *Foreign Policy-Making in the Middle East* (New York: Praeger, 1977).

Mutawi, Samir A., *Jordan in the 1967 War* (Cambridge: Cambridge UP, 1987).

Porath, Yehoshua, *In Search of Arab Unity, 1930–1945* (London: Frank Cass, 1986).

Seale, Patrick, *The Struggle for Syria*, 2nd edn (London: I. B. Tauris, 1986).

Tibi, Bassam, *Arab Nationalism* (London: Macmillan, 1981), trans. from German.

Economies and Oil

Amin, Galal, A., *The Modernisation of Poverty: A Study of the Political Economy of Growth in Nine Arab Countries* (Leiden: E. J. Brill, 1980).

Ibrahim, Ibrahim (ed.), *Arab Resources: The Transformation of a Society* (Washington: Center for Contemporary Arab Studies and London: Croom Helm, paperback 1983).

Issawi, Charles, *The Economic History of the Middle East and North Africa* (London: Methuen, paperback, 1982).

Kerr, Malcolm H. and Yassin, El Sayed (eds), *Rich States and Poor States in the Middle East: Egypt and the New Arab Order* (Boulder, Colorado: Westview, and Cairo: The American University Press, paperback 1982).

Mabro, Robert, *The Egyptian Economy 1952–1972* (Oxford: Clarendon Press, paperback 1974).

Odell, Peter, *Oil and World Power: Background in the Oil Crisis*, 3rd edn (Harmondsworth: Penguin, 1974).

Owen, Roger, *The Middle East in the World Economy, 1800–1914* (London: Methuen, paperback 1981).

Sampson, Anthony, *The Seven Sisters: The Great Oil Companies and the World They Made* (London: Hodder and Stoughton, 1975).

Sayigh, Yusif, *Arab Oil Policies in the 1970s: Opportunities and Responsibilities* (London: Croom Helm, 1983).

Sayigh, Yusif. *The Arab Economy: Past Performance and Future Prospects* (Oxford: Oxford UP, 1982).

The Middle East in World Affairs

Brown, L. Carl, *International Politics and the Middle East: Old Rules, Dangerous Game* (London: I. B. Tauris, 1984).

Cordesman, Anthony H., *The Gulf and the Search for Strategic Stability* (Boulder, Colorado: Westview, 1984).

Dawisha, A. and Dawisha, K. (eds), *The Soviet Union and the Middle East: Policies and Perspectives* (London: Heinemann, 1982).

Halliday, Fred, *Threat from the East?: Soviet Policy from Afghanistan and Iran to the Horn of Africa* (Harmondsworth: Pelican, paperback 1982).

Heikal, M. H., *Sphinx and Commissar: The Rise and Fall of Soviet Influence in the Arab World* (London: Collins, 1977).

Monroe, Elizabeth, *Britain's Moment in the Middle East, 1914–1956* (London: Chatto and Windus, 1963).

Quandt, William B., *Camp David: Peacemaking and Politics* (Washington DC: The Brookings Institution, paperback 1986).

Quandt, William A., *Decade of Decisions: American Policy towards the Arab–Israeli Conflict 1967–1976* (Berkeley and Los Angeles: University of California Press, 1977).

Sich, Garry, *All Fall Down: America's Fateful Encounter with Iran* (New York: Random House and London: I. B. Tauris, 1985).

Index